DISCARD

LENIN AND
THE TWENTIETH CENTURY

HOOVER ARCHIVAL DOCUMENTARIES

General editor: Milorad M. Drachkovitch

The documents reproduced in this series (unless otherwise indicated) are deposited in the archives of the Hoover Institution on War, Revolution and Peace at Stanford University. The purpose of their publication is to shed new light on some important events concerning the United States or the general history of the twentieth century.

LENIN

AND THE

TWENTIETH
CENTURY

A BERTRAM D. WOLFE
RETROSPECTIVE

COMPILED AND WITH AN INTRODUCTION BY
LENNARD D. GERSON

FOREWORD BY
ALAIN BESANÇON

HOOVER INSTITUTION PRESS
STANFORD UNIVERSITY   STANFORD, CALIFORNIA

Hoover Press Publication 293
© 1984 by the Board of Trustees of the
   Leland Stanford Junior University

First printing, 1984

Manufactured in the United States of America

88 87 86 85 84   9 8 7 6 5 4 3 2 1

Library of Congress Cataloging in Publication Data

Wolfe, Bertram David, 1896–1977.
  Lenin and the twentieth century.

  (Hoover archival documentaries)
  Includes bibliographical references and index.
    1. Lenin, Vladimir Ilích, 1870–1924—Addresses, essays,
lectures. 2. Heads of state—Soviet Union—Biography—
Addresses, essays, lectures. 3. Revolutionists—Soviet
Union—Biography—Addresses, essays, lectures.
4. Communists—Soviet Union—Biography—Addresses,
essays, lectures. 5. Communism—Soviet Union—Addresses,
essays, lectures. 6. Soviet Union—Revolution, 1917–1921—
Influence—Addresses, essays, lectures. 7. Soviet Union—
Politics and government—20th century—Addresses, essays,
lectures. I. Gerson, Lennard D. II. Title. III. Title: Lenin
and the 20th century. IV Series.
DK254.L4W593 1984   947.084'1'0924 [B]   84-8931
ISBN 0-8179-7931-X

Contents

Preface

Bertram D. Wolfe (1896–1977) was one of America's foremost authorities on Soviet history and politics. Several generations of students in dozens of countries acquired their first understanding of the events and personalities that have shaped modern Russia from Wolfe's landmark study, *Three Who Made a Revolution*. The twelve essays on Lenin and Leninism published in this volume were written during the last decades of Wolfe's long life and reflect the unique blend of personal experience, thorough scholarship, and ideological commitment that informed all his writings. These essays, nine of which appear in print here for the first time, do not constitute an integrated or complete biography of Lenin.* It was Wolfe's intention to write such a book, a sequel to *Three Who Made a Revolution*, but death claimed him before he could complete this project.

I was guided by two major considerations in compiling this collection of Bertram Wolfe's essays on Lenin. First, I wanted to present material that would not already be familiar to Wolfe's many readers and students. Only two of these essays were published during Wolfe's lifetime; one appeared posthumously. These previously published articles focus on such central matters as Lenin's concept of the party and Wolfe's final assessment of Lenin's place in history. Not to include them would have greatly diminished the scholarly value of the anthology. My second consideration was to stress the period after 1914, the point at which *Three Who Made a Revolution* ends. Wolfe wanted to tell the story of Lenin and the Bolsheviks in power. He did not live to complete this task, but these essays suggest the direction his research and thinking on the subject were taking him.

Bertram Wolfe's hitherto unpublished essays on Lenin are published verbatim. Wolfe was a master stylist, and no alterations have been made in

---

* Occasional phrases and passages did appear in some of Wolfe's published writings, but the essays have never been published in their entirety.

the text of his original manuscripts. Only a few silent corrections have been made to correct an occasional typographical error. Footnotes have also been renumbered in some of the essays to incorporate information that was originally contained in notes inserted into the text by the author. Readers interested in consulting the originals of these and other unpublished writings by Bertram D. Wolfe on Lenin and the Russian Revolution will find them in the Bertram D. Wolfe Papers, Boxes 16–22, at the Hoover Institution Archives, Stanford, California.

This project was undertaken at the request of Dr. Milorad M. Drach-kovitch, archivist and senior fellow at the Hoover Institution, as part of the Hoover Archival Documentaries series. I am pleased to express my gratitude for his encouragement and support. The Earhart Foundation made it possible for me to spend a year as a visiting scholar at the Hoover Institution on War, Revolution and Peace to pursue this and other research projects, and I am most grateful for its sponsorship. Special thanks are due to Mrs. Ella Wolfe, who provided much valuable information about her late husband's career. These essays will stand as a valuable contribution to history and a tribute to her husband's memory.

Foreword

The reason why Ludendorff agreed to allow Lenin's return to Russia in April 1917 is that he knew nothing of the nature of Bolshevism. The reason why Lloyd George, Edouard Herriot, and Mussolini recognized the Soviet regime in the 1920s is that they did not understand what it was. The reason why Roosevelt allowed Stalin to take over half of Europe in 1945 is that he did not know what Stalin was going to do with it. The reason why Eisenhower and John Foster Dulles wanted the liberation of Europe, but did not know how to take the opportunity to accomplish this task between 1953 and 1956, is that they did not accurately gauge the political situation of Stalin's heirs. And the reason why de Gaulle, Kissinger, and Carter believed in détente is that they had an incorrect view of the USSR and of its objectives.

Most of communism's successes occur because the adversaries of communism are incapable of making a precise and realistic evaluation of it. We would like to believe that the Soviet regime is not as bad as all that, or that it will change and improve. If our statesmen are social democrats, they think that communism will evolve toward social democracy. If they are liberals, they predict a Soviet liberalization. If they are conservatives, they see, behind the USSR, eternal Russia, a great power with its inalterable imperial goals and respectable interests. Policies formulated on such assumptions are all the falser for their appearance of being true. And these policies have consistently failed. Thirty years after the death of Stalin and sixty years after that of Lenin, the Soviet Union continues to act in conformity with its genetic code and to strive for the same goal: the destruction of capitalism and the construction of socialism; in other words, it seeks the transformation of the entire world into a world modeled on the original cancerous cell of communism. Western policies have in fact contributed to the success of the Leninist plan. They have all resulted in helping along the Soviet state's wish to form an atmosphere of confidence, according to which it would become more liberal or would peacefully take its place among the great powers. The Soviet state takes whatever one gives it and, having become stronger through Western aid, appears more threatening than ever.

The statesmen who have had the instinct or the intuition to understand what goes on in the communist world have been few and far between. It is too far removed from the ordinary conditions of humanity. Just as no one believed the Hitlerian Holocaust because no normal man could imagine such a thing, so also has communism clothed its operations for sixty years in the covering of unbelievability. It is normal that statesmen do not immediately understand what is happening. They are surrounded by experts, but there are few really competent experts in Sovietology, and those that are competent are far removed from the seats of power.

It is not an exaggeration to state that in no country, at any time, can one find more than ten persons capable of understanding the mechanisms of the Soviet regime and of formulating an accurate political analysis that can be recalled without blushing several years later. Moreover, these persons occupy positions on the sidelines of power. To have an accurate intuition of communism, one must have been very close to it, either physically through prolonged contact or morally by having yielded to its seductiveness for a certain time. One who passes through such an apprenticeship is far from the center of decision making, out on the sidelines, and it is rarely possible to come back to the political and academic establishment from such a remote position. Moreover, the wisdom accrued in this experience is not easy to pass on. Those holding positions of power do not want to learn from it; they prefer to stick to their customary mode of thought. So what one finds is a center of power, occupied by the statesmen, diplomats, newsmen, and those academics whose Sovietology is of the mainstream sort; and then, on the periphery, a few men, filling modest posts, who are compromised by their past. They know what is happening, but they have enormous difficulties in being heard.

Their situation has never been as bad as it was in the 1940s. The usual incomprehension of the USSR became even more total since the West's preoccupation with Hitler made it almost respectable to be blind to the nature of the Soviet Union. Nearly all anti-Nazi intellectuals felt obliged to be friendly toward the "country of the Soviets." During this period, four extraordinary men saved the honor of free thought. George Orwell was the first. An Englishman, he had been a volunteer with the Spanish Republicans. A few weeks in Barcelona, where he saw the anarcho-syndicalist POUM (Workers' Party of Marxist Unification) liquidated by the Soviet-Spanish secret police, were all his insight needed to enlighten him. In an instant, he came to understand communism to its depths. Arthur Koestler was the second. A Hungarian, he had served as a Comintern official. After escaping from one of Franco's prisons and from a French refugee camp, he found shelter in England, where he bravely confronted his past and wrote an epic account of what he had seen. The third was Boris Souvarine, a Frenchman, a founder of the French Communist Party and a Comintern delegate. Although opposed by most of the well-known intellectuals in Paris, he was able to publish his admirable *Stalin*. The fourth was Bertram Wolfe, an American. He was from the working class, or more specifically from workers in the printing industry. Moving from the labor movement to communism, he was drawn into the shadowy administration of the Comintern. As soon as he worked his way free, morally and physically, he went to work on his masterpiece, *Three Who Made a Revolution*, which, from the moment of its publication in 1948, was considered a classic and served to educate an entire generation.

We would like to be able to say about these four men what Churchill said about the fighter pilots in the Battle of Britain: "Never in the field of human conflict was so much owed by so many to so few." But these four men were not able to prevent the catastrophes that could have been avoided had their knowledge been taken into consideration. Nonetheless, they make up a tiny but unshakable core of clear conscience in the Western world.

Following the war and after the deceptions brought by the peace, several American universities founded well-financed and well-staffed research centers that accomplished some remarkable work. At Harvard, Columbia, and other centers, these were the halcyon years of Western Sovietology. Studies carried out in this period fully corroborated the conclusions reached by the pioneers of the preceding generation.

Communism is simple, and when one understands it, one understands it entirely. But this understanding requires a continuous effort, because communism is not part of an ordinary person's experience and it is not enjoyable to live for very long "through the looking glass." If the effort slackens, the understanding disintegrates completely. This is what happened in America, as in Europe, because of détente, which brought a spate of sophisticated theories about the Soviet regime, suggesting such developments as a forthcoming liberalization of the regime, the convergence of Soviet and Western society, political pluralism, and economic modernization. These theories were astute, brilliant, and unfortunately without any basis in reality. Today, after the painful deceptions of the past decades, specialists are rereading the classic works of Wolfe and are finding with astonishment that they are as fresh as always. The reason is that the Soviet regime has not changed.

Lennard D. Gerson has prepared this edition of Wolfe's essays. His Introduction describes the evolution of Wolfe's thought and characterizes the various expressions of this thought that appeared in Wolfe's lifetime. He explains why he chose from among the many available works the twelve essays that appear here. These essays were written at different times and treat different topics. But they nevertheless constitute a homogeneous work because like the multicolored bands of the spectrum they all passed through the prism of a single, focused mind.

So we find in this work the usual qualities of Bertram Wolfe's works: stylistic clarity, exact analysis, thorough documentation, and solid judgment. We also find here what we cannot find in more recent works by other authors: familiarity with the men and events being discussed. This is a book that is not the product of book learning. We find instead the reflection of a charming personality, whose vitality, curiosity, good will, and incorruptible integrity appear throughout these pages. It is as much a first-person account of the intellectual history of this generation of Americans as it is a history on the USSR.

There would be no point in criticizing these essays by comparing them to what Schapiro, Ulam, Lazitch and Drachkovitch, Heller, Malia, and Pipes—to mention only a few scholars—wrote at later dates. It is to be expected that scholarship makes some progress and that new points of view appear. History is a cumulative discipline. But it might help to understand these essays by pointing out that they implicitly pose three questions that one finds in all profound analyses of Leninism and, as well, suggest answers to these questions.

1. *The relationship between the Russian past and the Soviet regime.* Here is a question that had fueled discussion and debate for sixty years, as evidenced by the recent exchange between Solzhenitsyn and Richard Pipes. On the eve of the First World War, Russia was nearing a "great revolution" on the English (1642) and the French (1789) models. By "great revolution," we must understand the fall of the old regime and the progressive passing of power to civil society and its representatives. This great revolution had been ripening in Russia ever since the abolition of serfdom in 1861. It had almost succeeded in 1905. It did succeed in February 1917. But after the symbolic moment when the tsar was displaced, events took an altogether different course and broke completely away from the classic examples of England and France. Because of its weak condition, civil society was unable to assume leadership—worn out, disorganized, and destroyed as it had been by the war. Bertram Wolfe rightly underscores the overwhelming responsibility that this absurd war must bear. Power fell into the hands of a disciplined party, unified by ideology. It placed itself in the position that Russian society should have occupied, reconstituted the state around itself, and began to work to create a utopia.

So the Soviet regime is not a new regime, comparable to what was set up in England, the United States, and France from the eighteenth to the nineteenth centuries. Soviet power has as its objective, and as its only source of legitimacy, to bring about what its ideology promises: communism.

The Russian legacy contains a number of formulas for taking and holding power, some forgotten, others still in use. Any of them could be used again. The Mongols, Ivan the Terrible, Peter the Great, and Nicholas I had perfected efficient techniques of governing. The Bolsheviks used these techniques. But since their goal, in contrast to the goal of the old Russian state, was utopian and unattainable—because communism does not exist—they were obliged to use the most cruel techniques and to push them to hideous extremes.

Here is one example: in 1913, the secret police had only a few hundred regular members, and the number of persons in prison did not exceed 70,000. Today—not to mention the Stalin era—the KGB has half a million members, and there are four million persons in the Gulag.* We find the same disproportion in comparing Ivan the Terrible's *Opritchnina* with Stalin's purges or the construction of St. Petersburg with the first five-year plans.

Moreover, bolshevik power needs support from other sources. It put to its own use Russia's traditional nationalism, but it remained the master of the alliance. Bolshevism did not work for the goals of nationalism; instead, nationalism served the goals of bolshevism. Nationalism is a disguise of bolshevism, not the reverse.

Subsequently, it is a major error to visualize a continuity between Russia and the USSR. Power, in appearance, is Russian; in reality, it is communist. The West has made the same error with regard to Mao's China and the German Democratic Republic, supposedly the continuations, respectively, of imperial China and militaristic and bureaucratic Prussia. Every state that becomes communist moves into the same relationship with its past; ideology dresses up the past and makes it a caricature in order to work toward radically new goals.

2. *The relationship between Marxism and political Leninism.* How does Leninism differ from Marxism? The answer is ambiguous because it is always possible to find elements both of Leninism and of its refutation in Marx's writings. Marx himself was several men: a philosopher and an economist, each deserving a niche in European intellectual history; a liberal, who inspired the civilized social democracies of Western Europe; and finally, a Jacobin and a pre-Leninist, pushed in this direction by his authoritarian, systematic, and dogmatic tendencies.

---

* According to an official report submitted by the U.S. Department of State to Congress, dated February 9, 1983, "the Soviet forced labor system, the largest in the world, comprises a network of some 1100 forced labor camps, which cover most areas of the USSR. The system includes an estimated four million forced laborers, of whom at least 10,000 are considered to be political and religious prisoners."

Moreover, Lenin always covered himself with countless quotations from Marx, sincerely believing that he was the faithful interpreter of his master. And it is on this specific point that we find Lenin's decisive originality: his absolute, total, and blind confidence in Marxism. What for Marx remained open, subject to scrutiny and further research, became for Lenin an intangible *result*, a body of doctrine given the imprimatur of "science," which "explains everything."

From this act of faith we can draw the elements of political Leninism:

(1) The idea of the party. The central idea of the party is that its members share absolute knowledge as well as the promise that this absolute knowledge has revealed: socialism. The party does not represent the working class; it represents the interests of socialism for the working class, which because of its nature cannot understand its own will. The central committee does not represent the mass of the party members; it represents the interests of socialism for the party members, who are not fully aware. And not even Lenin himself is responsible to the party or to the working class; he is responsible to the idea of socialism, being the only person to understand it completely.

(2) The program. One must build a political apparatus capable of seizing power from the state, and then one must use the power of the state to destroy anything in material society or in the imagination that opposes the realization of socialism.

Given the elevated status of absolute knowledge, Lenin's first real task was to build a stable synthesis of the conspiratorial and clandestine party created by Russian populism and the simplified Marxism of the Second International. Once he brought about this synthesis, Lenin tolerated whatever party divisions or exclusions that were necessary to keep the synthesis pure. At the end he was almost alone, but he had succeeded in preserving the germinal cell of communism.

He had his chance due to the extraordinary circumstances of the war and the fall of the tsar. On the one hand, he encouraged the decomposition of society and state as much as possible; and on the other, he preserved his party from this decomposition in order to be able to thrust it forward as a central core around which the state could be reorganized. The Russian people in the end resigned themselves to the bolshevik state out of the lassitude of anarchy. Lenin's project had succeeded.

And it was at this moment that it failed. Lenin's idea was that the role of the state was limited to being the midwife of socialism. But socialism has never developed, and all the social classes, including the working class, have gone in a direction opposite to that foreseen by Lenin's ideology. What could be done? Well, the communist state must punish the mother in order to save the baby. It must destroy capitalism (i.e., classes, culture, religion, the market, and all that was real in Russia) and build socialism. Moreover, it was necessary that this construction appear as the spontaneous result of the laws of history, discovered by the doctrine. By controlling information, education, and the minds of the people, the state would act *as if* socialism existed. And this is how the legitimacy of the party and the truth of its ideology were confirmed.

Only one condition is necessary to be able to destroy (in fact) and to build (in imagination): being in power. As long as the party stays in power, it can build socialism—in a year, in a thousand years—but if it loses power, socialism will vanish like a bad dream, and everyone will notice that (in fact) the task of building it had never even been begun.

The fundamental rule of political Leninism, therefore, is to stay in power. Here is an example of how far it will go to adhere to this rule: the demographer Mikhail Bernstam judges that between 1917 and 1921, the USSR lost fifteen million people through famine, massacre, and typhus, in spite of the Hoover Mission, which saved about seven million people. These losses were more than five times the numbers lost during the war, whose very horrors had justified the bolshevik coup d'etat. Did this enormous suffering affect Lenin? Not at all, as long as the demographic catastrophe did not turn into a political one. It was because of the political threat that Lenin changed his tactics. Indeed, the first rule of Leninism has as a corollary a second one: compromise. When continuity of power is in jeopardy because the state is exercising its ideological program too rigidly, the program simply has to be put aside for a time. Once the state has solidified its power, it will wait for the favorable moment to repudiate the compromise and pick up with its programs where it had left them. A classic example is the peace of Brest-Litovsk. Lenin imposed on the party the concession of yielding half of the Russian Empire to the class enemy in order to preserve bolshevik power in an area having the form of a state. Later, he got back the other half. Another example is the New Economic Policy (NEP). Lenin imposed on the party the concession of giving up direct control over the villages in order to end the demographic hemorrhage and to rebuild to a minimal degree society and the economy. The goal of the NEP was not to help the Russian people but to grant relief to the party, which was in a perilous situation. In exchange for getting some temporary autonomy, the Russian people would have to support the party, to permit it to regain its strength and become capable, after a few years, of ending the compromise and taking total control of the villages, which is what Stalin did with collectivization. Compromise has the further advantage of causing the Western class enemy to believe that the bolshevik regime has changed, that it is evolving, becoming more liberal, and therefore that it must be *helped*. So the West ends up supporting Leninism until the latter is strong enough to repudiate the compromise. The equivalent of the NEP in foreign policy is détente.

3. *The relationship between Leninism and universal history.* Some men believe that they have a doctrine that explains all of world history, the secret of the origin of evil, and the solution for wiping it out entirely. These men organize and take power in order to build the best of all worlds. This is an old dream, but in the twentieth century this dream has been realized.

Leninism today controls 40 percent of the world's population. Wherever it dominates, one finds strangely identical phenomena. Everywhere are the same decrepit cities, the same sullen populace, the same miserable countrysides. Everywhere the posters, the loudspeakers, the newspapers, television, and the schools trumpet what Pasternak called "the inhuman domination of the imaginary and the magical power of the dead letter." From Vietnam to Cuba, the "wooden language," monopolistic, uniform in its grammar, its style, and its rhetoric, rises as a parody above the old Babel of tongues. The communist world is fragmented in opposing political entities, but communism is not thereby weakened. It continues to expand, and we do not know whether or not it will reach over the entire world.

What do we find if we look for the causes of this remarkable development? A simplistic doctrine, clearly false, but able nevertheless to win over new converts; a political practice that is extraordinarily simple, yet continues to seduce men to intellect. Behind both the doctrine and the practice are Lenin and his works, an intellectual jumble, a one-dimensional personality without real culture, without even the shocking vices that gave some dimension to Hitler and Stalin. We come up against a mystery.

Bertram Wolfe asked himself these three questions all his life, and the essays published here present subtle answers to them.

The first essay reproduced here emphasizes that Russia was a weak point in the Western world, a fragile society beaten down by a war that was too long and too harsh. Wolfe accepts the liberal version of the Russian revolution: Russian society foundered at the moment when it was freeing itself and was ready to bound ahead. It sank in port. But Wolfe accepts in part Berdyaev's vision: thanks to the revolution, archaic versions of power and of the Russian mentality came back to life.

The other essays analyze with finesse and remarkable thoroughness the different aspects of political Leninism. The relationship between Gorky and Lenin shows how the artist in revolt and the revolutionary militant have superficial resemblances and fundamental differences. Lenin was scornful of Gorky's sentimental humanism and religious impulses. But Lenin understood that he could use these characteristics for the revolution. Gorky was "useful." Chapter 9, "1921: Lenin's Change of Course," is an exceptionally precise and lucid study of the two rules of Leninism: stay in power and be willing to compromise. The compromise rule is illustrated by Lenin's willingness to change course in revolutionary tactics—the role of the Comintern, the national and colonial question, the NEP, etc.—without affecting his immutable strategy. Wolfe notes correctly that the NEP was a political, not an economic, turnabout. It was not a question of improving the welfare of the population but of profiting from economic détente to reinforce the party's discipline and making it capable of putting an end to the NEP. Such tactical deviation is worthwhile politically only if the party is in charge and if the deviation is reversible.

The last essay is a noble reflection on the general significance of Leninism for the history of the twentieth century. Bertram Wolfe led most of his contemporaries in understanding that the central problem was not Stalin but Lenin. On this point he was right and Boris Souvarine, who attempts in a way to "save" Lenin, is wrong. Stalinism was the logical development of the principles of Leninism.

Due to his irreplaceable knowledge of men and events, his clear and supple mind, and his moral courage, Bertram Wolfe was able to go as far as one could go in his era to understand the mystery of Leninism. But the Western world refuses to understand it, and it remains an even greater mystery, before which Bertram Wolfe was as helpless as his successors.

ALAIN BESANÇON
Professor of History, Ecole des Hautes Etudes en Sciences Sociales, Paris

Introduction

It is not true that the end justifies the means, for the means themselves determine the end that will be reached insofar as an end is ever reached. Indeed, that end is no more than the sum of the means used. Thus do evil means corrupt even the noblest end and degrade it . . . Moreover, the ends are at best in the future but the deterioration of character and the infamy of deeds are in the present.—BERTRAM D. WOLFE

Bertram D. Wolfe was a young man of 21 when Lenin and the Bolsheviks seized power in Petrograd. What little Wolfe knew then of Russia, he had gleaned from the great works of nineteenth-century Russian literature. Wolfe, like most Americans, was completely ignorant about Lenin, beyond his opposition to the Great War. Yet Wolfe, who was full of revulsion against the unprecedented violence of World War I and strongly opposed U.S. involvement in the horrible slaughter in Europe, was deeply stirred by Lenin's decision to pull Russia out of the conflict in the same year that the United States entered it. Wolfe was sure that the rulers of revolutionary Russia sought to abolish war, an evil that he had been taught was unthinkable in the civilized twentieth century. Wolfe saw a beacon of hope shining from the Kremlin towers and opened a generous line of credit to Russia's new rulers, as yet unknown to him. It was a credit that was not exhausted until 1929 when a prolonged argument in Moscow with Stalin caused Wolfe "to write off the spiritual investment of a decade as a total loss."[1]

Wolfe was one of the founders of the American Communist Party, but, as he admitted many years later, he came to communism "without rightly knowing what [it] was."[2] He learned Marxism "by dint of sheer stubbornness" and did not begin a serious study of Lenin's works until the mid-1920s. Nothing that Wolfe saw or heard in Russia during his first pilgrimage there in 1924 to attend the Fifth Congress of the Comintern shook his faith in the land of victorious proletarian revolution. He spoke only a few words of tourist Russian and had only a superficial knowledge of Soviet Russia's economic and political life. "My eyes were blinded by red bunting and banners," he told a group of students some five decades later, "my ears filled by the orations of Zinoviev and other Bolsheviks and the playing of the Internationale after each oration."[3]

Never one for the purely administrative or organizational side of communist party life, Wolfe was by temperament and ability best suited for writing, teaching, and speaking. During his years in New York as a leader of the American Communist Party, Wolfe served as National Agitprop director, the head of the Workers' School, and editor of the *Communist*. Wolfe did not view the American party as a mere appendage of the Russian party and was outspoken in his criticism of those among his fellow revolutionaries who had "their feet in America but their heads in Europe." Wolfe showed his independent streak when he became the maverick advocate of "American exceptionalism." This was the simple notion that the United States was not Germany, Italy, or the Soviet Union. Conditions in the United States were different from those elsewhere and the Communist Party, if it was to become a successful working-class party, had to be "Americanized" in its ways and aims. Wolfe urged his comrades to become more familiar with U.S. institutions and ways of thinking. Much to the dismay of his foreign-inspired comrades, Wolfe wrote a pamphlet in 1926 to commemorate the 150th anniversary of the American Revolution. It was important, Wolfe said, that Communists not reject this heritage:

> We need not go abroad for all our revolutionary traditions. Some of them at least we can find in a body of American tradition. We are the inheritors of the Bill of Rights today . . . It is time that the American working class began to "discover America" and its body of native revolutionary traditions.[4]

It was Wolfe's resistance to Stalin's efforts to turn the American Communist Party into an obedient and unquestioning tool of the Communist Party of the Soviet Union (CPSU) that led to his break with Moscow and the "Stalintern." Sent to the USSR in late 1928 as the U.S. representative to the Executive Committee of the Comintern, Wolfe fought strenuously but in vain against Stalin and his flunkeys to preserve some measure of independence for the American Party. Fortunately for Wolfe, Stalin had not yet perfected his methods for permanently silencing his opponents, and after several months of ugly confrontations with the bolshevik leaders, Wolfe was given permission to return to America. Looking back a decade later on his break with the Stalin-controlled Comintern, Wolfe could only "marvel at the blindness (in its essence blind loyalty and a reluctance to believe the worst until it was rubbed into our noses) which prevented our breaking earlier."[5]

Together with hundreds of his like-minded comrades, Wolfe was soon expelled from the American Communist Party. Though greatly disillusioned by his close-up view of the new Stalinist regime in Russia, Wolfe did not quickly loose faith in the programmatic goals of communism. The focus of his political activity during the 1930s was the Communist Party of the USA (Opposition). The Communist Opposition, whose program Wolfe wrote in 1932, stood for the same goals as the official party, namely, the proletarian dictatorship, the abolition of private property, and the defense of the USSR against assaults from the capitalists. But its tactics and methods were rooted in the conviction that "those who build a Communist movement in any country must know that country. They must adapt their tactics to the special conditions of that country. Else they will never build a Communist movement at all."[6]

Yet after his bitter experience in Moscow, communism gradually lost some of its pull for Wolfe. Communism remained his creed, and, as always, he took politics seriously, but striving for proletarian revolution no longer consumed the whole of his energy. In particular, Wolfe wanted to forget Russia and what amounted to a lost decade of his life. He made his living teaching at a New York City prep school and as a freelance writer. Although Wolfe wrote occasional articles and book reviews for the Communist Opposition and lectured at its New Workers' School, most of what he published during those years dealt with Mexico and Latin America, a part of the world with which he had long been fascinated. Wolfe was silent about events in Russia. It was not only that he had an aversion to writing about any subject that he did not fully understand, but all that he had witnessed during his six-month sojourn in Moscow left such a bad taste that he vowed never to write on that country. It was just too painful a subject for him ever to think of again.

Not until Bukharin was put on trial in 1938 in the last of the Moscow show trials did Wolfe break his silence on Russia and publicly denounce Stalin and the purges. "Anyone who fails to raise his voice unequivocably," he said, "makes himself a guilty accomplice by his silence." Anyone who "justifies [the purges] has bathed his hands . . . in the blood of the innocent victims." Stalin was a political gangster whose deeds

> made infinitely harder the task of those of us who love the Soviet Union and would make the world understand its wonders of achievement . . . [Stalin] has murdered his comrades in arms, spewed such filth upon their names and on the fair name of the Russian Revolution that all of us feel unclean even to have to discuss this vileness. Today we can only help the Soviet Union if we succeed in making clear that Stalinism is the very opposite of what we are aiming at and defending.[7]

Wolfe retained his faith in the historic mission of the working class to liberate and transform mankind. He was still a Communist, but an honest one. Honesty, he believed, was not just a bourgeois virtue. If the working class and its leaders lost respect for human life and integrity, "then humanity itself is doomed to retrogression, rebarbarization, degeneracy, and self-destruction." Those who still believed in communism, he said, must "deal with scrupulous cleanliness, clarity, decency and honesty, and maximum working class democracy with the problems of our own working class."[8]

Wolfe believed in a Leninist "golden age," and his remedy for the damage done by the "arch wrecker" Stalin was "to build on the line that Lenin taught": "no leader cult, no unanimous decisions, no dictatorship from above, no falsification of history." Only by returning to what he thought was "Lenin's line" could the honor of the Russian Revolution be redeemed. Wolfe viewed the Russian purges, not as a cause for despair, but as a "cause for harder, cleaner, better, more revolutionary work."[9]

The Nazi-Soviet Pact in 1939 proved to be the ultimate betrayal for Wolfe, as it was for a generation of American Communists and communist sympathizers. The leaders of the Soviet state, who Wolfe had once thought would show mankind how to abolish war and lead the way to an age of universal peace and freedom, had paved the way for yet another world conflict. It had taken Wolfe a long time, indeed, he admitted, too long, to recognize the painful truth about Soviet communism. His disillusionment complete, Wolfe set out to re-examine the tumultuous events in which he had been caught since he first gave credibility to Lenin and the Bolsheviks. In 1939, he signed a contract to write an intellectual and biographical history of the Russian revolutionary movement. He thought at first that the project would take only a few years to complete, but it took almost a decade. Years of painstaking research and study taught Wolfe "the unreliability of witnesses and even documents, the need to master the Russian tongue and thought and culture, to search for the truths of the defeated, check them against the truths of the victorious, the available documentary records, and the inherent probabilities in the evaluation of each person and event."[10]

When it was published in 1948, Wolfe's *Three Who Made a Revolution* was immediately recognized as a masterpiece of the historian's craft. *Three Who Made a Revolution* was among the first books to strip away some of the Soviet mythology and reveal the real-life outlines of Lenin, Trotsky, and Stalin. In middle age, Wolfe had found a new vocation as a student of Russian history, politics, and culture. Henceforth, Wolfe was "doomed," as he put it, "to be bogged down in the Pripet Marshes like any other invader of Russia."[11]

Three Who Made a Revolution has endured as one of the classic works of Russian history. With more than 500,000 copies in print, the book has been translated into more than a score of languages, none of which pleased its author more than the Russian *samizdat* version. But even as he put the finishing touches to his first book on Russia, Wolfe realized he faced a serious problem. In *Three Who Made a Revolution*, Wolfe was able to take the story of Lenin and the Bolsheviks only to the outbreak of World War I. It was a book, Wolfe said, that "dealt with life lived in a narrow and deep channel whereas any continuation would involve a number of volumes since the picture widened to include a world war, two revolutions in Russia, the history of a regime, an analysis of its character, attempts at world revolution which would carry the story to many lands, etc., etc." Wolfe decided to undertake this much larger enterprise "as if I were to live forever or might wake up tomorrow morning to find myself dead."[12] He devoted more than a quarter of a century to his study of the Bolshevik's seizure of power and the regime Lenin established and Stalin perfected, publishing separate books and articles along the way whenever he was satisfied that these contributions could live a life of their own and be submitted to the judgment of his peers.[13] But the completion of a unified and cohesive biography of Lenin was sidetracked by a variety of other research and teaching obligations. Finally, in his last years, Wolfe returned to the biography of Lenin that he had started in 1939. He realized that his physical resources were failing and he wanted to write about Lenin one last time "before signing off."

Lenin and the Twentieth Century, as Wolfe planned to entitle the work, would tell "the story of a great man, his influence on the course of the history of his land and time, and his impact upon the history of the twentieth century." Before applying the label "great" to any historical figure, Wolfe said, the historian must demonstrate that history would have turned out very differently had not the individual appeared on the scene. Lenin was a history-making man because he changed the world into which he was born beyond recognition. Without him there would have been no bolshevik movement and no October Revolution. And without him, Wolfe concluded, the world might well be a less bleak and dangerous place than it is today. For Lenin was the architect of the historically unprecedented totalitarian state. Once an uncritical admirer of Lenin, Wolfe had blamed the wicked Stalin for everything that had gone wrong with the Russian Revolution. Years of study of Lenin's life showed Wolfe how wide of the mark his earlier assessment of the founder of bolshevism had been. Wolfe challenged the view that the epoch of Stalinist despotism and repression constituted a sharp break from Leninist traditions and practices. Much of the latter-day Stalinist totalitarianism, Wolfe argued, was implicit in the Leninist embryo. Lenin paved the way for Stalinism not only by devising the political system that made Stalin's tyranny possible but also by steadily advancing Stalin to posts of ever greater prominence and power in the party and the state. Wolfe's emphasis on the totalitarian element in Lenin's thought and actions remains his most important contribution to our understanding of the Soviet system.

Wolfe's long-awaited sequel to *Three Who Made a Revolution* remained unfinished at the time of his death in February 1977. The renowned author's papers and manuscripts were donated to the Hoover Institution on War, Revolution and Peace, where Wolfe spent his last years as a senior research fellow working on his study of Lenin and writing his own autobiography.

Among Wolfe's papers are a number of chapter-length studies and shorter essays that he wrote over some 35 years as part of his ongoing study of Lenin and the Russian Revolution. Together, the twelve examples of Bertram D. Wolfe's scholarship published here offer a mosaic of Lenin's life and an assessment of his historic significance as seen by one of America's most thorough and respected students of Soviet history, a scholar, as one of his contemporaries put it, "who will be remembered and honored as long as respect for truth prevails among those engaged in the study of the contemporary world."[14]

NOTES TO INTRODUCTION

1. Hoover Institution Archives, Bertram David Wolfe Papers, Box 1, File 1.

2. Bertram D. Wolfe, *A Life in Two Centuries* (New York: Stein & Day, 1981), p. 375.

3. Bertram David Wolfe Papers, Box 53, File 12.

4. Ibid., Box 23, File 7.

5. Ibid., Box 1, File 1.

6. Ibid., Box 24, File 12.

7. Ibid., Box 25, File 24.

8. Ibid.

9. Ibid., Box 23, File 25.

10. Stanford University News Service, press release, February 22, 1977.

11. Bertram David Wolfe Papers, Box 1, File 1.

12. Ibid.

13. Among Wolfe's books on Soviet history and politics were *Six Keys to the Soviet System* (Boston: Beacon Press, 1956); *Khrushchev and Stalin's Ghost* (New York: Praeger, 1957); *Marxism: 100 Years in the Life of a Doctrine* (New York: Dial Press, 1965); *Strange Communists I Have Known* (New York: Stein & Day, 1965); *The Bridge and the Abyss: The Troubled Friendship of V. I. Lenin and Maxim Gorky* (New York: Praeger, 1967); and *An Ideology in Power: Reflections on the Russian Revolution* (New York: Stein & Day, 1969).

14. Leonard Schapiro, in Wolfe, *A Life in Two Centuries*, p. 11.

1

LENIN:
THE RUSSIAN BACKGROUND

Russian despotism grew up in the immensity of Russia, as a response to the boundlessness of the Eurasian plain, the need to bind that vastness together in a single bureaucratic system, and to set up Russia's huge armies for defense and conquest on all her open frontiers. The great Eurasian plain opposes few obstacles to frost and wind and drought, to migrant hordes and marching armies. In earlier centuries most of the plain was dominated by Asiatic empires, Iranian, Turkish, and Mongol. As the last of these disintegrated, Muscovy spread out from the opposite end of the plain, expanding steadily over several centuries to become the largest land empire in the world. History presents no parallel to its vastness. The Roman Empire at its height would have been lost in it. If we add together the three greatest continuous land empires of the modern world, China, India, and the United States, the three together do not equal the extent of European and Asiatic Russia.

From the beginning the body of Russia grew too fast for its soul. In the words of its great historian, Klyuchevsky, "the state swelled up, the people grew feeble." Throughout most of Russia's history, as is again the case today, the state was stronger than society.

The land was strangely silent. During the centuries when England had its Shakespeare and its Marlowe, Italy its Dante and its Petrarch, France its Corneille and its Racine, Spain its Cervantes and its Lope de Vega, Russia had no voice at all. There was virtually no lay literature and nothing that could be regarded as public opinion. Only in the eighteenth century did the silent land begin to find its voice. Then, in the nineteenth, full-throated, it astonished the world.

Throughout most of her history, marching armies and hordes of invaders caused the Eurasian plain to be sparsely settled, particularly where armies continually clashed near its frontiers. In the more thickly populated West, feudal tenure had grown up on lands that were well populated, where "every rood of ground maintained its man." It represented on the whole a system of mutual obligations between vassal and lord, rather than of subjects to a centralized state. But in the comparatively depopulated Russian plain there was always land to spare. Hence the chief problem of statecraft was the artificial creation of fixity. The aim of the powerful centralized state was to fasten each man in his place and his station in life by enforced decree, where the recruiting sergeant and the tax collector could find him in order to raise and supply the great armies that Russia required for the defense of her open boundaries and the expansion of her power. Even as feudalism was disappearing in Western Europe, Russia in the eighteenth century was just beginning to perfect and fix firmly its special type of bondage in an empire in which land was limitless and sparsely occupied and fixity a bureaucratic-military necessity, a mode of governing and of waging war.

When Russia at last became articulate and aware of itself and began to ponder that which made it different from the West, its first thought was of *raskreposhchenie,* generally translated *emancipation* but more accurately rendered *the loosening of the bonds,* those bonds by which the autocratic state tied each man to his place and to his station.

The main reason for the economic and political backwardness of this great land, despite its resources in human beings and in natural wealth, lay in the preservation of bondage until beyond the middle of the nineteenth century. In 1861, as originally he had been bound by decree of the state, the serf was now emancipated by Imperial decree, together with some portion of the land he had hitherto tilled in bondage. But vestiges of the bondage system lingered on until after the abortive Revolution of 1905, when a semi-constitutional order developed and society began to gain independence from and growing strength as against the autocratic state. During the year 1917, after the Tsar fell and the Provisional Government was set up, all the remaining bonds were loosened at once. "The freest government in the world," Lenin proclaimed it, even as he prepared to overthrow it and seize power for his dictatorship.[1]

Then, under Lenin and his successors, once more the state became stronger than society. Indeed, the state Lenin founded strove to become co-extensive with society. Society itself became completely atomized, with no non-governmental organizations, political parties, trade unions, or non-governmental press of its own.

Under the tsars the state had been powerful and autocratic, but it had concerned itself primarily with a monopoly of political power, although, for reasons which we shall consider in a moment, it made frequent excursions into the economic field. There were many aspects of life in which the tsars could not, and did not, seek to interfere. Thus, for all its might, it was still a limited despotism, that is, a despotism that limited its intervention to certain aspects of life, ignoring others. How Lenin came to the conclusion that there was no aspect of life that he should not seek to control and direct, how and why he overthrew the "freest government in the world," how the widespread yet in many senses still limited despotism of the tsars was replaced by the totalitarianism of Lenin and his successors, what there was in Lenin's character and doctrine that made him aspire to the total organization and total direction of life, is the central theme of our story.

We are prone to think of classic despotism or autocracy as essentially conservative, as seeking in the main to preserve the status quo. Yet Russian autocracy had a more fluctuating and irregular history. In the course of its development into the greatest land empire in the world, the duchy of Moscow had many times to battle for its very existence with the technologically more advanced countries of the West. At such junctures, the problem of the autocracy changed from that of preserving the status quo to that of "modernization" or "Westernization" by oriental-despotic methods for the purposes of meeting the technically superior foe. In each such crisis, the state became an innovator, the primary propelling agent of economic transformation for the purposes of conserving its power and waging desperate war. Each such propulsion was as ruthless as it was sporadic, a revolution from above which always strained the resources of a poor but populous land beyond its limits, raised armies of unprecedented size, put formidable burdens upon a given generation of Russian people, and set obstacles to any attempt on their part to evade their burdens by escape to the depopulated frontiers of the empire.

Such periods of extreme exactions and exertions, of which the reign of Peter the Great (1682–1725) is in some sense a model, were likely to be followed by periods of reaction, lassitude, and stagnation, until the next military emergency. Thus did Russian autocracy fluctuate between a conservative holding operation to maintain the status quo and an active, if one-sided, policy of revolutionizing Russia forcefully and despotically from above for the purposes of power and war. Lenin was to picture his regime at times as modelled on the paradigm of the regime of Peter the Great, which had "westernized" Russia by the methods of "oriental despotism."

> . . . our task [wrote Lenin] is to teach ourselves the state capitalism of the Germans, to imitate it *with all our might,* not to spare *dictatorial* methods in order to hasten the copying of Westernism by barbarous Russia, not shrinking from barbarous methods of struggle against barbarism.[2]

The greatest industrializer of Russia prior to Lenin and Stalin was Peter the Great. Overnight, alongside the cottage industry, he created a great textile and clothing industry to produce uniforms and sails for men of war, and a great iron and steel industry to produce bayonets, cannon and other munitions.

Later tsars met similar crises in similar fashion. Thus it was in the nineteenth century that the failure of Russia's massive armies of illiterate serfs to acquit themselves well in the Crimean War against the diminutive armies of the freer West caused Alexander II to abolish bondage by *ukaz.* Like the industrialization of Peter, this was a "revolution from above." Again in the closing years of the nineteenth century, for the logistics of modern warfare, Alexander III (1881–1894) and Nicholas II (1894–1917) backed Count Witte, onetime railway stationmaster, in the great construction of Russia's railways by the state, the absorption by the state of those lines which were privately owned, and the encouragement by subsidy of an iron and steel industry. Since Russia's banks by their size and their practices were unfit for capital investment, the Russian state became the great investment banker for heavy industry, too. The state's leading position in the economy (its possession of what Lenin would call "the commanding heights") was further strengthened by the conversion of industry to war after August 1914. What the Bolsheviks took over after 1917, even before Lenin had nationalized a single industry on his own, was the largest state economic machine in the world.

A characteristic formation of nineteenth-century Russia was the intelligentsia, a layer of Russian society to which by training and temperament Lenin belonged, though in the end he was to be the intelligentsia's undoing. The Russian term is derived from the Latin *intelligentia,* meaning intelligence. A whole stratum of Russian society applied this somewhat arrogant term to itself, considering itself to be the intelligence and voice of unthinking and voiceless Russia. Its members felt themselves alone and beleaguered in a land where neither court, nor nobility, nor merchants, nor peasants, were cultured or valued culture.

The Russian intelligentsia was something quite different from the educated and professional classes of the West, who by and large were integrated into their respective societies. Quite different, too, from the officials, technicians, managers, propagandists, artists, writers, spiritual policemen, and spiritual servitors of party and state in present-day Russia.

The first recruits for this unique layer of nineteenth-century Russian society came from a cultured minority of "conscience-stricken" sons of the landowning nobility who were repelled by the uncultured nature of the landowners as a class and who felt that their own privileges were built upon the foundation of the poverty and the dark ignorance of the Russian folk. Within a generation recruits were added from more plebeian layers of society, sons of priests and minor officials, publicists, and particularly seminary students, and various other groups extruded from an uncultured society in rapid transition yet structured in fixed medieval estates, in which they and their kind found no place and no understanding.

Coming thus from various social classes, its members nevertheless formed a class by themselves with a cohesion, a moral code and way of life, even a distinct appearance of their own. The peasants, who felt a latent antagonism and mistrust towards them, could instantly recognize an *intelligent* when they saw one, even if he came to them dressed in a peasant blouse. "They mainly do not see in us people," wrote one of the members of the intelligentsia, "we are for them monsters of human shape, without God in our souls."[3]

The intelligentsia was not held together by sharing a common relation to property or income level, nor by a common occupation or economic function or social origin of status, but by a common belief in the sovereign efficacy of ideas as giving meaning and shape to life, and by a common alienation from the existing society of their day.

They scorned practical work and the very thought of retaining a place, or making a place for themselves, in a society which was not in accord with their sovereign ideas and which they held to be a thing of evil. Their attitude towards all that existed in actual society was one of total rejection. Some of them were in love with the future and some with the past, but none with the present. The idealized past which the one group dreamed of restoring was as unreal as the idealized future which stirred the longings of the other.

The present, for its part, reciprocated by finding no place for them in its midst. They were—a characteristic Russian term—"superfluous men," and the best of them showed their virtue by being aware of their superfluity, thus misappraising themselves at the same time as they exalted themselves by their belief in the sovereign efficacy of their intelligence and their ideas. Thus the intelligentsia alternated between self-abasement and self-exaltation.

The Russian intellectual, or rather, to distinguish him from the familiar figure of the West, perhaps we should use his own term, the Russian *intelligent*, did not love his neighbor or his enemy, being alienated from both, but gave his love to abstract humanity. As Petrashevsky, an early landowner *intelligent*, put it, "Unable to find anything either in the women or in the men [around me] worthy of my adherence, I have turned to devoting myself to the service of humanity." From Petrashevsky, who founded the harmless discussion circle in which Dostoevsky was arrested when it was raided by the police, to Lenin who applied the death penalty to whole categories of men, the same formula applies. They tended to love mankind in the abstract, but to be indifferent, and often ruthless, in dealing with the fate of actual individual men.

The quest of the intelligentsia was a restless and unceasing one, for they took up one great idea after another in tandem fashion, the prevailing idea changing rapidly, several times in the same generation, sometimes as often as twice or more in a single decade. What they were searching for was a single and integral outlook that would give an answer to all the questions of life, reconcile theoretical reason with practical, unite standards of personal conduct with norms of justice, and give a philosophical basis for a regenerating social ideal. No idea less than a *Weltanschauung* was acceptable to them, and any idea they accepted, however unsuited, they turned into a *Weltanschauung*.

The questions they asked were as vast as the wide horizons of Russia: What is Russia? Why are we so different from Western Europe and from Asia? What is the meaning of our history? What is our destiny among the nations? What was the thought of the Creator concerning Russia's mission in history when he created our land? How do we inform our country with our sovereign idea and reshape it in the image of our ideal? How shall we serve the people and make up to them for their deprivations and our privileges? What holy truth is concealed in the people from which we must learn? Is a cultured class justified in the face of an uncultured mass? What lessons can we learn from the West and what is it Russia's destiny and duty to teach the West? How can we bring our backward country abreast of the present and propel it into the future which our thought foreknows?

Both government and intelligentsia borrowed from the West and each borrowing was in its own way one-sided. In a sense they were symmetrical opposites in their one-sidedness.

One of the advantages of technological backwardness is that the backward land, once it is institutionally and financially ready for that great spurt forward that is known as industrialization, can borrow the most advanced techniques without the many obsolete and obsolescent plants that burden the more advanced industrial country which serves as model. This technological borrowing, as we have already noted, was largely the work of the autocracy bent on making its armies and its heavy industry and transport adequate to cope with the superior if less numerous Western armies. But it was a one-sided acquisition of foreign techniques because the autocracy was not interested in borrowing ideas or general culture. It had no use for the spirit of inquiry and debate, the seedbed out of which science and industrial technology developed in the West. Still less was it interested in borrowing that individual initiative and independence from the state of economic and cultural activity, and that spirit of freedom which nourished and fertilized science and culture.

When the intelligentsia turned to the West, on the other hand, it was precisely ideas that it borrowed. But it did so with a one-sidedness of its own. At least until after Lenin took power into his hands, and with it responsibility for government, industry and war, the intelligentsia had no interest in technology, weaponry, or the practical application of ideas.[4]

The intelligentsia borrowed one idea at a time and, while the particular idea was in vogue among them, made it sovereign with an attachment that was fanatical and complete. The borrowed idea was invested with a single-minded passion with which it was not normally or naturally held in the West, a passion more suitable to the creation of a powerful, emotion-charged literature than to a series of rational conclusions.

Moreover, the borrowed idea was taken out of the context in which it was only one hypothesis among other rival hypotheses and in which its truth was regarded as tentative, relative, and subject to question. The idea was adopted without its shadings and qualifications, without the surrounding ambience of challenging, competing and offsetting ideas, without the faintest notion that one gets the most out of a hypothesis by challenging it. There was no feeling for the "free marketplace of ideas" that nourished and corrected and gave perspective to thought in the West. Skepticism was un-Russian, and in any case excluded one from the fraternity of the intelligentsia.

Even the natural science, or philosophical idealism or materialism, when they became the rage in Russia, was each in turn treated as if it were a theological dogma and a moral shibboleth. One who rejected science, or one who when Darwinism was in vogue turned to Lamarck, was not to be argued with, reasoned with, or corrected, but was treated as morally suspect and reprehensible and cast out from the intelligentsia as unworthy. One cannot really understand the tone of Lenin's discussion of even such abstruse questions as matter and energy, perception and thought, in his book entitled *Materialism and Empiriocriticism,*[5] if one does not take into account the quasi-religious emotion, moral passion, and exclusivist one-sidedness with which the Russian intelligentsia invested its ideas. Each idea was made over into a jealous god brooking no rival; into an absolute; an *alleinseligmach-endes* dogma or total and all-embracing creed from which alone can come salvation. One did not stake one's scholarly reputation on an idea (the highest stakes played for in the West); one staked one's soul.

Since all impulses toward forward movement in Russia had come from above, and since in the depths of the people there was only incomprehension for this new social layer of cultured Russians, at first the intelligentsia turned to the Autocrat with petitions, suggestions, and plans for the making of Russia. Indeed, Catherine II and Alexander I were in their fashion intellectuals, but intellectuals tainted and transformed by the possession of power.

The great reforms connected with the emancipation of the serfs also came from the autocracy, from Alexander II, against the opposition of his nobles.

But the members of the intelligentsia were by temperament extremists so that even such sweeping reforms as Alexander's seemed meager and unsatisfactory to them. Moreover, there was one reform that the Autocrat would not contemplate, namely the granting of some initiative to society, or to that narrow layer of society which called itself "the public" and called its opinion "public opinion." For this, the Autocrat was convinced that Russia was not ripe and, by its nature, not even suited.

When the intelligentsia began to meet together to discuss their extreme ideas and urge them upon the Russian state, the answer they received was prohibition by the police, arrest, denial of the right of residence in the two capitals, Moscow and St. Petersburg, or deportation to some remote part of the land.[6] Beginning as dreamers and would-be reformers, they were constantly punished for mere dreaming and discussing, and virtually forbidden to dream. Thus they were driven into rebelliousness, a mood so general that before long the very words *student* and *intelligent* tended to become synonymous with rebel or revolutionary.

Half in fear, half in desperation, they turned to the unlettered, uncomprehending folk to gain support for their maximalist ideas against the autocracy. Spurred by a false and wish-fulfilling image of the peasant mass, they indulged in demagogy, flattery and incitement of the people against the very foundations of their culture and traditions. When it was already perhaps too late, one of their number, Sergei Bulgakov, was to write in *Vekhi* in 1909, "Revolution is the spiritual child of the intelligentsia and consequently its history is a historical judgment on that intelligentsia." If he had added to the maximalism of the intelligentsia the stubborn unyieldingness of the autocracy, the impotence and corruption surrounding the last autocrat, and the strains of a war that put arms into the hands of the peasants, his verdict would have been more complete. But it was not like the intelligentsia, even when sobering up, to credit other factors for the making of history besides the sovereign power of ideas.

As the intelligentsia turned to the folk for support against the autocracy, their attitude was, as always, compounded of self-abasement (worship of the folk as the repository of truth and virtue) and self-exaltation (worship of themselves as the possessors of the one sovereign idea—whichever it was at the moment—without which the people would perish).

"Socialism will triumph," wrote one of their number, Chaadaev, "not because it is right, but because we are wrong." "The thirst for culture," Dostoevsky proclaimed, "is an aristocratic thirst." The adjective was meant to be demeaning.

With a greater sense of irony and a less extremist temperament, Turgenev described the relation of intelligentsia and folk in this bit of dialogue:

"The cultured Russian stands before the muzhik, makes a profound reverence and says, 'Heal me, for I am perishing of moral corruption.'

"And the muzhik makes a reverence no less profound, replying, 'Help me, I am perishing of ignorance.' "

The great novelist Tolstoy, deserting art in his later years, set it down that "a pair of boots is more important than all your madonnas, and all your refined talk about Shakespeare."

Thus the nihilistic attitude towards culture and tradition and the exaltation of the production of material things above the works of the spirit were prepared by the knights of the spirit themselves in the course of their crusade for the salvation of Russia and the folk. Bolshevism did not invent, it merely adapted, used, and misused, the spiritual nihilism that characterized the nineteenth-century intelligentsia.

When their efforts to enlighten and petition the Autocrat were so rudely rebuffed, and their efforts to rouse the people received no comprehension or answering echo, they became yet more reckless and irresponsible in their dreams, for the practicality or feasibility of which they did not need to concern themselves since there was no prospect of fulfillment.

Thought and feeling, unable to run over into action, accumulated like a dammed-up stream. Over and over they solved in agonizing theory problems that in practice they were forbidden to touch. Against the dam a turbulent stream of successive "solutions" flowed and were blocked, while the potential behind the dam rose steadily higher and higher.

The salvation of Russia and of the world was to come through a succession of philosophies; through natural science; through the literature of social criticism; through non-resistance to evil; through a return to primitive Christianity; through emptying the spirit of all its possessions, physical and cultural; through the village commune; through the religious truth hidden in the folk; through love of the people and going to the people; through the rejection of government and law; through anarchism; through agrarian socialism; through Marxism—whatever the gospel of the moment, its disciples adhered to it utterly, were ready to live by it, die for it, remake the world completely according to its blueprint. In its ardor and frustration the entire intelligentsia took as its device the words of Dostoevsky, "In all things I go to the uttermost extreme; my life long I have never been acquainted with moderation."

They lived in the most tenuous contact with their environment and actual reality, acquiring the power of living by ideas alone. Since their ideas could not lead to political action, they flowed into literature and thought where the comparatively mild, limited, and inept tsarist censorship found it impossible to restrain them.[7] They developed what one of their number, Nicholas Berdyaev, has called "a thoroughly true-to-type intolerance" of all and an intolerance no less intense of deviation from the prevailing sovereign idea of the moment, a deviation which they condemned as renegade. "Only so," continues Berdyaev, who, after exile by Lenin from Russia in 1922, acquired some ability to see the intelligentsia from without while remaining a part of it, "only so could it preserve itself in a hostile world, only thanks to its fanaticism could it weather persecution and retain its characteristic features."

Though the intelligentsia became avowedly atheistic, their atheism, like other dogmas, was charged with religious emotion and had a religious quality. Paradoxically, atheism arose in them out of a love of God which would not permit them to believe that He could allow such evil and suffering as they beheld. They were not prepared to accept so humble a solution as incomprehension of His ways, nor admit that divine goodness could permit unalloyed evil and atrocious suffering, so they ended by rejecting Him with the same fervor with which they had formerly accepted Him. Just as they had believed that the Autocrat on the throne, with a simple *ukaz*, could change the world from evil to good, and when he failed them they rejected him, so it was with God. Thus total rejection of the world around them led to total rejection of anything transcending it, leaving them only their sovereign ideas to live by.

Their fanaticism served as a surrogate for their older faith and was invested with many of the same religious qualities. They made a gospel of their particular brand of salvation. They possessed singleness, exclusivism, dogma, orthodoxy, heresy, renegation, schism, excommunication, prophets, masters and disciples, authorities, vocation, asceticism, readiness to sacrifice one's self, others, and the existing world to their doctrine. They offered a total attitude towards and a total explanation of the world, and they possessed the ability to suffer all things in order to bear witness to their faith. Not to be a materialist, when materialism was sovereign, was, as we have noted, to be morally suspect rather than intellectually mistaken. Heresy or rival doctrine was worse than ignorance or error; it was apostasy.

So to a Lenin, Marxism would not be an hypothesis or a theory of history and social development, but a science, or rather, *the* science, all-demanding, all-explaining, and all-absorbing. Lenin talked and thought and worked and contrived revolution during every working hour, and in his dreams, as one of his onetime associates wrote, "he dreamed only of revolution."

An *ipse dixit* of Marx or Engels was to Lenin an irrefutable proof. To doubt even one of the patristic utterances was a sign of moral turpitude and an enlistment in the service of evil. In his big book ostensibly treating of some philosophical questions of the natural sciences, he wrote: "In this philosophy of Marxism, cast from a single block of steel, you cannot eliminate a single basic premise, a single essential part, without deviating from objective truth, without falling into the arms of bourgeois-reactionary falsehood."

NOTES TO CHAPTER 1

1. Lenin referred to this freedom in four separate articles or addresses. The passages are reproduced in his works, 3rd Russian ed., 20:76; 4th Russian ed., 24:4 and 61; 25:333.

2. *Pravda*, May 9–11, 1918, reprinted in Lenin's *Collected Works*, 27:307. Except where otherwise stated, the 4th Russian edition of Lenin's works is used throughout this essay. Only where this edition omits something is the 3rd or 5th used. Italics, here as throughout, are in Lenin's original. The German "state capitalism" which Lenin refers to here (elsewhere he calls it German war-time state socialism) is the system of the organization of the German economy for military purposes during the First World War.

3. Mikhail Osipovich Gershenzon in *Vekhi* (St. Petersburg, 1909). *Vekhi* (Landmarks), a symposium, was the most complete stocktaking the Russian intelligentsia ever took of itself when some of its most articulate members were sobered into reflection by the turbulent experiences of 1905.

4. To be sure, there was occasionally a dissenting voice among intellectuals who thought that their use of ideas should be "practical" and "constructive" and involve systematic application to the "dirty work at home." But such isolated voices were silenced by scorn or drowned in a chorus of disapproval. They were greeted with epithets, *philistine, bourgeois,* or even *turncoat.* Only in the twentieth century, particularly after 1905 and during the patriotic upsurge of the first year of the First World War, were such constructive elements numerous enough to make their presence felt. And then, when the problem arose of appealing to the masses in uniform, the constructive section of the intelligentsia was no match for the destructive section in the simplifying field of demagogy. This helps to explain the weakness of the liberal and democratic parties in the year 1917.

5. This excursion of Lenin into philosophy takes up 346 angry and scornful pages, making up the entire fourteenth volume of his *Collected Works.* For its meaning in his political struggles within his faction, see the author's *Three Who Made a Revolution* (New York, 1948), chap. 19, "Lenin as Philosopher."

6. The Petrashevsky circle, for example, met to read and discuss the utopian socialist fantasies of Fourier. Though these involved no change in or challenge to the regime, but merely the thought of setting up little colonies of perfect living, the members of the circle were seized and sentenced to death, the death sentence being commuted only at the last nerve-wracking moment with, as is well known, a permanent effect on the spirit of its most famous member, Dostoevsky.

7. The tsarist censorship was more severe with the works of Auguste Comte than with those of Karl Marx. *Das Kapital* was published legally in Russian translation, the first translation into any language, because its abstruseness and physical bulk showed that it was meant for scholars and the educated, not the masses.

2

A PARTY OF
A NEW TYPE

*He keeps chiseling—chiseling at the same spot—finally he chisels through.
People become aware that a man has a high opinion of himself, that he gives
orders—that's the main thing, he gives orders; consequently he's bound to be
right, and one is compelled to obey him. All our schematics established themselves in just this way.*—TURGENEV IN *Smoke*

Wer einst den Blitz zu zünden hat muss lange—Wolke sein.—NIETZSCHE

The age of total wars called for new leaders. Men of modest aims, transaction
and compromise—the reasonable, knowing, sagely cynical moderate men
who had played their parts in the concert of Europe according to the view
that *politics is the art of the possible*—were not suited to the total mobi-
lization of body and spirit and the waging of war "until final victory."
Needed now were reckless spenders of lives and treasure, men of supernal
energy, uninhibited demagogy, "charismatic" attributes.[1] The crisis that was
to overwhelm Russia in the third year of the war was in great measure due
to the refusal of an unimaginative and unimpressive tsar and a domineering
and unloved tsarina to dismiss their aging retinue of routinary bureaucrats
and favorites and put at the helm new men equal to the new tasks. In
Austria-Hungary, too, an aging, moldering court paralyzed the war effort
until the monarchy crumbled.[2]

But in most lands, those who had blundered into the war gave way to
those who could wage it. The men who would dictate the treaties at Brest
and Versailles seemed a different breed from those at the helm in 1914.
Where an old leader was not replaced it was generally because he showed
the ability, like the nation, to go through a transformation.

All institutions were transformed, from industry, which became in essence
war industry, to finance, which worked not with calculated revenues and
expenditures but with astronomical deficits, from the church of the Prince
of Peace, which learned to bless the sword, to the social democracy, which
replaced class struggle by civil peace and sacred union. Whether their deaths
were timely or not, gone forever was the world of Jean Jaurès and August
Bebel.

From Revolution and Reality: Essays on the Origin and Fate of the Soviet Union, by Bertram
D. Wolfe. Copyright 1981 The University of North Carolina Press. Reprinted by permission
of the publisher.

In its way, history was kind to these two in letting them die before their day had quite ended. The others groped in the new darkness—grieved, shocked, robbed of certitudes, demoralized to their depths. They might wave flags or marshal self-justifying quotations, but something essential had gone out of their simple faith in class struggle, internationalism, peace, and socialism.

All but one! Lenin did not have to change his temper, nor his theories. Since the Russo-Japanese War and its aftermath of revolutionary unrest, he had held that war was the fruitful mother of revolution. Far from despairing, he was possessed by a new rage . . . and a new certainty. Rage at the great party of Marx, Engels, Bebel, and Kautsky, which he had expected to lead the international struggle in war as in peacetime. Certainty that the bourgeoisie, having begun this universal war, would never be able to end it. War was the begetter of revolution; world war would beget world revolution. Not "they," but the revolution would end it. That revolution with which he lived day and night, which possessed his waking hours, and of which in his sleep he dreamed—it would come in *his* time, out of *this* war.

"Great historical questions," he had written in 1905, "are settled only by force."[3] The thought had pleased him so much that on a number of occasions he repeated it. When the Balkan Wars came in 1912 and 1913, hope stirred in him that the war might spread, at least to Russia and Austria-Hungary. This would be a "very useful trick for the revolution in all of Eastern Europe," he wrote to Gorky, "but it is hardly likely that Franz Josef and Nikolasha will give us this pleasure."[4]

Not for him was the foreboding with which Marx and Engels had contemplated the prospect of universal war. Nor the dismay and disillusion which oppressed French and German socialists when they failed to prevent it. Now had come a time, Lenin wrote, "for heavy hob-nailed boots."[5] In these boots, he prepared to step from the Russian onto the world stage, to offer his analysis, outlook, tactics, ideas, his "rockhard, irreconcilable" temper, his personal leadership, as the only proper ones to the "newest age of wars and revolutions."

We must now take a closer look at this unique leader whose ideas and methods, whose moral code, whose attitude toward the civilization into which he was born, toward his native country, and toward war itself, have contributed so profoundly to the shaping of our age.[6]

Vladimir Ilyich Ulianov was forty-four and at the height of his powers. In a way peculiar to his self-confident, authoritative temperament and deeply Russian milieu, he had been "old" since his middle twenties. All memorialists agree to this, as do his own writings. A. N. Potresov, close colleague of Lenin's earliest political career and member of a *troika* with him from 1895 to 1903, falters when he tries to describe "the young Lenin," for "he was

young only in his passport."[7] Even in that early time there was the bald
dome with the thin fringe of dark-reddish hair, the sparse reddish moustache
and beard, the "unyouthful hoarse voice" enunciating certitudes, judging
people, selecting, admonishing, mocking, annihilating, binding to himself a
little band of respectful followers, many of them older than he, who regarded
him as the Russian folk regard a wise and revered elder. Before he was out
of his twenties, they were calling him Starik—"The Old Man." "The Old
Man is wise," they would chuckle exultantly, even when the wisdom lay in
some not-too-scrupulous polemical thrust or maneuver. Lenin accepted the
title Starik as if it were the most natural thing in the world for an authoritative
young man to be thus addressed by his contemporaries and elders. Many
of his early letters he begins, "Starik writing," or ends with the signature,
Starik. Even to Gleb Krzhizhanovsky, intimate comrade-in-arms since 1895,
who had lived near him in Siberian exile for seventeen months and one of
the only two political persons whom Lenin addressed by the intimate second
person singular ty, he nevertheless would open a letter with "Starik writing"
and close with "Ves' tvoj Starik" (All yours, the Old Man).[8]

Furthermore, this youthful "patriarch" was addressed by the members
of his circle—many of them older and longer in the movement than he—
not by his first name and patronymic (Vladimir Ilyich would have been the
customary method of address), but by his patronymic alone (Ilyich). When
his followers spoke among themselves about him, they called him Ilyich,
too. His youth, and the supposed equality of comradeship in the socialist
movement, made this form of address strange. No other Russian political
leader was called so. Not even Plekhanov, older by a decade and a half and
honored by all—Lenin included—as the "Master" and the "Father of Russian Marxism," was ever addressed or referred to as Valentinovich, in place
of Georgij Valentinovich. In many a Russian village, there was a respected
elder addressed thus by patronymic alone, as a mark of intimacy, respect
and affection. In Lenin's case the element of intimacy was lacking, for who
would dream of slapping Ilyich on the back or expect to be slapped on the
back by him? Both the Ilyich and Starik were signs of his authoritative and
charismatic predominance, a socialist leader of a different sort with followers
of a different sort. Furthermore, both titles reveal, perhaps without their
users being conscious of it, how deeply his group was saturated with habits
inherited from the Orthodox Russian folk. Stranger still, and to the sensitive
a little repugnant, even Krupskaia called him Ilyich, as if she were a worshipful disciple, not his wife.[9]

A second trait setting Lenin apart from his associates was his absorption
with the mechanics and dynamics of organization. In a world where most
intellectuals were in love with ideas, and accustomed—whether by temperament or the pressure of bitter circumstances—to a gap between dream

and deed, Lenin was an *organization man*, indeed, *the* organization man, of whatever movements he planned or took part in. He was an enemy alike to the slippered sloth and to the dusk-to-dawn discussion of the Russian intellectuals, as well as to the "spontaneous" and "unreliable" flare-ups, subsidings, and conception of the Russian masses' own interests. All his life he was at work on a machine to harness the force of the waves and tides, to convert their fluctuating, unreckonable rise and fall into a single stream of energy. It was his aim, as he wrote, "to collect and concentrate all the drops and streamlets of popular excitement that are called forth by Russian conditions . . . into one single, gigantic flood." Tidily, yet passionately, he assumed the task of "choosing the people who are necessary and verifying the practical execution of decisions." In a world of intellectuals who lived by ideas, organization was his idea. "In its struggle for power, the proletariat has no other weapon but organization." "*Now* we have become an organized party, and that means the creation of power, the transformation of the authority of ideas into the authority of power, the subordination of the lower party organs to the higher ones." Amidst men dedicated to dreams, organization was his dream. "Give me an organization of revolutionaries," he cried, echoing Archimedes, "and I will turn Russia upside down."[10]

When, at the so-called Second Congress, which was called to form a party, delegate Popov spoke of the future Central Committee in liturgical language as a "Spirit, omnipresent and one," Lenin cried out from his seat, "Not Spirit, but *Fist*."[11] Before there was a party congress or a central committee, Lenin was already dreaming of this, his fist, which would hold all reins in its grasp, control all levers and springs of action. In 1902, a year before the congress, he wrote:

> The Committee should lead *all* aspects of the local movement and direct *all* local institutions, forces and resources of the party. . . . Discussion of all party questions, of course, will take place also in the district circles, but the *deciding* of all general questions of the local movement should be done only by the Committee. The independence of the district groups, it follows, would be permitted only in questions of the technique of transmitting and distributing. The composition of the district groups should be determined by the Committee, i.e., the Committee designates one or two of its members (or even those not members of the Committee) as delegates to such and such a district, and entrusts these delegates with *setting up the district group*, all the members of which should be in their turn confirmed . . . in their positions by the Committee. The district group is a local branch of the Committee, receiving its powers only from the latter.[12]

Thus the Central Committee was to be the brain, the local organizations the limbs; the committee would decide, the locals execute; the committee would designate and confirm the local leaders in their posts, then the local leaders would in due course become delegates to a congress which would approve the Central Committee which had designated them. Such a Central Committee would be spirit and fist in one.

To his associates (as distinct from his admiring followers) there was something disconcerting in this zealotry of centralization. Yet their minds were on other aspects of the movement, its doctrine, its theory, its journalistic exposition. Organization was an unattractive concern. Not unwillingly, they handed over its practical burdens to this self-appointed, dedicated expert on organization. For their part, they dreamed of the day when Russia would know sufficient liberty so that the masses of workingmen might form their own organizations and democratically control and designate their central organs, which would then serve and obey rather than utilize and command the working class. But in the meanwhile Russia was police-ridden, and proper socialist organization was well nigh impossible. "Whether this revolutionary practice," Potresov was to write later, "which had not been so much experienced as thought up in the head of its future organizer, was really the practice which corresponded with the aims and methods of international social democracy, it was still difficult to judge." Later Lenin's associates "had to pay dearly for this misunderstanding."

The others might dream of the day when Russia would be free enough for the workingmen to organize freely and freely select their officials and determine their own program. Then the party, they thought, would become a simple instrument of the class, its creature and its servant, willing, expert, and dedicated to the task of helping the working class to achieve its own aims and its own freely decided goals. But Lenin did not see it that way. This was to him not Marxism, but a species of treason to Marxism. This was "bourgeois politics," as he wrote in one of his most uncompromising, and to his colleagues most incomprehensible, early utterances: "The task of the bourgeois politician is to 'assist the economic struggle of the proletariat.' The task of the socialist is to make the economic struggle assist the socialist movement and the victory of the revolutionary labor party."[13]

Could authoritarianism go further? To the question, do the workers exist for the party or does the party exist for the workers, Lenin had already found his sui generis, uncompromising answer.[14]

At first Lenin did not have the faintest idea that his concepts of organization and of the relation of the Central Committee to party and party to class were to set him apart from his fellow Marxists and embroil him in a lifelong war with them, which would end on opposite sides of a barricade.

He had always regarded Plekhanov as his teacher and one of the two greatest Marxists (Kautsky being the other). Until 1903 he looked on the Marxists of his own generation as peers and partners. From 1895 to 1900 he formed a troika or "triple alliance," as he called it, with two close comrades, his future Menshevik opponents, Martov and Potresov. It was the first of a series of a dozen triumvirates which he was to set up in the course of a lifetime to give the cover of collective leadership to his strongly original ideas on organization and his de facto one-man leadership. But this first troika differed from all the subsequent troikas in one respect: despite Lenin's headstrong self-assurance and confidence in the correctness of the least of his ideas, there was about this first troika a sense of equal partnership which would be lacking in all the others.

While in exile in Siberia, where he was until early 1900, Lenin worked out in meticulous detail plans for a Marxist journal to be published abroad and smuggled into Russia. His "triple alliance" would associate with itself the prestige and wisdom of that older generation, led by Plekhanov, which had been living in foreign exile since the beginning of the eighties. That would give the new journal an editorial board of six—three "elders" to give prestige and theoretical wisdom, three "youngsters" to supply practical organization, editorial and clandestine distribution activity.

The elders, Plekhanov, Axelrod, and Vera Zasulich, living out their home-sick lives isolated from Russia, were delighted with this energetic young man with a practical bent for organization. To be sure, there was a nasty moment when Plekhanov, taking it for granted that he would be the editor of the new journal, found that Lenin had come to the same conclusion about himself. Plekhanov was haughty, Lenin in a "rage" or "fury," a kind of overwhelming storm such as would well up in him from the depths of his being at intervals throughout his life.[15]

In a report to his faction, "How the Spark Was Nearly Extinguished,"[16] a document which takes up twenty-five pages in his *Collected Works* and is written in language more suited to a Russian novel than a political report, Lenin told how he had been "enamored" of Plekhanov, and "had courted him out of the great love I bore him. . . . Never, never in my life," he continued, "have I regarded any other man with such sincere respect and reverence . . . never stood before anyone with such humility, never been so brutally spurned. At times I thought I should burst into tears." But neither veneration or love, nor grief or humility suggested to him that Plekhanov, and not he, should be the editor. "My infatuation disappeared as if by magic . . . An enamored youth received from the object of his love a bitter lesson: to regard all persons without sentiment; to keep a stone in one's sling."

At that moment, the "youth" grew up. He never spoke of himself as a youth again. On the granite of his character, the lesson then engraved would last a lifetime. Three years later, when he was outvoted at a party congress on the organization question, he would show that he could "regard without sentiment" not only the "elders" but the other two members of his trium-virate as well. In 1900, however, the "lovers' quarrel" was still patched up with a cold agreement to live together "without infatuation"—with Lenin having his way.

Iskra would be printed in Germany, where Lenin lived, not Switzerland, where Plekhanov made his home. Lenin's wife was to be its secretary, keep the confidential addresses, code, uncode, develop the invisible ink, handle correspondence with the underground, consult with Lenin, and, on his order, dispatch items of correspondence to the others. Lenin assumed the burden of rewriting correspondence from Russia into articles, the tasks of answering most of them, assigning themes to the other editors subject to their approval, nagging contributors, dummying, proofreading (usually with Martov's help), cutting, arguing with authors to get revisions. He wrote the exhortations and instructions to the agents in Russia, developed the apparatus for smuggling, dispatched escapees and exiles to become agents, selected people to come abroad, be briefed by him, and return again to Russia. His fellow editors were grateful that he took upon his single shoulders these ungrateful tasks. Thus, from the outset, Lenin was master of the *apparat* which he himself had conceived.

He was better than any of the other five at his self-chosen chores. Plekhanov had a wider-ranging mind and more learning in Marxist theory, Vera Zasulich more concern with the sufferings of the masses, Axelrod more respect for the autonomy and dignity of the workers' organizations; Martov was a better journalist, Potresov a better provider of funds—mostly from his own private inherited fortune. But Lenin was the systematic, doctrinaire thinker on organization questions and the fulfiller of his own doctrines.

Moreover, it was he who had conceived an especially large, indeed unique role for their journal. Plekhanov, Martov, or Potresov could have edited it, too, but it would have had another character. On the masthead was the old message of hope from the Decembrists to Pushkin: "Out of the spark (*Iskra*) shall come the flame." To Lenin this was more than a figure of speech. *Iskra* was to be "an enormous pair of bellows that would blow every spark of popular indignation into a flame." It was to be "not only the collective agitator but the collective organizer." It was to become the guardian of the purity of doctrine, the destroyer of rival revolutionary theories (heresies in Lenin's mind) and rival movements (enemies to him). It was to be "the scaffolding" of an all-Russian revolutionary party, the convoker of a unifying and homogenizing all-national congress, for the party that should issue from it must be not only unified but uniform, not only integrated but systematized, rigorously intolerant of variety, pluralism, multiformity, whether in ideology or structure.

Iskra's "network of agents" must become the vanguard and elite of the revolutionary movement. They must "devote to the revolution not only their spare evenings, but the whole of their lives." They must make revolution their profession and be professional in their revolutionary skills. No mere vendors or distributors of a clandestine journal, they must "introduce strict division of labor in the various forms of work," become "accustomed to fulfilling the detailed functions of the national (All-Russian) work . . . , test their strength in organization of various kinds of revolutionary activities . . . , form the skeleton of an organization . . . sufficiently large to embrace the whole country"; they must be sufficiently self-assertive, ubiquitous, and omnipotent to "utilize" every flare-up of discontent in "every layer" of society, whether zemstvo, or student, or peasant, or worker. The aim of the journal was "to gather a clandestine circle of leaders and to set in motion the greatest possible mass." Clearly this was a not a group of newspaper distributors, but a party. More than a party, for a party might embrace all who agreed with it. The network of agents would be "the officers' cadres" of future armies, which it would lead in a storm attack against the citadel of tsarism. Their work for the paper "would serve as an exact measure of the extent to which . . . our military activities [17] had been firmly established. . . . This degree of military preparedness can be created only by the constant activity of a regular army. . . ." Not an ordinary army either, but an officer's corps, capable of expansion at any moment of unrest into the general staff of a multitudinous host. "The paper will bring forward not only the most competent propagandists but the most skillful organizers, and the most talented political leaders, who will be able at the right moment to issue the call for the decisive battle, and to lead that battle."[18]

While the other editors thought of themselves as agitators and propagandists, ideological guides and teachers, who told *Iskra* readers what to think and believe, only the rough-hewn, repetitive, audacious articles signed *Lenin* told them what to *do* and how high a value to set upon themselves and their routine-seeming work. In due course he elaborated all these articles into an epoch-making brochure called, after the celebrated utopian novel of Chernyshevsky, *Chto Delat'?* [What is to be done?].

Was ever a journal given so large a role in history? No wonder the *Iskra* agents in their narrow-horizoned, suffocating underground were attracted to this wise, old-young man. Here was a dream that gave one's smallest tasks enormous meaning. A dream that took one's breath away. Here was a commander one could trust, follow, worship. Even his amoralism seemed engagingly attractive when he wrote instructions on how to circumvent rival tendencies and journals, how to be sure that "our people" are elected as delegates to the coming congress, how to put "ours" into committees by taking advantage of police arrests of "theirs." With the representatives of other socialist groups, some older and better organized than the Iskrists, like the adherents of *Rabochee Delo* [the Workers' Cause] and of the Bund (the Jewish Workers' Union), he wrote: "Be wise as serpents and gentle as doves."[19]

By building an *apparat* for *Iskra* within the general revolutionary movement, Lenin was thus building a machine of personal loyalty to himself alone among the six *Iskra* editors. Though they did not yet know it, among the Iskrists there were already Leninists.

By 1903 the Iskrists had succeeded in establishing their ideological ascendancy—thanks chiefly to the prestige of the learned Plekhanov—and their organizational predominance—thanks chiefly to the detailed plans and directives of Lenin. They had managed to sidetrack or blow up all rival plans for a nationwide socialist congress. Now *Iskra* invited all local and national groups to send delegates to a congress it was calling. Out of respect for an abortive congress held in 1898, all of whose members had been arrested by the police, the convention called by *Iskra* was designated the "Second Congress." But its announced aim was to found a single, all-Russian, socialist party, on the basis, or so the *Iskra* editors intended, of *Iskra*'s program.

At the congress the Iskrists had a safe majority, all right. Lenin had seen to that. The Iskrist majority held together while they worsted rival tendencies. Then they themselves fell to quarreling over what seemed a trivial difference in the definition of a party member.[20] When Lenin was outvoted on this organization question, his fury knew no bounds. In one of his famous rages, he split the *Iskra* caucus, convoked a faction meeting of "true Iskrists," posting guards to keep out his fellow *Iskra* editors—except Plekhanov, who for the moment was siding with him. It was only two years since he had written to Martov that he would henceforth "regard all persons without sentiment and keep a stone in his sling." How well he had learned his lesson!

Could this be the unifying congress that was to give birth to a single, all-Russian party? Lenin was the first to realize that it had given birth to two parties instead of one; that the clash of temperaments concealed differences on organization, on relation of the party to the working class and to society, on the nature of the revolution itself—differences so profound that they could be resolved only by one faction's destroying the standing of the other. It took his five associates of yesterday, as it did the Russian underground, more than a decade before they realized it, too. During that decade, Lenin was often forced by party public opinion, including that of his own faction, to work together with those whom he thought of henceforth as ineluctable enemies, but no pretense at unity for tactical reasons ever caused him to give up his faction organization or alter his unique views one iota.

Though he had his slight majority for only a brief interval during the congress, his awareness of the power and propaganda impact of words caused him to arrogate to his faction the term *Bol'sheviki* (Majorityites), and to dub his opponents *Mensheviki* (Minorityites). Ineptly they accepted his label, coming to wear its stigma as a badge of pride. Actually, at the congress itself, the vote on which the Iskrists split into two factions, that on the "definition of a member," was 23 for Lenin against 28 for Martov, a clear majority for the "Minorityites." Only at the end of the congress, when a number of delegates had already left or withdrawn in protest, did Lenin manage to muster 19 votes on the personnel issue[21] against 17, with three abstentions. Even then he did not have a majority of those present and recording their vote, while his 17 was a mere third of the original congress. Between 1903 and 1917 his opponents would most of the time have the majority of the organized behind them, but Lenin clung to the power-redolent name which gave his faction and his deeds prestige among the inexperienced.

When the congress adjourned, there were three central organs: the editorial board of *Iskra*, consisting now of Lenin and Plekhanov[22] (who for the next ten years was to waver between Bolsheviks and Mensheviks); a Central Committee, handpicked by Lenin, to function underground in Russia; and a Party Council, made up from the first two. Within a year Plekhanov broke with Lenin because of his merciless attitude toward the other old editors, and Lenin lost his post on the central organ. His Central Committee broke with him because of his "splitting tactics," thereby becoming in his eyes "worse than Mensheviks." The Party Council, of course, turned against him. Then the underground let him know that it wanted "unity."

Unshaken, he picked himself a new troika of men who had not even been at the congress, nor been elected to anything. And he managed to gather twenty-two random signatures for an endorsement of what he had done and contemplated, the twenty-two including his wife, his sister, and himself. But he called this scratchpile faction group by the large name, "Bureau of the Committees of the Majority." Like all future troikas and faction committees, it was an emanation of his own person, handpicked from those who were willing to agree to the letter with a position which in his strong-minded, self-confident solitude he alone had elaborated. To the secretary of this new handpicked "Bureau of the Committees of the Majority" he wrote: "For God's sake, don't trust the Mensheviks and the Central Committee [his own handpicked Central Committee of yesterday] and put through unconditionally, everywhere, and most decisively, split, split and split."[23]

But whatever the future might hold in store, in 1903, when the "unifying" Second Congress adjourned, it was Lenin and his wife who held in their hands all the threads which led to the underground agents and hence to the localities in Russia. As one of his opponents was to tell me years later: "Though Lenin was virtually isolated abroad where everyone had been able to follow the Congress fight closely, he had all the connections with Russia and we had none."[24]

Thus did Lenin in his first big test prove himself a master of the twin arts of organization and power—power for the Iskrists within the many-colored socialist and revolutionary movement, power for himself and his faction in the underground. In 1917, when power was lying loose in the streets, he would demonstrate his skill in using his machine to seize power in the state and hold on to it. So was his belief to be confirmed that it did not matter how many he lost in the course of building the party machine, so long as the machine remained effective and those he won accepted his organization conceptions and his leadership.

Marx had been vague on how the working class takes power, deliberately silent on what it would do with power once it had it. In Lenin, however, he had an innovative disciple who was theoretician, technician, and virtuoso of organization and power. His speciality was the how rather than the why or what. Conspiracy, centralized organization, military discipline, the ability to stir, manipulate, and coalesce the sources of discontent for one's own power purposes—a technique and indeed a technology for the art and science of taking power, of devising the instruments of seizing, holding, wielding, and maximizing power—what are these if not the levers of modern revolution? Here indeed was a revolutionist of a new type, determined to form what he himself would call "a party of a new type," to make, as it turned out, a revolution of a new type. In 1903 his five associates of the *Iskra* editorial board contemplated the fury of his dictatorial centralism with uncomprehending wonder. In 1917, it would be the world's turn to stare and wonder.

For the three years from 1900 to 1903 the six editors of *Iskra* had been using a common vocabulary: *Marxism, orthodoxy, socialism, working class, party, central committee, member.* Plekhanov had written, and they had all approved, a common Program.[25] But at the congress their confident, self-chosen band of leaders had been rent in two over *the definition of a member*! It dawned on them then that every word they had been using in common was subject to directly opposite interpretations.

Factionalism has a logic of its own. It compelled five of the editors to ask for the first time how they could ever have permitted these strange organization doctrines to be uttered in their name by their specialist on questions of organization. And it led Lenin to invent for the other five a new heresy undreamed of by Marx: "Opportunism in the organization question." For this "deviation" he invented an entire new language of re-probation, derision, and condemnation: *khvostism* ("tailism," dragging at the tail instead of leading); "cringing before spontaneity"; "slavish kow-towing to the backwardness of the masses"; "dragging the Party backward";

glorifying unpreparedness and backwardness; "bourgeois trade unionism in the organization question," etc. etc. (All these expressions are culled from the rich new vocabulary of disparagement and abuse which Lenin introduced in his ground-breaking *What Is to Be Done?* Some of the terms are further analyzed below.)

It was "only" a question of organization (since they still kept the common program). Only a question of organization, but what a gulf it opened! Of course, both Lenin and his opponents appealed to Marxism, for both sides looked on Marxism as truth and science. But here as elsewhere, Marxism is ambiguous. Among these champions of orthodoxy and slayers of "revisionism," one text from the sacred canon could be made as probative as another. Alongside Marx's certitude concerning his own theoretical ideas, there was his insistence that ideas play only a minor role in history, as a reflection of more fundamental self-acting material forces. Though Marx fought ruthlessly for the supremacy of his own doctrine in the International, always he insisted that in the long run the working class itself would elaborate its own "consciousness" and organization, while "doctrinaire sects" would be outgrown or absorbed into mere servants of mass workingmen's parties. "The Emancipation of the working class must be conquered by the working class itself," wrote Marx as the first point in the "Statutes of the International Workingmen's Organization." And, even as he criticized the unity of Lassalleans and Marxians in Germany which had taken place without his advice, based on a program which seemed to him unsound, he nevertheless wrote: "Every step of a real movement is more important than a dozen programs."[26] By virtue of the very conditions of its life, he thought, the working class would develop its own revolutionary consciousness. From its increasing numbers and urban concentration, its mounting polarization at one pole of society, its ever-grander struggles and deeper experiences, its growing humiliation, degradation, despair, and indignation, it would generate its own mass working-class party, correct its own errors, coming at last to the point where "the conditions themselves would cry out: *Hic Rhodus! Hic salta!*" The "class *in* itself" would become a "class *for* itself," would elevate itself to the ruling class and revolutionize society.

If one goes from isolated texts to the overall context of Marx's thought, or if one takes the mighty German movement which Marx and Engels (and until August 1914, Lenin, too) regarded as the model, there can be no doubt that Marx assigned a decisive role to the spontaneous development, the self-organization, the *class* consciousness, the conditions of life and experiences of struggle of the working class. But in less than three years, from 1900 to 1903, Lenin put out quite a body of literature in the name of *Iskra* and "orthodox" Marxism which made it crystal clear that he did not share Marx's confidence in the working class.

The first peculiarity that strikes one in Lenin's doctrine is its extreme centralism, coupled with its extreme distrust of the rank and file of his party and the local organizations.

"What is bad," Lenin asked defiantly when he was in control of the central organ of the party, "What is bad about the complete dictatorship of the Central Organ?"[27]

Chided with suppressing party democracy, Lenin answered for himself and his band of professional revolutionaries: "They have no time to think of the toy forms of democracy . . . but they have a lively sense of their *responsibility* and they know by experience that to get rid of an undesirable member, an organization of real revolutionaries will stop at nothing."[28]

This is surely one of the most unresponsive answers in the whole of political literature. Lenin argues that under the conditions of police spying in Russia, party democracy is a "useless and harmful toy." But the context reveals that even in a free country the chief function of party "democracy" to him is to provide "the general control, in the literal sense of the term, that the party exercises over every member," a control which enables the party to decide whether to assign to a member one function or another, or to get rid of him altogether as unfit. It is his thought that in the context of illegality, democracy can be completely replaced by the mutual trust of socialists in each other, the absolute trust of all in the self-selected leading committee and in the ability of the latter to get rid of those who cannot be trusted.

Even more uncompromising is Lenin's championing of "bureaucratic centralism" as against the democratic autonomy of the primary or local organizations and their democratic control over the center. This *bureaucratic centralism* he considers appropriate to a socialist party in any country. The language of his celebration of "bureaucratism" is prickly and rough-hewn, but its meaning is startlingly clear: "Bureaucratism *versus* democratism, i.e., precisely centralism *versus* autonomy, such is the principle of revolutionary social democracy as against that of the opportunists. . . . The organization of revolutionary social democracy strives to go from the top downward, and defends the enlargement of the rights and plenary powers of the central body. . . ."[29]

It was impossible for this power-centered man to imagine that he would not be in control of the center. To Lunacharsky he said:

> "If we have in the CC or in the Central Organ a majority, then we will demand the firmest discipline. We will insist on every sort of subordination of the Mensheviks to party unity . . ."
> I asked Vladimir Ilyich:
> "Well, and what if it should turn out after all that we are in a minority?"

Lenin smiled enigmatically and said:

"It depends on the circumstances. In any case we will not permit them to make of unity a rope around our necks. And under no circumstances will we let the Mensheviks drag us after them on such a rope."[30]

Not until Lenin had been bombarded by his opponents over half a decade for his rejection of party democracy did he finally seek to conceal somewhat his arch centralism and aversion to any democracy down below. Then he coined his celebrated term, *democratic centralism*! Even after he was in power and no longer could give as justification the tsar's police, in the third year of his rule he defined that self-contradictory term as "meaning only that representatives from the localities gather and choose a responsible organ. . . . The responsible organ must do the administering."

When Lenin's concept of democratic centralism was transplanted to the Communist International, its formulation read:

The main principle of democratic centralism is that of the higher cell being elected by the lower cell, the absolute binding force of all directives of a higher cell to a cell subordinate to it, and the existence of a commanding [*vlastnogo*, i.e., endowed with or clothed with power] party center [the authority of which] is unchallengeable for all its leaders in party life, from one congress to the next.[31]

Lenin's idea of what should be "centralized" and what "decentralized" would be comical were it not for its tragic implications for Russia and for communism. In his "Letter to a Comrade on Our Organizational Tasks," Lenin wrote:

We have arrived at an extremely important principle of all party organization and party activity. In regard to ideological and practical *direction* the movement and the revolutionary struggle of the proletariat need the *greatest possible centralization*, but in regard to *keeping the center informed* about the movement and about the party as a whole, in regard to *responsibility* before the party, we need the *greatest possible decentralization*. The movement must be led by the smallest possible number of the most homogeneous groups of trained and experienced revolutionaries. But the largest possible number of the most varied and heterogeneous groups drawn from the most diverse layers of the proletariat (and of other classes) should take part in the movement. And in regard to each such group the center of the party must have always before it not only exact data on their activities, but all the fullest possible knowledge of their composition.[32]

If we add to this the rule which prescribes that the "committee should lead *all* aspects of the local movement . . . direct *all* local institutions, forces . . . decide all general questions" and leave "independence to the district groups only in the questions of the technique of distribution," then Lenin's conception of hierarchical centralism becomes terrifyingly clear. All power, all command, all decision should be with the center ("the district group receives its powers only from the latter") but the duty to carry out, obey, and report should be "decentralized" and accorded as a "privilege" to every local organization and individual member and even to party sympathizers.

Afraid that his readers might not get its full implications, Lenin, as was his wont, repeated it all again, with only slight variations and different underscorings:

> We must centralize the direction of the movement. We must also (and we must *for this reason*, for without the informing of the center its leadership is impossible) decentralize as much as possible the *responsibility before the party* of each individual member, of each participant in its work, of each circle which forms part of the party or inclines to it. This decentralization is the necessary condition for revolutionary centralization and *its necessary corrective* ... nothing else but the reverse side of *the division of labor.* ... In order that the center may not only give advice, persuade, and argue (as has been done up to now), but may really direct the orchestra, it is essential to know exactly who is playing which fiddle and where; who, where, is learning to master which instrument or has mastered it; who, where and why, is playing out of tune (when the music begins to grate on the ear); and who, how and where should be transferred to correct the dissonance, and so on.[33]

From the outset Lenin's "center" was self-appointed. He began with himself, then gathered around him those who agreed with him. Again and again he removed players from his orchestra when *their* playing grated on *his* ears, gathering others more in harmony with his directing. Thus his "Leninist" center was self-perpetuating.

The same ideas reappear in the years of comparative open activity between 1907 and 1914, when *Zvezda* and *Pravda* were legal journals and the Bolsheviks could elect deputies to the Duma. The ideas continue during the six months of 1917 when Russia, in Lenin's words, was "the freest country in the world." And they continue when Lenin holds power in party and country. At first he sought to justify his centralism before its critics by pointing to the harsh conditions of a conspirative, underground movement, but in time it became clear that it sprang from the deepest necessities of Lenin's temperament, his confidence in himself and his pessimistic view of the dependability of his fellow men. He has been compared to a schoolmaster commanding his pupils (by Edmund Wilson) and to a general commanding an embattled army (in his own figures of speech on military discipline). Here, in any case, is "a revolutionary of a rare type: a revolutionary with a bureaucratic mind,"[34] for whom the complete centralization and control of activities is—of all things—the road to a stateless utopia!

Hence Lenin's Archimedian cry for an organization of revolutionaries "to turn Russia upside down" did not cease when Russia was "turned upside down." Then as before Lenin repeated the cry of "organization, organization, organization." In power, as when fighting for power, he said: "Our fighting method is organization." But now he had something new to "fight" for. To the old dream of *centralized organization of the party*, which he did not for a moment abandon, he added the new dream of *total organization by the party*. Of what? Why, of Russia. Its industries and its agriculture, its feelings and its thoughts, its habits, even its dreams, total organization of slackness, of the waywardness of will, of deeds and desires. "We must organize everything," he said in the summer of 1918, "take everything into our hands."[35]

When, to the authoritarian trend inherent in an infallible doctrine, possessed and interpreted by an infallible interpreter who ruled an infallible party, from above, infallibly, Lenin added the further dream of an authoritarian organization doctrine and a party and state machine vested with exclusive and unique power and imbued with the determination to "organize everything, take everything into our hands"—totalitarianism was inescapable.

This ambition totally to organize everything was actually inherent in his doctrine and his spirit from the start. We have only to read attentively the outbursts against "spontaneity" and "elementalness" in the first "Leninist" pamphlet (*What Is to Be Done?*) to see that the longing to give ordered and organized form to the spontaneously developing life of the masses was always at the heart of Lenin's thought. After he had taken power he would write in 1920, "Petit-bourgeois spontaneity is more terrible than all the Denikins, Kolchaks and Yudeniches put together."[36]

If it seems strange in a "democrat" to distrust the rank and file of the party and the local organizations, it seems stranger still in a socialist to express distrust of the very class whence "proletarian consciousness" was to issue and whose destiny it was to achieve socialism. But Lenin thought this distrust necessary and obvious. "Cut off from the influence of the Social Democracy," he wrote in his first signed article for *Iskra*, "the workingman's movement becomes petty and inevitably bourgeois."[37]

That dictum, only a single sentence in his first *Iskra* article, became the central thought of *What Is to Be Done?* There he spelled out his distrust, underscored it, repeated it tirelessly and monotonously.

An entire chapter is devoted to distinguishing between "The Spontaneity of the Masses and the Consciousness of the Social Democracy." The distinction between *spontaneity* and *consciousness* is worth pondering, for it brings us to the core of Lenin's spirit. The Russian word *stikhijnost'* means both spontaneity and elementalness. *Soznatel'nost'* is ordered and order-producing consciousness. Lenin opposed the two words to each other as one might light and darkness. The elemental and spontaneous were incorporated in the working class and the masses generally. It was the way they thought, felt, fought, when they had no guidance from "consciousness." Consciousness was the party. The party without leadership over the masses was mind without body. The masses without the leadership of the party was body without mind.

As his emphasis on centralism as against democracy had led him to invent the heresy of "opportunism in the organization question," so now his emphasis on consciousness as opposed to spontaneity led him to invent the heresy of *"slavish kowtowing before spontaneity."* The language is strange, the idea of the heresy stranger still. "Kowtowing" is the act of worship by which the devout in the Russian church prostrate themselves before a revered image. To call it "slavish" and "shameful" makes it clear that Lenin regards it as evil. But why? Because the working class, left to itself, without the tutelage of the party, will never in its life attain to so much as the conception of socialism! Socialism turns out not to be, as Marx believed, the quintessential thought of the proletariat, but a doctrine understood, possessed, and propagated by an intellectual elite. Hence to look to the working class to work out its own salvation, to seek only to serve the working-class movement rather than to take it in tow, is in Lenin's eyes to renounce revolution and socialism. Lenin describes this as dragging behind the working class instead of dragging it after you. This is the heresy of *khvostism.* Thus Lenin's distrust of "spontaneity" and his heresy of "tailism" are bound up with his distrust of the working class.[38]

In the introduction of *What Is to Be Done?* Lenin apologizes—for the first and last time—"for its numerous literary shortcomings." Actually, it has no "literary" form at all. It does not develop its ideas, it proclaims them, repeats them again and again, *hammers* them home. Repetition of his main points, not merely until they sink in, but until they "condition" the reader, hypnotize him, take possession of him, take on the air of indisputable truisms; this was, in speaking as in writing, a characteristic of Lenin's styleless *"style."*

He took a backward glance at the yesterday of the Russian working class. Their struggles had not made them socialists, nor could any amount of experience in struggle ever turn the working class into a socialist class or a consciously revolutionary one. For this there was needed a vanguard of professionals, professionals of theory, organization, and consciousness, professionals who made revolution their profession. There had not been, there was not,

> nor *could there be* social democratic consciousness in the workers. This can be brought to them only from the outside. The history of all lands testifies to

the fact that alone by their own forces the working class is capable of working out only a trade union consciousness. . . . But the teachings of socialism have grown out of those philosophical, historical, economic theories which were worked out by the educated representatives of the possessing classes, the intelligentsia. By their social position, Marx and Engels, the founders of contemporary scientific socialism, belonged to the bourgeois intelligentsia, too. This is true for Russia also, where the theoretical doctrine of social democracy arose in complete independence from the spontaneous (elemental) growth of the workers' movement—arose as the natural and inevitable result of the development of thought among the revolutionary intelligentsia.[39]

The workers have to be "pushed from the outside." There has never been, nor can there be, enough of this "pushing from the outside." Conversely, to "flatter the workers, to arouse in them" a sense of distrust toward all who bring them political knowledge and revolutionary experience from the outside" is to be a demagogue—a unique, Leninist definition of the term—"and a demagogue is the worst enemy of the working class."[40]

Since there can be no talk of an independent ideology's being worked out by the workers themselves in the course of their movement the *only choice is:* either bourgeois or socialist ideology. There is no middle term (for no "third" ideology has been worked out by mankind, and furthermore, in a society torn by class contradictions in general there can never be an outside of class or above class ideology). Hence *any* diminution of socialist ideology, any *departure* from it, signifies by that very fact a strengthening of bourgeois ideology. But the *spontaneous* development of the workers' movement leads precisely to its subordination to bourgeois ideology . . . for the spontaneous workers' movement is trade-unionism, etc., is *nur Gewerkschaftlerei* [the German term for trade unionism pure and simple], and trade unionism means precisely the ideological enslavement of the workers to the bourgeoisie.[41]

Class political consciousness can be brought to the worker only from *the outside,* that is, from outside the sphere of relations between workers and bosses. The sphere from which alone it is possible to derive this knowledge is the sphere of the relation of *all* the classes and strata and the state and the government—the sphere of interrelations among *all* classes. Therefore, the question, what is to be done to bring to the workers political knowledge, cannot be answered . . . by "go to the workers." To bring to the *workers* political knowledge, the social democrats must *go into all classes of the population,* should send *in all directions* the detachments of its army.[42]

We [what Lenin chooses to italicize is always of special interest] must take upon ourselves the task of organizing such an all-sided political struggle under the direction of *our* party. . . . *We* must develop from the practical activists of the social democracy such political leaders as will be able to direct all the manifestations of this all-sided struggle, be able at the necessary moment "to dictate a positive program of action" alike to rebellious students, and to dissatisfied zemstvo figures, and discontented religious sectaries, and indignant school teachers, and so on.[43]

Aided by historical hindsight, we can see that Lenin was driving at a party that was to direct not only the working class, but the entire populace, a party that would conceive as its duty to "dictate the positive program" of every class of society. That *dictate* was no empty figure of speech to Lenin became clear from the outset of his career. When he was still a member of the *Iskra* editorial board, he explained once in a memorandum to his colleagues that he proposed to show every kindness to the peasantry, "but not yield an inch" in our "maximum program." "If the peasants do not accept socialism" when the dictatorship comes, we shall say to them, "It's no use wasting words when you have got to use force." On the margin of this memorandum Vera Zasulich wrote: "Upon millions of people? Just you try!" When he and his party came to power, that is just what they did try.

It was to be neither a party "of" the entire populace nor "of" the working class. It was to be a carefully selected elite, offering itself as leader, director, guardian, *for* the working class and for all the discontented from religious sectaries to zemstvo councillors.

> The economic struggle against the bosses and the government does not in the least require—and therefore such a struggle can never give rise to—an all-Russian centralized organization, uniting in one general attack each and every manifestation of political opposition, protest and indignation, an organization consisting of revolutionaries by profession and led by the real political leaders of the entire people.[44]

Thus *stikhijnost'*, spontaneity, the natural liberty of men and classes to be themselves, was the enemy and opposite of consciousness. In Marx spontaneity and consciousness coincided, for though Marx had his own idea of consciousness, he thought that historical experience would be the connecting link to bring the proletariat to that "consciousness" in the course of its struggles. But for Lenin, spontaneity and consciousness were irreconcilable opposites. The party did not give expression to the consciousness of the class, but itself possessed that consciousness as its own infallible possession which it must inject into, impose upon the class. The party was the institutional organization of consciousness which needed the elemental or spontaneous movement, its rebelliousness and its numbers, to give it force, even as a General Staff needs an army. But it is the General Staff which possesses military science, does the planning of battles and campaigns, gives orders, decides on offensives and retreats, and—where General Staff and political party are one and the same—decides on objectives as well. The army is needed to provide numbers, muscle; the General Staff is the brains. What general worthy of his stripes would let his army determine its own tactics and actions? That way lay chaos. He must drill the army, give it experience under fire, keep it in a fighting mood, train it to obey automatically and completely, harden it by fire, supply officers for every detachment, discredit and eliminate the willful and insubordinate.

Obviously we have gone a long way from the original Marxist conception of a party of the working class, growing more and more inclusive as modern industry and experience develop, engendering more and more solidarity and consciousness in the course of its repeated struggles. To Lenin the crowd was but a rabble, its spontaneous thoughts and feelings mere false understanding, unless it could be turned into a disciplined, obedient force by officers who alone knew the aims and the art of war.

One question remained to be answered, and this Lenin did not altogether spell out. Yet, if we wander through the repetitive pages of his brochure, to this question Lenin gives answers again and again. *Who were these revolutionaries by profession?* From what class or classes would they be recruited? To what class would they belong?

If "consciousness" comes not from the working class but only from outside, if its bearers and formulators are "by their social position educated representatives of the possessing class, the intelligentsia," then it is clear that the members of his elite band would come chiefly from those layers of society which had it in them to master this doctrine, namely the students and the intellectuals.[45] True, by becoming professional revolutionaries they were in a certain sense declassing themselves—but not thereby becoming members of the working class. Rather they would withdraw from their professions and economic functions, withdraw from the existing "classes" of society and from society itself, live in its interstices as masters of a profession new in history, the profession of revolutionary. They were not to be part of the present at all, but its challengers—bearers of the future, which they and they alone foreknew.

As a concession to the "working-class" element in Marxist theory, Lenin acknowledged that "the best of the workers" might also attain to this consciousness. Russia in due time would beget its own "Bebels," and, he hoped, many of them. But they too would have to leave the factory and the workbench, be extruded from their class, in short, declassed:

> The worker-revolutionary for full preparation for his job must also become a professional revolutionary.... A worker-agitator who shows any talent and is at all "promising" *should not* work in the factory eleven hours a day. We must see to it that he lives on party support, that he should be able in time to go over to an underground status.[46]

Even when Lenin was in power and exercising the "proletarian" dictatorship, he repeated this judgment: "It is understood that the broad masses of the toilers includes very many people who . . . are not enlightened socialists and cannot be, because they have to work at hard labor in the factory and they neither have the time nor the possibility to become socialists."[47]

Among professional revolutionaries, whether declassed representatives of the propertied classes or declassed workers, "*all distinctions as between workers and intellectuals* must be obliterated."[48] This classless band of priest-guardians must "form a clandestine group of leaders, to set the largest possible masses in motion," become the leader and "dictate the program" to all the discontented of all classes, and lead them all in an all-Russian struggle against the existing order.

There was yet another sense in which Lenin held his organization of classless professional revolutionaries to be "the vanguard" of a particular class, the proletariat. When his opponents accused him of being nothing but a nineteenth-century revolutionary conspirator like those of the old *Narodnaia volia*, Lenin answered proudly:

> The very idea of a militant centralized organization, which declares determined war upon tsarism, you describe as *narodovolist*. . . . No revolutionary tendency that seriously thinks of fighting can dispense with such an organization . . . a powerful, strictly secret organization which concentrates in its hands all the threads of secret activities, an organization which must of necessity be centralized.[49]

Yes, in all these things he was a *narodovolets*, and "flattered" to be so described. Like them, too, he sought "to recruit *all* the discontented and hurl this organization into decisive battle . . . that was their great historic merit." Only two mistakes did the *narodovoltsy* make, and only in these did he differ from them. Their first mistake was not to realize that Russia would and must develop modern industry and modern capitalism, and with this a modern proletariat. Their second mistake, which followed from the first, was to believe that the main mass of discontented, the *main battering ram* to use against the gates of the fortress, was the peasantry. But the industrialization of Russia and the teachings of Marxism combined to show that the main mass force to be used as a battering ram, more concentrated, more organized by the barracks discipline of the factory, more accessible to the teachings and leadership of Lenin's elite—*that main* battering ram was the working class.

Herein lay the heart of Lenin's "Marxism." Namely, this made it essential that his elite, regardless of class origin, should proclaim itself the "vanguard of the working class." *This* made it so essential for the vanguard of society to claim recognition as the vanguard of the class which must in turn be recognized as the vanguard class in society. For this his vanguard must penetrate the working class, enter into its "essentially bourgeois" trade unions, indoctrinate it with the vanguard doctrine which was at the same time, whether the proletariat accepted or rejected it, the "proletarian" doctrine. For this it must seek to guide and control the workers' struggles, divert them from their "spontaneous" purposes to its conscious purpose, manipulate and utilize their number and penetrate their organizations for the aims of the vanguard elite, "dictate to them a positive program of action," force their organizations to transcend their natural aims and limitations, inject into the working class "from outside" the "consciousness" of the revolutionary mission assigned to it by its vanguard, by Marx, and by history.

Indeed, the workingmen and their organizations would be measured by this standard, a standard developed outside their movement and in opposition to its "spontaneous" aims, a standard impossible for the workingmen themselves to develop under any circumstances. For the workers, "consciousness" was neither more nor less than *acceptance of the leadership*, guardianship, guidance, program, and decisions of this elite band of professionals of revolution.

Thus Lenin's vanguard was the vanguard of the proletariat by definition. Its doctrine was the doctrine of the proletariat by definition. And its organization was the "highest form" of organization of the working class by definition.

He who regarded himself as the most orthodox of orthodox Marxists could rightly claim that the party he was to build was a party of a new type, which Marx and Engels would have been astonished to contemplate. It was not only new and unique; it was exclusive. For while there might be many parties with differing programs, even many rival parties all alike claiming to be socialist, there was room in any society for only *one* party to be *the* vanguard of the working class and then the vanguard of the "ruling class" and the vanguard of society.

There have been attempts to find "predecessors" and "influences" for Lenin's conception, in Babeuf and Blanqui, in Pestel, Nechaev, Tkachov, Chernyshevsky.[50] But when all of these, or the relevant fragments from their writings, are added together, they do not make Lenin's theory or practice. He is unique as its begetter, systematizer, developer, realizer in life, and—what gives it its great importance—the architect of its successful seizure of power.

Such a classless elite might well seize power, not as Marx had foretold, where the economy was most advanced and the working class most numerous, organized, cultured, and "conscious," but just as easily, nay more easily, where the economy was backward, the workers neither "mature" nor "conscious," and all political organization of all parties and classes rudimentary.

Once in power, it might continue to hold power in the name of the proletariat, since it was the vanguard of the proletariat by definition and self-proclamation. It might dictate to the rest of society in the proletariat's name, and dictate to the proletariat as well in the proletariat's name, for the vanguard knows best.

Moreover, this vanguard-elite theory would make it possible for restless intellectuals to seize power in the name of the proletariat in lands where the proletariat was in its infancy. In the name of this doctrine, Mao Tse-tung could seize power "for the proletariat" by means of peasant armies in an overwhelmingly agrarian land of rudimentary industry. Ho Chi Minh might do the same in a land where the only workers were plantation hands and craftsmen plying their ancient trades. All that was needed was opportunity and will plus the acceptance of the idea of the Leninist *apparat*.

Once in power, they could do as Lenin, and after him Stalin and Khrushchev: use the "proletarian power" to rule society as a whole, including the proletariat, for, as Lenin put it, "just because the revolution has begun, that does not mean that people have turned into saints." Far from it. One of the important duties of the "proletarian power" is "to resist the inevitable petit-bourgeois waverings of these proletarian masses." Indeed, one of its first tasks is to combat the demoralization which war and the party's own war against the Provisional Government had introduced into the masses. "Only by an extraordinarily difficult, prolonged, stubborn road can we overcome this demoralization and conquer those elements who are augmenting it by regarding the revolution as a means of getting rid of their old shackles by getting out of it as much as they can."[51] Surely, a proletarian party of a new type!

NOTES TO CHAPTER 2

1. *Charismatic attributes.* In this essay, as in my *Communist Totalitarianism*, I have used the term *charismatic* in the sense given to it by Max Weber in "Die drei reinen Typen der legitimen Herrschaft."

In its original sense, *charisma* meant the grace of God, manifested by prophets, priest-kings, divinely inspired rulers and leaders, upon whom God has conferred his grace or guidance. In the course of history many peoples have held their rulers to be divine, or divinely inspired, chosen, guided, or otherwise endowed with magical or transcendentally derived qualities. The "Divine Right of Kings" and the sovereign who is head of the church of his realm (*rex et pontifex maximus*) are survivals into recent times of charisma in this primary sense.

The great service of Max Weber has been to call our attention to a nonrational and nonbureaucratic element in the leadership and rulership of some who do not think of their powers as derived from a transcendental or a magical source. He has extended the term *charismatic* to qualities and dimensions of leadership and rule in societies which consider themselves "modern," "rational," bureaucratically or constitutionally regulated. As used by him, the term serves as a distinction between two basically different types of leadership and rule in modern movements and great-state societies. On the one hand, there are the ordinary rulers, leaders and officials who hold their places by virtue of some established procedure or practical qualification, and who display in general the "rational" and workaday talents which ordinarily go with men in such offices. On the other hand, there are those leaders and rulers who—however they acquire the position—exhibit in their leadership an added dimension which is nonrational (or supra- or infrarational), depending on some quality in their persons which is felt as magnetic, contagious, stirring, overpowering, a quality which inspires in their followers powerful emotions and fanatical devotion. There is something about the latter type of ruler or leader which, whether for good or evil, surpasses the common light of every day, makes incandescent the multitudes listening to his word, calls forth unquestioning and fanatical obedience to commands, induces a surrender of individual reason and the normal moral code of the individual in favor of the reason and the code proclaimed by the charismatic leader or ruler. It is a quality which makes for disciples rather than mere attentive subordinates and fuses around the person of the charismatic leader a *movement* of followers and idolizers. Max Weber thus finds charisma not only in prophets but also in fanatically followed and idolized war leaders and in urban "great demagogues."

Weber's extention of the term *charisma* and the adjective *charismatic* to types of leadership and rule (*Führerschaft und Herrschaft*) whose possessors do not feel that the source of their powers is transcendental and whose followers do not feel it to be transcendental either, has evoked critical reactions in those who (like Professor Carl J. Friedrich of Harvard) find the extension improper, not to say blasphemous. Such objectors would allow charisma to Jesus and His Disciples, to the prophets and the saints, and perhaps to some of the successors of Peter. Not to be parochial, they would allow it to a Mohammed, too, since he and his followers believed that his powers of prophecy, prescription, command, and leadership in war and statecraft came from Allah. But they would deny the term to a Lenin or a Hitler, the first of whom surely, and the second presumably, believed neither in God's grace nor in God.

Max Weber, who bluntly, even proudly, proclaimed that he was tone deaf in religion as others are tone deaf in music, did not ease matters any when he wrote: "It is clear that the expression *charisma* is here used in an entirely value-free sense. The manic seizure of rage in the Nordic Beserker, the miracles and revelations of any hole-in-the-corner prophet, the demagogical gifts of a Cleon, are to sociology as much 'charisma' as the qualities of a Napoleon, a Jesus, a Pericles."

To the religiously sensitive, the second triad (Napoleon-Jesus-Pericles) is likely to be as offensive as the first.

However provocative or Puckish this juxtaposition may seem, there is need in sociology, history, and political thought for a term both to cover and to call our attention to that special dimension in some leaders and rulers not to be found in functional, bureaucratic, practical, prosy, uninspired and uninspiring, sometimes competent and sometimes bumbling, everyday leadership and rulership. Weber has given us such a term, serviceable in social and political analysis and historiography. We must be careful to indicate its different varieties and different approaches to itself, and be aware that it is not an absolute but a matter of more or less; we must perforce leave it to theology and religious feeling to decide whether in a given case its source is transcendental. Nor can one (as Dr. Friedrich has suggested to the writer) content oneself with a diversity of special terms for each special case: "military leadership," "demagogic leadership," "totalitarian leadership," "demonic leadership." For despite the illusions of our age concerning its "rationality," there appear today, with increasing importance, leaders and rulers who have this special irrational dimension or quality for which some special term is needed.

What, for instance, shall we say of a Gandhi, who did not himself claim that his gifts were from God, but whose simple journey to the sea clad in a homespun loincloth and armed with a ladle to scoop out one spoonful of water from the sea and wait for the sun to turn it into salt, could arouse an entire people to a frenzy?

Or what shall we think of a Shamyl, leading from his mountain peaks and deep ravines his little band of Moslem tribesmen in a war which held off the armies of mighty Russia for three decades (1830–61)? He believed in his own transcendental charisma, as did his followers. He thought of himself as the next great prophet after Mohammed, invincible, invulnerable, obligated to enforce his rule with ruthless severity since through him Allah spoke. Even outsiders wrote that he "exuded a mystical aura of leadership." Men—and women and children—died willingly in his Holy War, confident that they would awake that very day in Paradise. But to the Russian armies hunting him down like a wild beast, he was not even one of Weber's "hole-in-the-corner prophets," only a guerrilla leader, a mountain bandit, an enemy of the true faith and the truly charismatic Sovereign, Autocrat by divine right, by sacred charismatic inheritance through the royal blood, by holy anointment and patriarchal coronation, Defender and Head of the True Faith and dread absolute ruler over Holy Mother Russia. Yet Nicholas I did not possess charisma in Weber's sense and Shamyl did.

In the present work I have further extended the term as used by Weber. He used it to cover three types (the religious leader and prophet; the warrior leader; and the "great Demagogue"). But as the present essay suggests, modern total war called for and elevated to leadership a new type of war leader who is no warrior, no leader of armies in the field, but a *civilian* war leader. He sweeps aside the everyday politican when the latter proves incapable of developing the high emotion and energy, and inspiring the fanatical devotion, which total war requires. A Lloyd George replaces an Asquith; a Clemenceau takes over from a succession of Vivianis, Ribots, and Painlevés; a Churchill supplants a Chamberlain; a de Gaulle seizes the standard from the feeble hand of Pétain or a Darlan, who does not know how to raise it high enough to gather Free France around it. This replacement is not necessarily a matter of greater competence or even greater energy, though of course competence and energy help. It is primarily a matter of greater "appeal," a stronger belief in one's "mission," somehow communicated to multitudes.

Since for millions nationalism has been an *ersatz* or *quasi* religion, and for other millions Marxism has served as a surrogate for a lost transcendental faith, while for yet other millions this function has been fulfilled by a mixture of nationalism and Marxism called national socialism or national communism, it is not surprising that these movements have tended to invest their leaders with an aura of quasi-religious feeling. There is no more difficulty here in the use of the word *charisma* than there is in the use of the word *religion* for the prefix *quasi* is as readily understood in the one case as in the other, and the attributes of charisma, though hard to define, are not difficult to perceive in their possessor.

When the Leader of such a movement dies, a special problem arises which does not exist for ordinary "rational" organizations, everyday political parties or ordinary legitimate governments—the problem of the succession. When a charismatic Leader dies, a vacuum remains at the heart of his movement and his state until the problem of the succession is solved. Thus these movements and institutions which already exhibit so many quasi-religious features have now to develop yet another feature: namely, a sort of apostolic succession. In the first chapter of *Three Who Made a Revolution* I noted among these quasi-religious features: singleness, exclusivism, dogma, sacred and infallible doctrine, orthodoxy, heresy, renegacy, schism, inquisition, purge, confession, excommunication, prophesy, prophets, disciples, vocation, asceticism, chiliastic expectation, redemption, the readiness to suffer all things for the sake of the faith.

But what if no other charismatic person be at hand among the disciples or lieutenants? For a movement whose members are sufficiently close in their banding together and in their separateness from the rest of society and its criticism, any successor, by the mere fact of his reaching the vacant post, may be made to appear to possess some semblance of the necessary attributes. Or else there may be a struggle for the succession until another such Leader appears, or until the movement is fragmented and disintegrates.

For a movement-in-power there is a special means employable to fill the gap, when a suitable charismatic successor is lacking. Since its monopoly of power and of doctrine gives it a monopoly of all the springs and levers of organization, communication and manipulation of public feeling and thought, it has proved possible for such a movement-as-state to manufacture a synthetic pseudo-charisma in a successor who, until he came to power, may have seemed to the masses and even to his close associates to be no more than "a grey blur." If the genuine Leader may be said to possess only *ersatz*-charisma in the transcendental sense, then this synthetic fabrication is *ersatz* to the second power.

Since one of the laws of a dictatorship-in-permanence seems to be that the Dictator normally surrounds himself not with original thinkers and questioners or men of independent intellectual and emotional force, but with disciples, faction lieutenants, yes-men, able but faithful executors of his will, the constantly recurring need to build up some hitherto colorless lieutenant into another Leader of more than natural size and attributes, another master of everything and infallible interpreter of infallible doctrine, becomes an ever more difficult task. There seems to be a built-in tendency to a downward trend in the charismatic or demonic attributes: after a Lenin comes a Stalin, after a Stalin a Khrushchev, after a Khrushchev . . . ?

2. The tragedy of Russia in wartime came not so much from the fact that the tsar, under the influence of the empress, persisted in selecting for the symbolic

"leadership of the nation" a doddering Goremykin and then a contemptible Stuermer, men who lacked not merely magnetism but elementary competence, and in Stuermer's case even common honesty. Much more serious was the fact that both the empress and Nicholas himself were convinced that the tsar possessed charisma in the primary, sacred sense—the grace hereditary in the royal blood, in the divine guidance of the autocrat of Holy Russia, in the leadership of the true faith, and the literal love and reverence of his people. This was augmented in their eyes by Alexandra's certitude of a special divine guidance vouchsafed through the "Man of God," Rasputin. Neither the "public," nor the other members of the royal family, nor the more serious cabinet ministers, nor the Duma, nor the urban crowd, nor, as it turned out in the end, even the peasants, felt in Nicholas any charismatic spark. There were some at court who felt the "charisma" of Rasputin, but many more thought of him as demonic, or merely dissolute, and an unexplainable evil influence on the sovereigns.

3. V. I. Lenin, *Sochineniia* [Works], 9:111. From 1905 to 1907 and again during the war, Lenin's writings abound in hymns to force (the official English translation usually says "violence") and terror. The passage cited appears again and again in varying contexts but always with a touch of exultation. Lenin manifestly rejoices that the Russian autocracy has "put the bayonet on the order of business." He foreshadows his boycott of the Duma elections and his future dispersal of the Constituent Assembly by expressing relief that "constitutional illusions and school exercises in parliamentarism are becoming only a screen for bourgeois betrayal of the revolution. . . . The really revolutionary class must then specifically advance the slogan of dictatorship" ("Dve taktiki sotsialdemokraticheskoi i demokraticheskoi revolyutsii") [Two tactics of the social-democratic and democratic revolution], 8:120. One interesting variant reads: "A revolutionary army is necessary because only by *force* can great historical questions be decided, and *the organization of force* in the contemporary struggle is a military organization (ibid., 8:527).

4. V. I. Lenin and A. M. Gorkii, *Pis'ma, Vospominaniia, dokumenty* [Correspondence, memoirs, documents] (Moscow, 1958), p. 91 (hereafter cited as Lenin and Gorky).

5. Again we catch a note of exultation. The passage reads: "If it was still possible to be satisfied with thin and weak soles when it was a matter of walking on the cultured sidewalks of a little provincial city, it is impossible to go without heavy, hob-nailed soles when you are marching into the mountains. Socialism in Europe has left the state of comparatively peaceful and narrow national limits" so that it is now "impossible to tolerate opportunism" in the day of the "hob-nailed soles." This passage leaves no doubt as to which era and way of struggle Lenin found more congenial (*Sochineniia*, 21:222).

6. Lenin is considered at length in *Three Who Made a Revolution*. Here only such features are touched on as seem most significant for an understanding of his role in the war and the October Revolution.

7. This and subsequent passages from Potresov are from the latter's article, "Lenin," in *Die Gesellschaft* (Berlin, 1927). For a Russian translation, see B. Nikolaevsky, *A. N. Potresov: Posthumous Collection of His Works* (Paris, 1937).

8. For letters to Krzhizhanovsky addressing him with the intimate pronoun, *ty*, and employing the pseudonymous title *Starik*, see Lenin, *Sochineniia*, 34:113–14,

127, 186–88. One letter is extant showing that for a brief period Lenin also felt close enough to Martov so that they addressed each other as *ty*. But with their first political disagreement, Lenin switched to the formal *vy*. There was only one other Bolshevik besides Krzhizhanovsky (we must, of course, except the members of his immediate family, two sisters, a brother, and his wife) to whom Lenin was to write *ty*, namely, Inessa Armand. But by that time he had had a difference with Krzhizhanovsky (in 1904 over the question of splitting the party). Thereafter, though the latter remained his faithful follower and Lenin wrote notes to him almost daily when he made Krzhizhanovsky the chairman of the State Planning Commission, the "Old Man" never used *ty* to him again. Once you had differed with Lenin on a political matter, all intimacy was at an end.

9. For a discussion of the overtones of the use of *Ilyich* and *Starik* as they affect a sensitive Russian ear, see N. Valentinov, *Vstrechi s Leninym* (New York, 1953), pp. 71–73.

10. Lenin, *Sochineniia*, 5:390, 435; 7:338–39.

11. *Leninskii Sbornik* [Collected Leniniana], 6:134 and 137; *Vtoroi ocherednoi s"ezd* [The second regular congress] (Geneva, 1903), p. 241. *Leninskii Sbornik* wrongly ascribes the speech to Rozanov instead of Popov. The *Sbornik* is illustrated with a reproduction of the handwritten notes which Lenin used for the interruption and for his subsequent speech. When a delegate spoke of the rights of party members, Lenin wrote in his notes, "*There are no rights* in party membership. RESPONSIBILITY." But the minutes show that he softened this when he said, "Independent even of rights, we must not forget that every member of the party is responsible for the party and *the party responsible for every member*" (*Vtoroi s"ezd* [Second congress], p. 254).

12. Lenin, *Sochineniia*, 6:211–15.

13. Ibid., 4:273.

14. There is an ambivalence about leadership and its functions even in democratic societies: how far shall the leader follow his followers, and how far seek to lead them? Perhaps in all Marxists, beginning with Marx himself, because they think they know what path and what doctrine the working class *must* choose, there is an unconscious germ of authoritarianism, an intention to indoctrinate, enlighten, in- struct, and direct, according to a preconceived formula. But most Marxists, again beginning with Marx himself, rejected any intention to dictate to the working class. They expected the working class to arrive at its own "consciousness" out of its own experiences, form its own mass parties, select its own leadership, write its own programs. At most the Marxists hoped consciously to serve as informed experts and thus reach official position and the chance to give leadership by virtue of such selection. It was the opponents of Marx, notably the Pole Makhaiski (Machajski) and the Russian Bakunin, who charged that Marxism aimed at a dictatorship by the intelligentsia, a new official class. Among Marxists, however, Lenin was unique in developing this authoritarian germ to full flower, unique in taking pride in it. It was only gradually in the development of their struggle with Lenin and Leninism that the more democratic socialists came to reject the authoritarian strain in the doctrine they had accepted. At the opposite extreme of the spectrum from Lenin

was Axelrod, whose organization doctrine genuinely anticipated the dissolution of the "elite party" in the future mass party of the working class.

15. Lenin's "rages" are discussed from time to time in Krupskaia's letters to his family as if they were a familiar thing to them. They are several times hinted at in her memoirs, where she describes how they are followed by periods of complete exhaustion and a desire only to doze or find solitude in mountain walks. The best analysis of these seizures of rage alternating with depressed exhaustion is to be found in Valentinov, *Vstrechi s Leninym* [Meetings with Lenin], pp. 182 and 210–12. Lenin acknowledges that he was "possessed" by such a "rage" during the controversies with his fellow Iskrists at the Second Congress. He writes of it apologetically in a letter to Potresov, dated Sept. 13, 1903 (Lenin, *Sochineniia*, 34:137–39). He also speaks of the rages which "possess" him in several letters to Gorky. In one such letter he angrily denounces Gorky for "God-constructions" ("Every God-worship is copulation with death"). Because it was Gorky, whom Lenin pardoned for many things and treated with special consideration as a writer useful to the cause, he delayed the sending of the letter until he had cooled off. Nevertheless, he sent it, with a lame apology, for Lenin by no means repudiated in his cooler moments the things he said in his rages. The admission and apology were omitted from the 4th edition of Lenin's works but may be found in Lenin and Gorky, pp. 105–9.

16. *Iskra* ("The Spark") was the name he had chosen for the journal.

17. And Lenin did not mean the word *military* to be merely figurative.

18. Lenin, *Sochineniia*, 5:8–12, 346–50, 355–56, 400–401, 410, 421–22, 431, 440–41, 442–44, 481.

19. Ibid., 36:80.

20. The verbal difference was trivial, but actually Lenin's definition envisaged a party of "professional revolutionaries" or a revolutionary vanguard elite, while Martov's was intended to be looser and more inclusive, making room for anyone who accepted the party's directives and the party's program. For an analysis of this point and other aspects of the congress, see *Three Who Made a Revolution*, chaps. 14 and 15.

21. The election of the members of the leading bodies.

22. Lenin's temporary majority elected Martov also to the editorial board, but he refused to serve because Axelrod, Zasulich, and Potresov had been excluded.

23. Lenin, *Sochineniia*, 34:252.

24. Rafael Abramovich to the writer.

25. It was to remain the common *Program* of both Bolsheviks and Mensheviks until 1919!

26. Karl Marx and Friedrich Engels, *Ausgewaehlte Werke* (Berlin, 1958), 1:360; 2:8.

27. Leon Trotsky, *Lenin* (New York, 1925), p. 43. But when Lenin did not have a majority in the Central Committee, there was no room in his thoughts for the idea of the "subordination of the minority to the majority." Then he would threaten to resign, to mobilize the party against the Central Committee, or even, as in November 1917, to "go to the sailors," i.e., mobilize the unruly, nonparty masses against the party.

28. Lenin, *Sochineniia,* 5:448.

29. Ibid., 7:365–66.

30. *Vospominaniia o Lenine* [Memories of Lenin] (Moscow, 1956), 1:313.

31. Lenin to the Ninth Congress, April 1920; and "II Kongress Kommunisticheskogo Internationala, Stenograficheskii Otchet" [Second congress of the Communist International, stenographic account], p. 576.

32. Lenin, *Sochineniia,* 6–221; cf. ibid., 7:365–66.

33. Ibid.

34. Alfred G. Meyer, *Leninism* (Cambridge, 1957), p. 98. Better, a revolutionary with a bureaucratic-military mind.

35. Lenin, *Sochineniia,* 27:477.

36. Denikin, Kolchak, and Yudenich were leaders of the anti-Bolshevik armies that tried to overthrow Lenin.

37. Lenin, *Sochineniia,* 4:343.

38. Ibid., 5:350 ff.

39. Ibid., pp. 347–48.

40. Ibid., p. 431.

41. Ibid., pp. 355–56.

42. Ibid., p. 392.

43. Ibid., p. 398.

44. Ibid., p. 410.

45. It is interesting to note that of the original *Iskra* six, four were from the hereditary nobility—Plekhanov, Zasulich, Potresov, and Lenin—while the other two, Axelrod and Martov, were *raznochintsy* from those "miscellaneous groups," neither noble, peasant, nor worker that did not belong to any of the basic classes or estates of traditional Russian society. All six were students when they became revolutionaries.

46. Lenin, *Sochineniia,* 5:441.

47. Ibid., 27:420. Lenin uses the term *katorzhno,* derived from the word *katorga,* hard labor in a juridical sense, i.e., penal servitude.

48. Ibid., 5:421.

49. Ibid., pp. 442–43.

50. Cf. "We must put the revolutionary party in the place that the mythical Tsar now holds in the eyes of our citizens" (*Zemlya i volya* [Land and liberty], April 1879).

51. Lenin, *Sochineniia,* 28:54; 32:222; 27:69.

3

LENIN AND
THE CLASS WAR

Because Lenin was a more profound human being than his successors—because his horizon was broader, his utopian faith deeper, simpler and more primitive than that of either Stalin or Khrushchev—a legend has grown up around him which Nikita Khrushchev has not been slow to utilize. Inside the Soviet Union, a hagiography, organized by the most powerful state machine on earth, has prepared for the masses an image of Lenin that obscures his single-minded ruthlessness in a haze of sentiment. The same hagiography has had its effect abroad, where many a bemused mind is made to believe that Lenin overthrew the Tsar and not the only democratic government which Russia ever possessed; made to forget that it was Lenin who laid the foundations of the one-party state, established the first totalitarian regime, introduced the terror, founded the *Cheka*—in short, built and set in motion the power machine into whose driver's seat climbed first Stalin and then Khrushchev.

When Khrushchev proclaims a "return to Leninism," there are many both inside the Soviet Union and abroad who are ready to believe that this means a return to mellow tactics, kindly human ways, gentleness and peace. But one has only to turn to Lenin's own words and the legend is dispelled. Though Lenin never hesitated to shift ground for tactical reasons, through every line he wrote runs a single, consistent thread of terrible simplification and demonic possession. The present article examines only one aspect of his thought, his idea of the class struggle, and limits itself to the early Lenin, before his ideas were implemented by the terrible instruments of power. Yet, it will suffice to restore the true outlines of Lenin's mind and conception.

From *Orbis*, Winter 1960, pp. 443–457. Reprinted by permission of the publisher.

I

When ordinary socialists, at the turn of the century, spoke of the class struggle, they meant little more than a struggle for social reforms, universal suffrage, labor legislation, social security, the development of unions and a party of labor, and the attempt to win men of good will from other classes to labor's side. The social revolution, as they saw it, was a long-range, profound transformation of the political, economic and social structure by a dominant Socialist Party after it had been entrusted with power. Force, as Friedrich Engels pointed out in the waning years of his life, was to be held in reserve to back up the will of the pro-labor majority in the event that a ruling minority attempted to hold on to power or stage a violent counter-revolution.

To be sure, there was a Left, Right and Center in socialism; there were the orthodox and the revisionists, the moderates and the extremists. But the orthodox battled only against attempts to bring Marx's theories "up-to-date." Even Karl Liebknecht called for no more than public opposition by the youth to militarization and Rosa Luxemburg for faith in the creative energy of the masses to be expressed in extra-parliamentary mass action and political general strikes.

Lenin, however, when he said "class war" meant *war*. He was sure, beyond the slightest doubt, that this war would be for the good of humanity. But first a considerable portion of humanity had to be dealt with by war in its literal, formal sense, and power over it had to be acquired by violent warfare. Thus, he promised:

> When we get into power, we will establish the dictatorship of the proletariat, although all development goes toward the abolition of the rule by force of one part of society over another. Dictatorship is a rule of one part of society over the whole of society, and moreover rule resting directly on force. . . . The question of the dictatorship of the proletariat possesses such importance that he who rejects it or recognizes it conditionally cannot be a member of the social democratic party.

It was not altogether impossible, Lenin speculated, that a tiny state, neighbor of a large one that had already established the dictatorship, might be so frightened that the members of its ruling class, "to keep their heads from being cut off," might yield power peacefully when they became convinced of "the hopelessness of further resistance." But he suggested that, even in the case of the little state which is overawed by its revolutionary neighbor: "It is much more probable that in the little states without a civil war socialism *will not* be realized, and therefore the *only* program of the international social democracy must be the recognition of such a war, even though in our ideal there is no place for force over men."[1]

Outside of these two qualifiers—that some men might save their heads by yielding power voluntarily and that the grim conflict was for the ultimate good of that part of humanity which deserved to survive—there was not a trace of the humanitarian, the sentimental or the metaphorical in Lenin's use of the term "class war." It was a war that was to culminate in "that furious or frenzied (*beshenyi*) class war exacerbated to the uttermost, which is called revolution."

Many attempts have been made to explain that strain in Lenin's character which prompted his unique attachment to the "furious uttermost." From his personal biography we can extract the experience of the hanging of his revered elder brother for an attempt on the life of the Tsar while Lenin was an impressionable adolescent. In his spiritual biography we can single out the ideological and psychological roots fed by the early writings of Marx in 1848–50. And among Lenin's Russian contemporaries we can trace the influence of Bakunin, Nechaev and Tkachov, of Chernishevsky and his followers, and of the "Jacobin" and Narodnaya Volya underground of the sixties and seventies.

The writings of Marx from 1848–50 were indeed resonant with cries for war and vengeance and hymns to terror and the fist. ". . . There is only one method of *shortening* the murderous death agonies of the old society, the bloody birth pangs of the new . . . ," Marx had written, "only *one means*— revolutionary terror!" Or: "We are without mercy, we demand no mercy from you. When our turn comes, we will spare no terror." Or again: "The workers must . . . force the democrats to carry out their present terrorist phrases. . . . Far from opposing the so-called excesses, the examples of popular vengeance against hated individuals or public buildings . . . we must not merely tolerate these examples but ourselves take over their leadership."

But there was another Marx. No sooner did it become clear that the storms of 1848 had passed than the more horrendous phase of the writings of Marx and Engels ended and Marx began his long journey into "scientific socialism." To be sure, there were moments when the two founders of socialism, like old warhorses, grew restless at the scent of powder. At no later period, however, did they return to their former exaltation of terror. By 1870, Engels was writing to Marx:

> From these perpetual little *panics* of the French . . . one gets a much better idea of the Reign of Terror. We think of it as the reign of people who instill terror. But quite the contrary, it is the reign of people who are themselves terrified. *La Terreur* is for the most part useless cruelties by people who are themselves frightened, perpetrated for the purpose of reassuring themselves. I am convinced that the blame for the Reign of Terror, Anno 1793, falls almost entirely on the over-nervous bourgeois acting the patriot, on the little philistine

petit-bourgeois soiling his pants out of fright (*kleinen hosenscheissenden Spiessbuerger*), and on the riff-raff mob, making a business out of the *terreur*.[2]

Such a quotation, like other statements by Marx and Engels expressing fear of general war, suited neither the needs nor the temperament of Lenin. But their early writings he engraved upon the tablets of his memory, citing them again and again to confound his fellow orthodox Marxists of the Menshevik camp. Thus was Marxism divided between the two schools of orthodoxy in Russia: Lenin clung to the early Marx while Plekhanov, and to an even greater extent Martov and Axelrod, turned for their favorite citations to the Marx and Engels of the last years. When the Mensheviks forced Lenin to pay heed to their quotations from Marx, he answered with an "orthodox revisionism" of his own: These texts, he claimed, were correct at the moment of their utterance but no longer applicable to the new age of imperialist war and social revolution—nor to Russia on the eve of a "bourgeois democratic revolution."

This latter claim led to much debate among Russian Marxists—a debate which was couched in the dates of the revolutionary French calendar. Was Russia on the eve of her 1789, 1793, or 1848? The use of the calendar of actual uprisings in France gave Lenin a decided advantage, for it made both wings of orthodox Marxism talk in terms of an impending violent upheaval. In the later writings of Marx, revolution was often a synonym for fundamental political and economic change. For the Russian Marxists, however, stirred by the memories of their own nineteenth century revolutionaries and the upheaval of 1905, revolution tended to become a synonym for street fighting, mutinies, chateau burnings and barricades. In these endeavors, Lenin could always outbid his competitors.

II

Just as he leaned on early Marxism to the virtual exclusion of the later body of Marx's thought, so Lenin inclined to the early and more primitive theory and practice of the Russian revolutionary tradition.

In the sixties and seventies, the peasantry was passive while a working class scarcely existed. One tendency among Russian idealists had been to "go to the people," to awaken and enlighten them by patient education and service, to stir in them a deeper sense of human dignity and the worth of the personality. Another group had sought to act in the people's name, to awaken them by deeds of sacrificial terror, or by a conspiratorial seizure of power from which vantage point the people could be dragged into the future. Lenin took his inspiration from the latter school.

The best critical summary of the fusion in Lenin of elements of primitive Marxism with certain elements of primitive Russian revolutionary tradition comes from the pen of the historian Michael Karpovich:

Leninist Bolshevism represented a unique amalgam of *certain elements* of Marxism and of the Russian non-Marxist revolutionary tradition. And, in the first case as in the second, Lenin took from the heritage of the past that which was *most negative* and *most obsolete*.

The ideological and psychological roots of Bolshevism have to be sought in the early Marxism of the epoch of the revolutionary communism of the middle of the past century, and in the Russian revolutionary underground of a Jacobin type of the sixties and seventies. In accord with the conspiratorial pathos of the Bolshevik movement, Lenin took from these two sources their authoritarian and sectarian-doctrinaire elements: the idea of dictatorship, the idea of a revolutionary elite, the belief in the omnipotence of revolutionary violence, the contempt for "formal democracy," the political amoralism and fanatical intolerance in the holding of revolutionary doctrine, which claimed the role of the all-embracing world view obligatory for everyone.

. . . The spirit of love of liberty was alien to Leninist Bolshevism from the outset and remained alien to it to the end. Its place was taken by the spirit of violence and compulsion. For the intrinsic worth and dignity of the human personality there is no place in Bolshevism: the human being is only a means to the attainment of the revolutionary goals which Bolshevism has set for itself. To those goals they are ready to sacrifice without doubt or hesitation not only individual human beings but whole social groups. The love of the people of the earlier revolutionaries is replaced by a "practical" approach to the popular masses. . . .[3]

Lenin never took pains to be consistent or systematic. He wrote as a political journalist, reacting to each occasion and each remark of his opponents. Yet his utterances on violence, terror and the class war form a coherent, consistent and cumulative whole. It is astonishing how early this side of his thought appears fully formed.

In the first issue of *Iskra* (December 1900) he wrote: ". . . With regard to tactics, Social Democracy does not tie its hands. . . . It recognizes all methods of struggle."[4] In the first issue of the theoretical journal *Zarya* (January 1901), he asserted: "Trial by the street is valuable because it breathes a living spirit into the bureaucratic formalism which pervades our government institutions."[5] In "Where to Begin" (*Iskra*, May 1901) Lenin discussed terror. "We have never," he said, "rejected terror on principle, nor can we ever do so." However, acts of terror should not be committed in isolation from the general struggle, but rather in close union with it, lest the most heroic and energetic be fruitlessly sacrificed, thus "weakening the fighting detachments upon which alone serious hopes can be placed." An organization was needed capable of combining all forces and methods of struggle and "supporting and utilizing every outbreak . . . for the purpose of increasing and strengthening the military force required for the decisive battle.""⁶ "Fighting detachments," "military force"—these were strange words for a journal that had just been founded to build an as yet non-existent party!

Next, in a quarrelsome address in June 1901 to the liberal opposition with which *Iskra* was supposed to be cementing an alliance, Lenin observed offhandedly in a footnote: "The *real* political training of the worker masses can be given them only through their manysided participation in the revolutionary movement, including open street fighting, including civil war with the defenders of political and economic slavery."⁷

In *What Is to Be Done?*, the programmatic pamphlet of Leninism published in 1902, he asked himself the question: "What type of organization do we require?" His answer was: "Regular, permanent troops . . . to take their place at the head of the crowd . . . and *merge* the elemental destructive force of the crowd with the conscious destructive force of the organization of revolutionaries." These "permanent troops" were nothing else but the network of *Iskra* agents (officers' cadres) and the local armies they are to gather around them: "An organization that is built up around this newspaper . . . will be ready *for everything*, from protecting the honor, the prestige, the continuity of the party in periods of acute revolutionary 'depression,' to . . . the carrying out of the *national armed insurrection.*"⁸

All the strong and specific formulations we have quoted thus far came from Lenin's pen prior to 1903. They were therefore published in the old *Iskra* (or in *Zarya*)—hence, in the name of all six editors, Plekhanov, Axelrod, Zasulich, Martov, Potresov and Lenin. When, in 1903–04, Lenin broke with the other five, he was able to express himself with even less restraint.⁹ Moreover, in the year 1904 the Russo-Japanese War broke out, putting, Lenin said, "the bayonet on the order of the day." And the year 1905, which began with Priest Gapon's peaceful workingmen's march to the Tsar and ended amid barricades in Moscow, convinced Lenin that he had been right all along. At the same time, the event raised his excitement to fever pitch.

Priest Gapon's procession marched, and was fired upon, on January 22.¹⁰ Living then in Geneva, Lenin, as soon as he saw the first foreign press reports, wrote an analysis which culminated in a call for "the immediate arming of the workers and all citizens in general, the preparation and organization of the revolutionary forces for the annihilation of the governmental power and institutions."¹¹ Then, in an article entitled "The Plan of the Battle of Saint Petersburg," he explained to his readers that Priest Gapon's procession and the firing on it by the troops were part of a carefully thought out plan by the Tsar to "call forth" an uprising in order to crush it and "teach the proletariat a lesson." The working class would not forget the lesson—"a military one"—that the era of armed uprising had come. The

proletariat would now "teach itself the art of civil war," for: "Revolution
is war. Of all the wars known to history, this is the only lawful, just,
righteous, truly great war. . . . The workers will arm themselves everywhere.
. . . Each one by himself will strain all his force to get himself a gun, or at
least a revolver. . . ."[12]

Now Lenin recalled the "Russian Jacobin" tradition of Chernishevsky
and Zaichnevsky, the celebrated appeal to the axe.[13] He wove it skillfully
into his comment by picking up the following "conversation reported by a
British correspondent" in Moscow:

> "Axes?" says one.
> "No, with axes you won't be able to do anything against sabres. With an axe
> you can't get to him, perhaps with a knife, but that is even less. No, what is
> needed is revolvers, at the least revolvers, but still better, guns."

"Such conversations," Lenin added, "are now taking place over all Russia
. . . and not stopping at mere talk. . . . From all the thought of the masses
. . . into the consciousness of the masses will come this conclusion: in war
it necessary to act according to the ways of war. . . ."[14]

He burned with impatience for the Russian masses to arm themselves
and engage in armed revolt. Instead, millions went on strike—millions who
had never heard of Bolshevism and Menshevism, of the "inevitably bourgeois" nature of their "spontaneous activity," or of Lenin's organizational
plan. From all throats rose an instinctive cry for unity of all opposition
forces against the government. From the "accursed distance" Lenin mis-
judged, or misprised, the longing for unity. He redoubled his efforts to
harden the split in the social democracy, to call a rump conference of his
faction, now an undoubted minority, which conference must claim that it
was the Congress of the Party, choose a "Central Committee" amenable to
his will, and set up an "Official Organ" to oppose *Iskra*.

Since he had broken with the old guard of orthodox Marxism, Lenin
was not scrupulous in his choice of the new men he picked personally, one
by one, to be his lieutenants. These included the philosophers Bogdanov
and Bazarov, the writer Lunacharsky, the engineer Krassin, his future Duma
floor-leader Alexinsky, none of whom he could regard as an "orthodox
Marxist." Neither Bogdanov nor Bazarov accepted "dialectical materialism." In philosophy they leaned on Kant rather than Hegel, and opposed
Mach and Avenarius to Plekhanov and Engels. Lunacharsky was to lay in
Lenin's intellectual nest the cuckoo egg of "God building." But at this
moment they were "useful," so he built with them, as he explained later to
Gorky, his tactical bloc "neutral on philosophy." Most of them were "softs"
who, by way of compensation, found his "rockhard" extremism tremendously attractive. To Litvinov, a true "hard" but a minor lieutenant, Lenin

wrote his praises of the new recruits, particularly Bogdanov, who is "working at everything, has attracted collaborators, devotes himself completely to finding a millionaire, with no little chance of success."[15]

His lieutenants inside Russia, including those he had handpicked for the Central Committee, could not but sense the rising tide of unity. This brought angry letters from him, full of "scorn" for those whom "the revolution seems to have made soft" instead of hardened. Had he lost control of the Central Committee and of *Iskra*? Then, in spite of Central Organ and Central Committee and *against* them, he would call the Congress:

> Our only strength is our open inflexibility and compactness of organization, in the energy of the offensive. . . . We have proclaimed a *split*, we will call for a congress of *Vperyodists*. We want to organize a *Vperyodist* party and to break, immediately break *any* and *all* relations with the disorganizers— and they talk to us of loyalty. . . . ! The Congress must be simple, short, not many people. A Congress for the organization of war.[16]

Though later the tide of unity was to overwhelm even Lenin, forcing him to work once more in the same party with the Mensheviks for a few years, by April 1905 he had managed to convoke his separate Congress. It was what Lenin wanted it to be: *"a Congress for war"*—war on *Iskra* and war on the government.

In a preliminary draft of the call for Congress, Lenin inserted the following points into the order of business: "organization, relation to the periphery, uprising, arming the workers (setting up workshops for making dynamite), agreements with the Social Revolutionaries for an uprising, support of the revolutionary peasant movement. . . ."[17] *"Workshops for making dynamite"* on the order of business of a socialist congress—even among the "rockhard" who but Lenin could think of that?

Just before the Congress, which finally convened at the end of April, Lenin personally translated into Russian a section of the memoirs of General Cluseret, entitled "On Street Fighting." This was intended as study material for the armed workers' detachments. In an outline of what the Congress should take up, he wrote:

a) Necessity for immediate preparation of an uprising.
b) Necessity for creation of . . . fighting organizations.
c) Necessity for multiplying organization in general: to organize the revolution.
d) Terror must in practice be fused with the movement of the masses.
e) Aim of the uprising: provisional revolutionary government, arming of the people, constituent assembly, revolutionary peasant committees.[18]

On Lenin's motion, the Congress duly decided to "organize an armed uprising, and to create for this purpose an informational and a leading apparatus . . . organization of special groups to secure and distribute arms, and the direct leadership thereof."[19]

By now, Lenin's "Marxist doctrine" was reduced (or elevated) to the single formula: *armed uprising*. In an article entitled "New Tasks and New Goals," he explained:

> This does not mean, of course, that it is in order . . . to neglect the systematic teaching of the truths of Marxism. No, but it is needful to remember that now an enormously greater significance is possessed by the preparation and teaching of military actions themselves, which will *teach* the unprepared precisely in *our* and completely in our direction. It is needful to remember that our "doctrinaire" belief in Marxism is strengthened now by the fact that the course of revolutionary events gives everywhere, and in everything, *object lessons to the masses*, and all these lessons confirm precisely our dogma. We are not speaking of renouncing dogmas . . . just the opposite. We are speaking of new methods of teaching the dogma. . . . We are speaking of how important it is now to utilize the obvious lessons of the great revolutionary events to teach no longer little circles but the masses our old "dogmatic lessons," for example, the lesson that what is needed is the active fusion of the terror with the uprising of the masses. . . .[20]

Lenin, of course, was right in this claim. He had not had to wait for the storms of 1905, or the holocaust of 1914, to advocate terror and systematic preparation of armed uprising. These elements of the Marxism of 1848–50 had been the core of *his* Marxism all along. Even in the suffocating years of the nineties and the quiet period from 1900 to 1904, this had been the sum and substance of his intransigence, his Jacobinism, his centralized conspiratorial, hierarchical and authoritarian conception of organization. In his claim in 1905, and more insistently in the period from 1914 to 1917, that his was "the only true" and orthodox Marxism there was not a trace of hypocrisy or vainglory. He wrote in the summer of 1905:

> Great questions in the life of a people are decided only by force. Once such a situation has been created, once the bayonet really stands as the first order of political business . . . then constitutional illusions and scholastic exercises in parliamentarism become nothing but a cover for bourgeois betrayal of the revolution. . . . The truly revolutionary class must then advance the slogan of the dictatorship.[21]

"Great questions in the life of the peoples are decided only by force!" Lenin was to repeat this sentence again and again, as the first axiom of his revolutionary geometry.

And what did one do in the years when "the bayonet was not on the order of business"? One organized "the cadres of the revolutionary army" that would be suited to the storms which must surely come. And one taught that capitalism must inevitably bring the years of the bayonet, as surely as the accumulating clouds bring a storm.

In the Resolution "On Armed Uprising" which Lenin prepared for his Congress of April–May 1905, he wrote:

> The Congress resolves . . . that by preparation of the uprising it understands not only the preparation of weapons and creation of groups, etc., but equally the accumulation of experience by means of practical attempts at individual armed attacks, for example, attacks of armed detachments upon the police and the army . . . on prisons, government institutions, etc.[22]

His organization in Saint Petersburg duly set up a "Military Committee" to accomplish these things, but Lenin soon became convinced that it was doing "nothing but discussing." Already armed bands were staging holdups and jail breaks, and murdering police in Poland and in the Caucasus. But they were not under the control of his organization. Was his organization good only for talk? His answer was unequivocal:

> The bomb has ceased to be the weapon of the solitary bomb-thrower. It has become a *necessary part* of the equipment for arming the people. . . .
>
> Preparation of bombs is possible everywhere and in all places. . . . No force can oppose the detachments of a revolutionary army which arms itself with bombs. . . .
>
> In this, frenzied energy is needed, and yet more energy. With consternation, by God with consternation, I see that there has been talk of bombs *for more than a half year*, and not a single bomb has yet been made.[23]

What could Lenin do "at the accursed distance" but write instructions so detailed that they could not be evaded, so simple that they could be followed by anyone, even without the guidance of his committee? The result was a notable document: "Tasks of the Sections of the Revolutionary Army." It was written at a moment when the Tsar was promising a constitution and large sections of the opposition were deciding to cease all attacks until they could see whether the Tsar's promises were genuine and meaningful. This, thought Lenin, was all the more reason to push for an uprising.

The detachments, he wrote, should have two related tasks: to engage in military actions on their own and to assume leadership over mobs. The detachments might be of any size, beginning with two or three. They must "arm themselves the best they can (guns, revolvers, bombs, knives, brass knuckles, cudgels, rags with kerosene to start fires, rope or rope ladders, spades for building barricades, barbed wire, tacks against cavalry, etc. and so forth). In no case wait for help from above, from outside, but procure everything themselves." They should select leaders or officers, work out signals to hang in their windows, agree upon cries, whistles, passwords, signs by which to know each other amid tumult or in the dark. Even before they had arms they could assume the leadership of crowds, "attack a policeman or a cossack that has gotten separated, and take away his weapons; rescue the arrested and wounded when the police are not numerous; climb on roofs or upper floors and shower stones on troops, boiling water, etc." They should start "theoretical studies" of the art of warfare (for this Lenin had translated General Cluseret). They could invite friendly officers and workingmen who had been in the army to teach what they knew.

But from the outset, they needed "practical training" as well. This should include procurement of weapons and explosives, selection of good sites for street fighting ("good for giving battle from above, for storing bombs or stones, etc., to pour acid on the police, etc."). Practical training should include espionage and reconnaissance to learn the layout of prisons, police stations, ministries, official institutions and banks, how they are guarded, to strike up friendships with guards and service personnel, locate supplies of arms, arsenals, etc. (Always there is the "etc. and so forth" at the end of virtually every sentence and catalogue of deeds of terror and daring, as if Lenin were afraid that he might forget something, or that overly servile and disciplined followers might not go beyond the letter of his instructions.)

"The aged, women, children, and altogether weak persons" had their work cut out for them, too. After all, how much strength does it take to spy on the enemy, to pour oil or acid or boiling water from a roof, to strew tacks before horses?

From the very beginning it is important not to limit one's self to mere preparatory work, but as soon as possible undertake "military actions" with the aims of: "1) training forces; 2) spying out the weak spots of the enemy; 3) dealing him partial defeats; 4) liberating prisoners (the arrested); 5) securing arms; 6) getting hold of resources for the uprising (confiscation of government funds, etc., etc. . . . for, without training *under fire* it is impossible to acquire the readiness for an uprising."

Since "the slogan of an uprising *has already been proclaimed* and the uprising has already *begun*" (did not Lenin himself issue the call and proclaim the "beginning of the uprising" three days after Priest Gapon's procession was fired upon?), it follows that "to begin attacks under proper circumstances is not only a right but the outright duty of every revolutionary. The killing of spies, policemen, gendarmes, the blowing up of police buildings, the liberating of the arrested, the seizing of government funds for use in the uprising" cannot be premature. Has not the Polish Socialist Party under Pilsudski already begun them? Why are we Bolsheviks lagging? To miss any opportunity now "is the greatest crime for a revolutionist . . . the greatest shame for anyone striving for freedom, not in words but in deeds." Those "democrats" who refuse to take part must be branded as quasi-democrats."[24]

These directives, and the train of thought which led to them, are unique in the history of modern socialism. Neither in the Russian social democracy nor in the entire International was there another man who could have conceived and issued these coldly calculated yet passionate directives. Engels, though he fought on the barricades in 1848, wrote much on military matters and delighted in the nickname, "The General," has nothing like it in his writings. The Marx of 1848, with his eulogies to terror, popular vengeance and the fist, seems but to be "unpacking his heart with curses" compared to these thoughtful, systematic instructions on acid from rooftops, tacks for horses' hoofs and kerosene rags to start fires. The ruthlessness of Nechaev, the romantic exaltation of banditry and barricade by Bakunin, the appeal of Zaichnevsky to the axe, seem mild by comparison. Here, in Lenin's doctrine, is the pedantry, systematization and scientific organization of terror.

Even the ardent Rosa Luxemburg, for all her exaltation of extra-parlia-mentary mass action and revolutionary general strike, rejected with aversion the acts of revolutionary banditry and murder of policemen committed by Pilsudski's armed detachments in Russian Poland, and the banditry soon to be committed under Lenin's leadership in Moscow and the Caucasus.[25] Up to August 1914, the overwhelming majority in every socialist party rejected both Lenin's organizational methods and his methods of waging the class war. Had they understood more fully what he was saying and realized that he meant every word, they would have been more outraged still.

But in August 1914 began the terrible years—four long years during which statesmen and generals treated their people as "human material" to be expended without stint or calculation in the pursuit of meaningless and unattainable objectives. Men learned to accept as an everyday affair the ruthless logic of mutual extermination. They learned to master their fear of death and their revulsion against inflicting it. They learned the law of the grenade, the shell, the rifle and the machine gun, of the few feet of mud gained and lost at the cost of X number of casualties. "They developed a monstrous indifference to suffering, their own as well as that of others." Universal war so brutalized European man that, in the words of Reinhold Niebuhr, it became possible to "beguile men into fresh brutalities by the fury of their resentment against brutality."

Lenin's technique of organization and his plans for "class war" began to seem less alien, to arouse less indignation. "Since it was a time of horrors," as Raymond Aron would write later, "at least let violence have peace as its objective, and as its enemy the civilization that had made the sterile carnage possible." Now that all the affairs of men were being subjected to the arbitration of bayonet and bullet, why not the nature of the "system" out of which the crisis had come? If Lenin still rejected peace in favor of having the world war prolonged and turned into civil war, this "fine point" of distinction was now less noticeable.

Thus, war was Lenin's opportunity, for it made his fantastic prescriptions for the class war seem more timely and natural. Before there could come that reign of what Churchill would one day call "the bloody-minded professors of the Kremlin," there first had to be the bloodbath of Flanders Field, where, as England's wartime leader, Lloyd George was to write, "nothing could stop Haig's compulsion to send thousands and thousands to their death against the enemy's guns in the bovine and brutal game of attrition."

NOTES TO CHAPTER 3

1. V. I. Lenin, *Collected Works* (Moscow, 1949), 23:57. It was this passage from Lenin's works which caused such a spate of commentary in the Western press on communism's "new line" of "possible social revolution without civil war," when Khrushchev quoted it at the 20th Congress. This in spite of the fact that Khrushchev, as a "good Leninist," made clear that it applied only to small states, neighbors of great states where communism had already won power.

2. Marx-Engels, *Ausgewählte Schriften* (Berlin, 1958), 1:98–99; *Nachlass* (Berlin, 1923), 3:267–68.

3. M. Karpovich, "Traditsii russkoi obshchestvennoi mysli," in *Sudby Rossii* (New York, 1957), pp. 22–24.

4. *Collected Works*, 4:345–46.

5. Ibid., p. 369.

6. Ibid., 5:7–9.

7. Ibid., p. 57*n*. The footnote reveals once more Lenin's contempt for the workers' own organizations and their struggles for their own objectives. The footnote reads: " 'The economic organizations of the workers,' says Mr. R. N. S. [Struve], 'serve as a school for the practical political training of the masses of the workers.' We would advise our author to be more careful in his use of the term 'practical,' so beloved by knights of opportunism. . . . Under certain conditions the industrial organizations may help very considerably toward their political training . . . under other circumstances they may help toward their political corruption. But *real* political training can be given to the worker masses only through all-sided participation in the revolutionary movement, including open street fighting, including civil war against the defenders of political and economic slavery."

8. Ibid., p. 481.

9. One curious episode suggests that Lenin may have been checked by his fellow editors on at least one occasion. In 1906, in an article on the "Lessons of the Moscow Uprising," Lenin wrote: "We could and should have surrounded the Malakhovs [Aide to the Commander of the Moscow Military District] with bomb-throwers. Long ago, in the old *Iskra*, the Social Democratic press pointed out that a merciless extermination of civilian and military leaders is our duty in a period of uprising." *Collected Works* (Moscow, 1947), 11:149. Manifestly, Lenin is quoting something

he wrote for the old *Iskra*. But the author has looked in vain for such a passage, as have the editors of his works. The nearest they could find to it is a passage which speaks merely of "systematic terror" but makes no mention of "extermination of civil and military leaders." [See Lenin's *Selected Works*, English ed. (New York), 3:350 and 589.] A possible explanation is that Lenin did, indeed, write such a passage on "extermination" for the old *Iskra*, but the other editors, or some one of them, going over the proofs, eliminated it. In any case, Lenin thought he had published such a passage, and from what we know of the six, he is the only one who could have thought of writing it.

10. On January 9, according to the Old Style Calendar in use in Russia until 1917. Throughout this article, the Western or Reformed Calendar is generally used, unless otherwise noted.

11. The article was dated Geneva, January 25, 1905. *Collected Works*, 8:79.

12. Ibid., p. 87.

13. Chernishevsky to Herzen: "Nothing will do here but the axe. Change your tone. Let your *Bell* stop calling the faithful to prayer and sound the tocsin. Call Russia to the axe." The famous declaration of his disciple Zaichnevsky, calling on the revolutionists to use the axe on the Tsar and his family and all who defend them, is too well known to require citation here.

14. Ibid., p. 88.

15. Ibid., 34:245.

16. Ibid., 8:122–24.

17. Ibid., p. 157.

18. Ibid., p. 162.

19. Ibid., pp. 336 and 342.

20. Ibid., p. 191.

21. Ibid., p. 111. Among the various repetitions of this "axiom," the best known is in Lenin's article entitled, "Revolutionary Army and Revolutionary Government," in which he writes: "A revolutionary army is necessary because only *by force* may be settled great historical questions, and the *organization of force* in the contemporary struggle is a military organization." (8:527.)

22. Ibid., 8:337.

23. Ibid., 9:258–59 and 315.

24. Ibid., pp. 389–93.

25. For an account of Lenin's use of armed bands and revolutionary banditry, see chapter 22 ("Arms and the Man") in the author's *Three Who Made a Revolution* (New York, 1948). For Rosa Luxemburg's attack on revolutionary banditry, see ibid., p. 375.

4

HOW LENIN PREPARED FOR AUGUST 1914

The power of the Marxist-Leninist theory lies in the fact that it enables the Party to find the right orientation in any situation, to understand the inner connection of current events, to foresee their course, and to perceive not only how and in what direction they are developing in the present, but how and in what direction they are bound to develop in the future.—HISTORY OF THE COMMUNIST PARTY: SHORT COURSE

In his youth Adolf Hitler cursed the fate that had put him on earth in a time of "quiet and order." The Balkan Wars came like a "first gust of wind." In 1914, "I fell down on my knees and thanked Heaven out of my overflowing heart."[1]

Not one to fall on his knees or thank Heaven, Lenin, too, watched hopefully for the Balkan Wars of 1912 and 1913 to spread to Austria and Russia. Between considering war beautiful and considering war "useful" there is a world of difference, yet neither attitude bespeaks a special love for peace.

If we examine Lenin's writings prior to August 1914, we are struck by the total absence of any concern with averting war. While congress after congress of the Socialist International made this concern its major preoccupation, while Bebel, Jaurès, and other European leaders filled whole shelves with their writings on war and made the air ring with their expressions of abhorrence, Lenin seemed unaware of the shadow darkening Europe. Or unconcerned. Or hopeful. His references to war prior to 1914 would not make even a thin pamphlet. But what little there is about war between nations, as in the case of his attitude towards war between the classes, reveals Lenin as unique in his generation.

In 1904, Japan went to war with Russia over Korea and Manchuria. Millions of peasants and workingmen were sent to far-off Siberia to fight and die. This elicited from a Lenin a May Day Manifesto, expressing the hope that combat at such a distance between autocratic Russia and "cultured and free Japan" would reveal the incapacity of the Tsar's government to wage modern war and would promote revolution in Russia.

The first defeats of his country (at the Yalu and Dairen) pleased him greatly, but he said nothing in print until the fall of Port Arthur. Then he broke into celebration:

The Russian forces have lost a whole army . . . 48,000 prisoners; and how many thousands more have perished in the battles before Kinchao and before the fortress itself? . . . The military blow is irretrievable . . . the Russian Pacific fleet destroyed once and for all . . . It is quite likely that the war will be prolonged but its hopelessness is already evident . . .

Yes, the European bourgeoisie has good reason to fear. The proletariat good reason to rejoice. The catastrophe of our worst enemy means not only the approach of Russian freedom. It heralds, too, a new revolutionary upsurge of the European proletariat . . .

Progressive, advanced Asia has dealt an irreparable blow to backward, reactionary Europe.

There is no talk against "progressive" Japan's carving up of China. Rather the contrary:

Ten years ago, this same reactionary Europe, Russia at the head, was upset by the breaking up of China by Japan, and united to deprive her of the best fruits of her victory . . . The return of Port Arthur to the Japanese is a blow dealt to all reactionary Europe . . .

That Port Arthur was a port of China does not concern him. His real hope from all these defeats is formulated in these terms: the mighty Russian giant has proved to be mere outward show (Lenin uses the word *mishura*— "tinsel"); with a lazy and corrupt bureaucracy, and with an ignorant and backward peasant mass, modern war with modern weapons "cannot be waged successfully."

As Lenin was to repeat during the World War, one of the "mighty advantages" of wars was that they "mercilessly reveal, expose and destroy much that is rotten, outlived, moribund in human institutions."

By its stupid and criminal adventure, the autocracy has gotten itself into a blind alley from which there is no exit except through the people themselves, and only at the expense of the destruction of tsarism . . . War of an advanced land with a backward one, as often in the past, has this time too played a revolutionary role.

The war, he hoped, was "far from ended." Every further step must bring fresh defeats and "bring nearer the moment of the new great war, the war of the people against the autocracy."[2]

The article on "The Fall of Port Arthur" thus contained the germ of the position Lenin was to develop in 1914. Though the war of 1914–1918 would clarify and develop many new aspects of his attitude, there was only one point in the article on the fall of Port Arthur which he would have to jettison. In 1905, he found Japan "cultured, progressive, and free." He had no word of criticism for Japanese imperialism and no word to say on revolution in Japan. In 1914, he would charge both camps with being imperialistic and would broaden his hopes from revolution in Russia to revolution in all the world.

In the Port Arthur article, he broadened his differences with other socialists. Both the Social Revolutionary journal, *Revolyutsionnaya Rossiya*, and the Menshevik *Iskra* called for peace to end the sufferings of the Russian and Japanese peoples. Both rebuked the French Marxist Jules Guesde and the English Marxist Hyndman for avowing sympathy with Japan. They reminded Guesde and Hyndman, and by implication Lenin, that the Japanese "had a bourgeoisie too." *Iskra* condemned Lenin for "speculating on the victory of Japan," and for its part called for "peace at all costs."

Lenin took refuge in the writings of Marx and Engels, who had taken sides in every "capitalist" war in their time, according to their judgment as to "whose victory would be more advantageous to democracy and socialism." It is "perfectly understandable," wrote Lenin, that Guesde and Hyndman, "these most consistent and decisive representatives of revolutionary international social democracy, have expressed without ifs and buts their sympathy with Japan, which is shattering the Russian autocracy." Though socialists are enemies of all bourgeoisies, "this enmity does not absolve them from the duty of distinguishing between historically progressive and reactionary representatives" of that class.

In 1914, Lenin would claim to be absolved from this duty of distinguishing between historically progressive and historically reactionary representatives of the bourgeoisie. In 1917, after the Tsar fell, Lenin would not even distinguish between revolutionary Russia, "the freest government in the world," and Wilhelm's Germany. He would do his best to obliterate all traces of the fact that in "the epoch of imperialism," as late as 1905, he had thus followed the practice of Marx and Engels and distinguished between "historically progressive" and "historically reactionary" bourgeoisies.

After his hymn of rejoicing at the fall of Port Arthur, Lenin scarcely mentioned the Russo-Japanese War again. He became absorbed completely in his "class war" against the Tsarist autocracy and in his war against all rival socialist movements. Only the disturbing news that there were behind-the-scenes peace soundings roused him to a fresh discussion of the war. Its sharp edge was directed not against the Tsar, but against *Iskra*.

The peace negotiations, he declared flatly, were being forced on the Tsar by his French bankers. They were trying to force him at the same time to make domestic peace by granting to "the liberal Russian bourgeoisie" a constitution and a limited monarchy.

Having painted this fanciful picture of the "peace plot" of the European bourgeoisie with the Russian Tsar and the Russian liberal bourgeoisie, he found it unexceptionable. The strong-minded Lenin was never one to doubt his own speculations, nor to permit others to doubt them. Since that's how things were, *Iskra* must now see how wrong had been its call for peace, its denunciation of Lenin for speculating on a Japanese victory, its slogan of "Peace at all costs."

> Now reality has shown that "peace at all costs" has become the slogan of the European stock exchange and the reactionaries . . . The phrases of the new Iskrists have turned out to be nothing but sentimental phrases, alien to a class viewpoint and to the calculation of the relation of the various forces . . . It is impermissible to demand only peace, for Tsarist peace is not better (and sometimes worse) than Tsarist war. It is impermissible to raise the slogan, "peace at all costs," only peace together with the fall of the autocracy, peace made by a freed people . . . i.e., not peace at all costs, but only and exclusively at the cost of the overthrow of absolutism. We will hope that, having understood this much, *Iskra* will also understand the impropriety of its haughty moral tirade against speculation on the victory of the Japanese bourgeoisie . . . Both the one conclusion and other were worthy only of a bourgeois democrat who judges political questions on a sentimental basis. . . .[3]

When peace came, Lenin was too busy with his efforts to develop armed detachments and an armed uprising to so much as take notice of it in his writings.

In the great debates of the Socialist International on war and militarism, Lenin took no part. Only at the Stuttgart Congress of 1907 was he a participant—behind the scenes. At that time, Martov for the Mensheviks, Lenin for the Bolsheviks,[4] and Rosa Luxemburg for the Polish Social Democracy prepared an amendment to Bebel's resolution. It was an amendment to an amendment prepared by Bebel himself. Actually it was Rosa who drafted it, introduced it, and spoke on it in the Congress. For Lenin, the important phrase was to be the one italicized below:

> Should war nonetheless break out, it is their duty to intervene in favor of its speedy termination, and *to do all in their power to utilize the economic and political crisis caused by the war to rouse the peoples and thereby to hasten the abolition of capitalist class rule.*

The italics were not in the original. The resolution, like all the International's compromise unanimous resolutions on war, was not very specific, but Lenin would make it work; repeating it during the Great War, he would introduce the italics and the one-sided emphasis. To Rosa, as to Martov and Bebel, war was in itself an evil, and the first half of the sentence, binding socialists to work for the speediest possible restoration of peace, was a serious pledge. But not to Lenin. In an article on the Stuttgart Congress in the Bolshevik paper *Proletarii* for October 20, 1907, he even then played fast and loose with the whole spirit of Bebel's resolution and with the first half of the very amendment introduced by Rosa Luxemburg in his name. The "essence" of the resolution, he wrote, is not in preventing the outbreak of war, but in using the crisis engendered by war for the acceleration of the overthrow of the bourgeoisie.[5]

In the same spirit Lenin had rejected the idea of ending the Russo-Japanese War ("not peace at all costs but only and exclusively at the cost of the overthrow of absolutism"). In the abstract, he recognized that it was "proper" to agitate against war and militarism, but merely as one of the ways of agitating against capitalism which was pregnant with war as storm clouds with rain. However, revolution, too, needed war in order to spread to all the ends of the earth. Revolution, too, was pregnant with war as the clouds with rain; hence, he was not going to spread mental disarmament and pacifism among the class that would have to wage it. A show of moral indignation against "war as such" was treason to the class that would have to fight the greatest and holiest of all wars in history. To pretend that war could be averted in either case, whether under capitalism or in time of revolution, was deception, philistinism, treason.

On March 29, 1913, when the Bulgarians had just taken Adrianople and the first Balkan War was drawing to a close, Lenin wrote optimistically that the war was "a link in the chain of world events signifying the collapse of the Middle Ages in Asia and Eastern Europe." Because the proletariat was too weak, "these tasks have been resolved by a war led by bourgeois and dynastic interests." It had been a progressive war, an important step in "the creation of unified national states in the Balkans, the overthrow of the yoke of local feudalists, the final emancipation of the Balkan peasants of all the various nationalities from the yoke of large landed interests." But the almost instantaneous regrouping in the Balkans that saw Turkey lined up with Serbia, Greece, and Rumania, in a new war against Bulgaria made mincemeat of Lenin's analysis, whereupon he said nothing more about the Balkan wars, although he now had a daily paper at his disposal and the kaleidoscopic conflicts continued into the autumn.[6]

As he had not been able to believe in the "stroke of luck" that would bring Russia and Austria into these wars, still less could he believe that the "more enlightened and progressive" German rulers were the main support of the Russian autocracy, not its enemy. Besides, the German Kaiser knew better than to give the German Social Democracy its chance at revolution. In *Pravda* of May 22, 1913, at the height of the tensions of Austria-Hungary, Russia, Italy and Germany over the Balkans, Lenin wrote in praise of the German Social Democracy, of the superiority of the Austro-Hungarian constitution to the Russian, of the Hapsburg pacific policy and enlightened attitude towards its Slavic population, and in scornful ridicule of the German Chancellor's talk of the war danger:

> The German Chancellor is frightening the German philistines with the *Slavic menace*. They are supposed to see that the Balkan victories have strengthened "Slavdom," which is hostile to the entire "Germanic world"!
>
> ... The German Social Democrats have exposed, and unceasingly continue to expose in their press, their speeches in parliament, and at their meetings, these hypocritical, chauvinistic fantasies. There is a state, say the Social Democrats, which has a Slavic majority population, and this majority has long been enjoying political freedom and a constitutional order. That state is Austria. To fear intentions of war from this state is outright stupid.
>
> Forced to the wall, the German Chancellor based his claim on the noisy demonstrations of the Panslavists in Petersburg. A fine proof! Munitions manufacturers, armor makers, cannon and powder makers, and manufacturers of other such "cultural" needs, want to enrich themselves both in Germany and in Russia, and, to fool the public, they mutually rely upon each other. The Germans frighten the Russian chauvinists, the Russians the German! And both the one group and the other are playing a pitiful role in the hands of the capitalists who know perfectly that of a war between Russia and Germany it is ridiculous even to think.[7]

If the "power of the Marxist theory" lies indeed in its enabling its possessor "to foresee the course of events," then Lenin was at that moment about the poorest Marxist in all Europe.

Whether because he thought it too good to be true or because he was a bad prophet, Lenin kept expressing doubt that general war was on the way. As tension mounted over the wars in the Balkans, as presidents, kings, premiers, and generals exchanged visits and reviewed each other's armies, as parliaments appropriated fantastic sums for arms, Lenin continued to be absorbed in his war with the Mensheviks to the exclusion of the prospect of war between the nations.

Of course, he read the papers and was aware of the war talk. In the autumn of 1912, with the Balkans ablaze, he wrote to his older sister, Anna, and his younger sister, Maria, in identical language: "I do not believe that there will be a war."[8]

More significant than his letters were his acts. Since until 1917, Lenin never had a chance to address a mass meeting, for him the most important public act was writing an agitational article. From January 22, 1912, until July 1914, he had at his disposal a legally published daily paper in Russia, the Bolshevik *Pravda*.[9] While all other socialist dailies in Europe were filled with alarms of war, exhortations to the masses to prevent it, protests against the mounting arms burden, veiled and open threats that war would bring revolution, *Pravda* all but ignored the subject. Lenin's ammunition was no longer directed mainly at the Tsar (the class war had died down in 1907), but at the Mensheviks, and particularly at those who were trying to find their way to a legal labor movement.[10]

On July 2, 1912, Lenin moved to the land which he himself thought most likely to become an enemy country if war should break out. He left France and perennially neutral Switzerland to move to Cracow in Austrian Poland. This was not to be nearer to the Balkans, where war began that autumn, but nearer to Russia, where *Pravda* was appearing as a daily.

There was yet another reason for his move, which he explained to Gorky:

> There will probably not be a war, and we shall stay here for the time being, taking advantage of the desperate hatred of the Poles for Tsarism.[11]

This reason is made still clearer by Krupskaya:

> Whereas the French police assisted the Russian police in every possible way, the [Austrian] Polish police was hostile to the Russian police as it was to the whole Russian government. In Cracow we could be sure that our letters would not be intercepted and that no one would spy on us.[12]

And yet more clear, because he wrote long after 1914, was the explanation of Jacob Hanecki (Ganetskii), real name, Jacob Fuerstenberg, who made the arrangements for Lenin's move:

> Austria-Hungary, with the active participation of Germany, was actively preparing for war with Russia. The Austrian Government for that reason was not interested in making easier the struggle of the Tsarist Government with the Russian revolutionaries. Counting on that, I was convinced that Lenin could without fear go to Cracow. In conversation with local political figures, who explained the situation in the government, I convinced myself that I was right and wrote Lenin to that effect.[13]

Lenin found that something like 4,000 exiles from Russian Poland were being accorded the same hospitality. He had no difficulty getting other Bolsheviks admitted to the country, including Zinoviev and his wife, Ilina, Inessa Armand, Bukharin, fresh from a Russian prison, Stalin, shortly to be arrested, Kamenev, Troyanovsky, all the Bolshevik Duma deputies, and many less-known underground workers. They were able to enter Austria-Hungary from Western Europe or from Russia, able to confer freely with Lenin, or with Lenin's current *troika* (Lenin, Zinoviev, and Kamenev). If they could outwit the Russian police, they were able to return from Austrian Poland to Russia without interference from the Austro-Hungarian authorities. In one case, when an underground agent from Moscow, who had come for literature to smuggle into Russia, attracted suspicion by his exaggerated, comic-opera, conspiratorial ways, the police actually came to Lenin to ask "whether he knew and would vouch for him."[14]

In Austrian Poland, Lenin managed to convoke a party conference from September 21 to October 1, with all of his Duma deputies except Samoilov, who was ill, and with two representatives from Moscow, one each from Saint Petersburg, Kiev, and the Urals, Troyanovsky as a delegate from the legal Bolshevik theoretical journal, *Prosveshchenie*, and such Bolshevik Poles as Hanecki and Domsky. Lenin, Zinoviev, and Kamenev were also present. If most of the delegates from the underground fell into the hands of the Russian police on their return, it was not the fault of the benevolent Austrian and Austro-Polish authorities but the fact that Lenin's pet delegate, the metalworker and Duma deputy Roman Malinovsky, was an agent of the Tsarist police.[15]

How long Austria had been thus hospitable to Russia's malcontent Poles I do not know, but it is clear that the hospitality to Lenin and his co-conspirators began on the eve of the Balkan wars, when Austria-Hungary and Russia stood ready to intervene. Thus did the Central Powers begin that political warfare which, in 1917, was to culminate in Lenin's celebrated journey through Germany in a sealed train.

Frightened by the outbreak of the Balkan wars, the leaders of the Socialist International called a special Emergency Congress in Basel for November 24, 1912, with no other order of business but the question of war. Lenin, entitled to be present both as representative of his party on the International Socialist Bureau (ISB) and as delegate, was not interested enough to attend. He contented himself with sending a Bolshevik delegation of second-raters, headed by Kamenev. At Basel there were 36 representatives from the various socialist parties and factions in Russia.[16] Lenin's five Bolsheviks were so busy with their faction war in the corridors of the Congress that not one of them took the floor on the war danger and measures to avert it. Lenin, for his part, expressed no interest in the question which had caused the emergency session. In a letter to Shklovsky, one of his five representatives, he rebuked them for not sending reports to *Pravda* while the Menshevik delegates had sent several articles to their legal daily, *Luch*. Still, he was "enormously pleased with the Basel results, for those idiots, the Liquidators, allowed themselves to be caught on the Initiative Group! These scoundrels (*svoloch'*—riff-raff, scum, no-goods) couldn't possibly have been trapped any better!!"

Lenin's only complaint was that his five delegates had not lobbied enough in the interests of the Bolshevik faction:

> The inactivity of our delegates, some inexplicable incapacity to open their mouths, has outraged me. After all, four or five *new how to speak German.*

Who did speak? With whom? How? About what? ... Yet agitation among the Germans is *very* important.[17]

Not a word on the war danger! On possible differences in the International. On measures to be taken or pledges to be entered into. All this was no concern of Lenin's.

Kamenev, for his part, wrote a report on Basel, which Lenin approvingly published in the Bolshevik journal, *Sotsial Demokrat*. The article showed how little importance Lenin and his followers attached to the struggle against war as such. That struggle seemed unreal to Kamenev as long as Tsarism endured:

> The Basel Congress could not conceal from itself the fact that the matter of assuring peace in Europe demands at least *one war*: a victorious war of all the people of Russia against the Romanov monarchy. But it was also clear at the Congress that, if this war is inevitable as a condition precedent to the solution of the problem of a stable peace, then a number of similar "wars" might be required for the actual solution of this problem.

For the rest, he was not moved by the French delegation's effort to have a general strike endorsed; he thought it important that the resolution of the International on the one hand should not "bind the Russian proletariat in any degree in the application of a general strike and insurrection," and on the other that the Russians should not make the specific revolutionary conditions in Russia a criterion for the tactics of the rest of Europe. Being entirely satisfied with the resolutions on war, he saw no need to propose amendments or so much as take the floor.[18]

Despite Lenin's large talk, *after 1914*, of internationalism, he really showed little interest in the International until it collapsed. From 1907 on he contrived to be his party's representative on the International Socialist Bureau (ISB), but he did not trouble to attend its sessions. When the great congresses were called, he was not interested either. The last such gathering he attended was that at Copenhagen in 1910. There he took a stand (in informal gatherings and commissions) on the Dutch Social Democratic Left, on the British Labour Party, on Cooperatives. But he did not take the floor at a plenary session, nor have one word to say on the question of war, which even then overshadowed all else. His real interest was in the squabbles taking place in the many-factioned Russian delegation. In the Russian meetings, he quarrelled incessantly with the others, raking up every difference that had arisen since 1900. Krzhizhanovsky's wife, who was present, records that she overheard the Menshevik Dan growl: "One against all! Lunacy! He is ruining the party. If only he would disappear or drop dead!"

"But how can one man ruin the entire party," she asked, "and all of you be so impotent against him that you have to call on Death to help you?"

"Because there is no other man in the world like him," she records Dan as snarling, "who is occupied twenty-four hours a day by the revolution, who has no other thoughts except those which are related to revolution, and who, even when he is asleep, sees only revolution in his dreams."[19]

Lenin took advantage of the Copenhagen Congress to go on up to Stockholm to meet his aging mother, who came especially from Russia for the reunion. Between them there had always been warm affection. It was the last time she was to see her son. And the Copenhagen Congress of 1910 was the last pre-war international gathering of any kind that Lenin was to attend—though from Switzerland, from Paris, and even from Cracow, the journeys were short.

The accelerating arms race and the mounting tension (Agadir, 1911; the First Balkan War, 1912; the Second Balkan War, 1913; the Austrian Ultimatum to Serbia, 1913; the Turkish Army Crisis, 1913–14; the Assassination at Sarajevo, June 28, 1914) caused the International to multiply its efforts. There were special conferences; ISB meetings; parliamentary conferences; conferences of heads of parties; congresses, regular and special. Lenin sent substitutes to the ISB meetings and major congresses, always refusing to attend himself. The assassination of the Archduke of Austria, Francis Ferdinand, filled the Empire in which Lenin now lived with its angry echoes, but nothing could budge him. Even on July 28, 1914, when Austria declared war on Serbia and the ISB called its last despairing conference, Lenin had no interest in attending. The emergency meeting in Brussels decided to hasten the date of the next international congress. For this intended congress, too, Lenin designated mere emissaries.

Actually, all Lenin's writings and acts up to 1914 show that he was with all his being a *Russian* revolutionary. To be sure, his Marxism gave him an abstract faith that revolution in Russia was a condition precedent to general European revolution. Had not Marx and Engels repeatedly said so? But his tremendous passions and narrow, powerful intellect were completely concentrated on Russian affairs. The battle with Tsarism, the battle with the liberals and democrats, the battle with the Social Revolutionaries, the battle with the Mensheviks, the struggle to split the Social Democratic Party and the socialist Duma delegation, the battle to make *Pravda* more powerful than *Luch*, the battle to achieve dominion over the masses and stir them for another armed uprising such as almost took place after the Russo-Japanese War in 1905—these are the real substance of Lenin's writings, his letters, his maneuvers and his thoughts, until August 1914.

Other Russians thrown into foreign parts took part in the socialist movements of their lands of refuge. Plekhanov became a leading theoretician of the International; Parvus a leader of the German Left; Trotsky was sporadically active in the Austrian Social Democracy; Rosa Luxemburg was the leader of parties or left factions in three lands (Poland, Germany, and Russia); Angelica Balabanoff became a beloved leader of Italian socialism. Most of the lesser Bolsheviks in France flocked into the French socialist party and trade unions. But not Lenin! Until his rather ineffectual attempts to participate during the war in the Swiss movement, always, whether he was in London, Zurich, or Geneva, he lived in a little Russian island of his own. Only in Cracow did he build up a faction among another people, the Poles, to split Rosa Luxemburg's party—but this was for the purposes of his Russian faction struggles, too.

His very refusal to carry out his duties as a member of the ISB were motivated by his Russian preoccupation no less than by his unconcern at, and unbelief in, the prospect of general war. Since 1904 the leaders of the Socialist International, particularly Bebel and Kautsky, had been trying to restore unity to the Russian party. Though he revered these two above all other living socialists, Lenin was no more minded to let them unify the party which he was determined to split, than he had been to let the revered Plekhanov interfere with his plans.

A number of considerations motivated the attempt of the German leaders to bring about Russian socialist unity. First there was their own experience: the upsurge of their movement after Lasalleans and Marxists had united. Then there was the German socialist fear of Tsarist reaction and Russian military attack, which could only be curbed or ended by a powerful, unified Russian opposition. Third, there was the vexed question of funds. The wealthy German party was quite willing to help its poor Russian brothers, but whom should they help? And what guarantee was there that the Russians wouldn't use the money to fight each other rather than the Tsar? Moreover, Mehring, Kautsky, and Klara Zetkin had been made trustees of certain "dirty monies"[20] obtained by Lenin through revolutionary holdups and through threats of physical force against certain wealthy heirs. These funds were to be held in trust until a unified party should emerge to establish a clear claim. Lenin was perpetually presenting evidence to his "Court of Honor" to prove that his committee was *the* Central Committee, his conferences *the* congresses of the Party, and that therefore he was entitled to the funds. The Mensheviks were just as constantly disputing his claim.[21]

Finally, Kautsky, as was his wont, advanced a theoretical consideration for the requirement of unity in the Russian party. In a resolution on the Russian problem, adopted by the ISB (as usual, with Lenin absent), Kautsky wrote:

In order that the working class may put forth all its strength in the struggle against capitalism, it is necessary that in every country there exist, vis-à-vis the bourgeois parties, only *one* socialist party, just as there exists only *one* proletariat.[22]

Though Kautsky could not foresee it then, Lenin would himself one day accept this theory, combining with it the dictatorship of the *one* party of the *unitary* proletariat, to outlaw all "bourgeois" parties, including liberals and democrats, agrarian socialists and Menshevik Social Democrats alike. For Lenin, too, held—more strongly and ruthlessly than Kautsky—that there was no room for pluralism: there was only one proletariat, and only one party entitled to be its vanguard. Large or small, that one party was wherever Lenin himself and two or three were gathered together to speak in its name.

In 1904, the Amsterdam Congress of the International adopted a resolution, presented by the German party, demanding that there should be only one socialist party in each land. A year later, Bebel asked Bolsheviks and Mensheviks to submit their differences to a court of arbitration over which he would preside. Reverence or no reverence, Lenin rejected Bebel's offer. In 1911, Kautsky, Mehring and Zetkin, as "fund trustees," called a unity conference. Lenin refused to attend. In 1912, the German Party offered to help with funds for the Duma election, provided unity could be achieved at least in the electoral contests. Once more, Lenin blocked the effort. After the election, through the activities of the police agent and Bolshevik Duma deputy Malinovsky, Lenin succeeded in splitting the Social Democratic Duma Delegation in two. For him, as for the police, this was a great achievement, for each of them, for differing reasons, desired to split every party institution.[23]

Thus in the years from 1912 to 1914, the years of the Balkan wars and the murder at Sarajevo, Lenin was more than ever determined not to go near an international conference. Having fended off offers of arbitration in 1904 and 1905 when his group was much weaker than the Mensheviks and the split still incomplete, he was not minded to accept Bebel's and Kautsky's or the whole International's intervention in 1912 to 1914, when things were going well. In 1912, he had convened his rump conference in Prague and had it arrogate to itself the powers and name of a Party Congress. The executive it elected he called the Central Committee. Thus he was no longer the leader of a group calling itself "Majorityites" (*Bolsheviki*), but spoke in the name of "the" party. Those who did not accept his, or its, decisions— Axelrod, Martov, Trotsky, Plekhanov, or whoever—were simply declared to be outside the party until they submitted to it.

When the International invited him to attend ISB meetings, or congresses, or special conferences on unity, Lenin told his intimates: "They only want to scold me . . . their interference now will spoil everything . . . I'm not going." When they proposed to arbitrate the differences in the Russian party, he anxiously inquired whether the decision of the arbitration court would be binding. If it should turn out favorable, he would use it for agitation; if unfavorable, he would ignore it. The International, he thought, should have no controlling voice over the life of his party or his faction. After 1914 he would severely criticize the Second International for having been a mere federation of parties with no centralized power. But that was when he was founding his own international. Wherever he was at the helm, authoritarian centralism was indispensable. But from 1904 to 1914 even the attempts of the International, to which Lenin belonged, to offer an "advisory opinion" aroused his anger.

That is how it came about that Lenin sent mere emissaries in his place to the International Socialist Bureau and delegations of second-string men to the great Congresses.

At the end of 1913, the ISB adopted another resolution inviting all Russian factions to send delegates and offering its "services" to bring about unity. Lenin had designated Kamenev to replace him on the ISB, but this time he sent a lesser, and tougher, delegate, Litvinov. All Russian factions accepted the proposal, except the Bolsheviks. In *Pravda* Lenin published the Bolshevik conditions for "unity"; those who wanted unity would find it by "rejoining" the party, i.e., his faction.[24]

In the spring and summer of 1914, the ISB made what proved to be its last attempt to unify the Russian socialist movement. Emile Vandervelde, Chairman of the Bureau, came personally to St. Petersburg and spent three days there interviewing Duma deputies and members of the major groups. According to Martov, who was living legally in St. Petersburg,[25] Vandervelde found faintly comic Lenin's emphasis on the underground when

the Pravdists received him pompously in their editorial office, posed for pictures with him, made appointments with him by telephone . . .[26]

On July 16 and 17, 1914, less than two weeks before the outbreak of the World War, the ISB called a conference of all Russian groups to come to an agreement on unification. Eleven groups attended. Among the delegates were Plekhanov, Axelrod, Martov, Trotsky, Alexinsky for the dissident Bolsheviks of the *Vperyod* group, Berzin, a Lett under the influence of Lenin, Lapinski for the Polish Socialist Party Left Wing (Levitsa), Rosa Luxemburg, Hanecki and others from the various factions of the Polish Social Democracy (Lenin had lined up the anti-Luxemburg faction in his camp), Mickiewicz-Kapsukas for the Lithuanians, who was to be one of the founders of the Communist International, Rubanovich of the Social Revolutionaries (in his capacity as a member of the ISB), the Menshevik Duma leader Chkhenkeli, and many more.

Once more Lenin failed to exercise his rights as a member of the ISB, ostentatiously staying away. He wanted to blow the detestable conference up from within, so he sent a delegation of three, headed by a new emissary whom he felt sure he could trust to carry out instructions to the letter. The emissary was Inessa Armand. She was French, not Russian, had lived many years in Russia, was a member of Lenin's party and of his leading group, and was virtually a part of his immediate family circle. For conspiratorial reasons, at Brussels she used the Russian name Petrova.

Petrova spoke French and English well, had a fair command of German, and, of course, Russian. Lenin wrote a lengthy report for her to read to the conference, which she read in French. As it takes up thirty pages of Lenin's *Collected Works* (20:465–95), it must have taken her more than an hour to read. He added several pages of *Zametki privés* "Private notes" (he was fond of using French and English fragments in his letters to her), telling her under what circumstances to take the floor and what to say. Krupskaya writes:

> The attempt, through the International Socialist Bureau to break up this line, to check the work, put Ilyich into a rage (*beshenstvo*). He resolved not to go himself to the Brussels unity conference. Inessa was to go. She was a master of the French language (French was her native tongue), she would not lose her head, hers was a firm character. She could be counted on not to yield. She was living [then] in Trieste, and Ilyich sent her there the report of the C.C., written by him, sent an entire series of instructions, how to conduct herself in such and such a case, thought out all details. In the delegation, besides Inessa, were M. F. Vladimirskii and N. F. Popov ... Inessa carried out her task bravely and with dignity.[27]

The police, like Lenin, were worried that unity might ensue. All the delegations voted for the resolution of unification, prepared by Kautsky, except the three Bolsheviks and the pro-Bolshevik Latvian, Berzin. These four stubbornly refused to vote. Kautsky and Huysmans pressed Inessa, but she remained firm. Nor did she weaken when Huysmans warned her that "whoever does not vote on the resolution is responsible before the entire International for the disruption of the effort to bring about unity, and it will be so reported to the [forthcoming] Congress at Vienna." Lenin was pleased with his emissary whom neither threats nor pleas had shaken.

The police were pleased, too. One agent reported that the failure of the Conference was due entirely to the firm and irreconcilable stand of the Bolsheviks. Another agent wrote:

> It is characteristic that Lenin avoided participation in the Conference although he was [personally] invited to attend ... The majority of the members of the

Conference were greatly disgusted with Petrova's report and speech, as no one expected that the impudence of the "Leninists" would reach such dimensions. Vandervelde, Rosa Luxemburg, Plekhanov, and Kautsky came forward with criticisms of [Lenin's, or Petrova's] report . . . All the orators were rather passionate, but did not help the situation . . .

Still, the police were worried enough to send instructions to all their agents who were secretly participating in all sorts of party conferences, "steadfastly and persistently to defend the idea of the complete impossibility of any organization fusion whatsoever, of [all] these tendencies, and especially of the union of the Bolsheviks with the Mensheviks."[28]

That summer of 1914 Lenin went to the country earlier than usual, for his wife was troubled with goiter and he believed that "mountain air cures the disease." Early in June he left with Nadya (Krupskaya) for Poronin. To his younger sister, Maria, he wrote:

Autumn is marvelous in the Tatras (the mountains near which we live in Poronin) . . . If it is fine this autumn, we shall probably stay here in the country through October.[29]

Once more there is no thought of, nor belief in, the imminence of war.

On June 28, the heir to the Austrian throne and his wife were shot in Sarajevo. A month later, on July 28, Austria declared war on Serbia. The International Socialist Bureau went into emergency session next day. Again Lenin was invited, but he did not leave Poronin. He contented himself with being "represented" by the Lettish Bolshevik Berzin, who had stood firm, shoulder to shoulder with Inessa Armand, in refusing to vote yes or no on the unity resolution. Though war had begun between Austria and Serbia, Lenin did not seem to realize that that meant world war. His mind was still absorbed with his own faction war. He had won control of the apparatus; he had seized the trade name of the party; he had split the Duma fraction; he was winning a preponderance of circulation with his *Pravda* in St. Petersburg. He was not going to yield all this—no, not even to the pressure of the entire International.

At the Emergency Conference of the ISB, nothing was further from their minds than Lenin and his split. They talked of war, the war that had begun, the broader war that was about to begin, turning this monstrous thing over and over helplessly in their minds. They voted a ringing manifesto, they collectively addressed a huge mass meeting in Brussels, they called for mass meetings everywhere. They expressed their unshakable resolve to maintain peace, to localize the war to Austria and Serbia, to bring pressure on both countries to settle their differences by arbitration.

If only they could hold off war until the coming great Congress scheduled for August 23 in Vienna! Perhaps there they could bring their international might to bear on the Great Powers. They advanced the date of the Congress from August 23 to August 9. Since Vienna was at war, they switched from Vienna to Paris.

Lenin not only boycotted the ISB Emergency Conference, he planned to boycott the Congress, too. As early as May 22, he had written to Karpinsky that he was sending him a credential as a delegate to the coming International Congress. And now, *after* war had broken out between Austria and Serbia, he wrote to another delegate he intended to send, G. L. Shklovsky:

> I have just found out that the International Congress has been transferred to Paris and set for August 9, New Style. I hope you will go?—and *as soon as possible*, to prepare yourself in Paris (Kamskii [Vladimirskii] was on the delegation in Brussels and he will bring you fully up to date on everything). Answer at once. A still more important question is whether Samoilov [the Bolshevik Duma deputy] will go. Will he be able to? It is quite probable that from Russia none of the members of the Duma will get there. Therefore it is obligatory that Samoilov goes. Best of all, arrange to travel with him . . . We are not going. In the ISB will be either Litvinov or Kamskii.[30]

In short, Lenin was still uninterested in the last frantic anti-war efforts of the International. Though Austria was at war with Serbia, he did not believe that Russia or Germany would get involved. He disbelieved in the possibility of the general war which had already, at that moment, begun. His instructions to Shklovsky had nothing to do with the concern of the Emergency Congress. Shklovsky was to bring himself up to date on the "unity conference" Lenin had sabotaged at Brussels. He was to get to Paris early so that he could begin buttonholing the Germans on the Russian faction fight. He must bring Duma deputy Samoilov (abroad to consult specialists because he was gravely ill), if Samoilov could possibly drag himself there, because a Duma deputy would give him an advantage over the Menshevik delegation and could present Lenin's version of the split in the Duma fraction.

Thus from the Extraordinary International Socialist Congress at Basel through the Extraordinary ISB Conference on the War Danger in late July 1914, and including the projected International Congress scheduled for August, Lenin obdurately boycotted every meeting of the International, for the sake of a freer hand in his own war, the war on the Mensheviks.

Why should he go to Vienna (or Paris) when Huysmans, Vandervelde and Kautsky were threatening to denounce his splitting activities before the entire Congress? Did not the Brussels Resolution say:

> No greater crime can be committed against the proletariat of Russia than to hinder the rallying of all its various groups into one single organism.[31]

What did he have to do at these "anti-war" congresses and conferences, when the war which filled the horizon, the war that really threatened him, the only war they seemed to him to be trying to block, was his war against the Mensheviks? Even the fact that the Congress could not be held in Vienna because there was war in Vienna did not clear his vision. Shklovsky and Karpinsky and Samoilov and Litvinov must go to Paris then, to fight the good fight against the Mensheviks in the corridors of the Congress.

But the International Congress could not be held in Paris either, for on August 1 Germany—the "unexpected"—declared war on Lenin's own native land. On August 2, Germany declared war on France. On August 6, Austria declared war on Russia. The war he did not believe in caught him in the Tatra Mountains, an alien in an enemy country. Clearly his Marxism had not enabled him to foresee the major event that was to prove the turning point of his life and his age, the huge event which on the morrow he was to declare had been "inevitable" all along.

NOTES TO CHAPTER 4

1. Adolf Hitler, *Mein Kampf,* Eng. trans. (New York, 1941), pp. 205–10.

2. Lenin, *Collected Works,* 4th Russian ed. 7:183; 8:31–39; see also 8:239; 21:184; 30:133.

3. Ibid., 8:238–40 and 448–51.

4. Martov and Lenin at the moment were not representatives of their respective factions, but delegates from a nominally reunited Social Democratic Party.

5. Lenin, *Collected Works,* 8:64.

6. Ibid., 19:19.

7. Ibid., 36:204–5. Leninist piety excluded this article from the *Collected Works* until 1957. Its omission from the 1st edition may have been an accident, for that edition was fragmentary and unsystematic. The 2d and 3rd editions (identical), "complete" in 30 volumes, should have carried it in vol. 16, immediately after the *Pravda* article of May 21, 1913, i.e., on page 407. The 4th edition, published during the period of Stalin's rule, "complete" in 35 volumes, omitted the article once more. After Stalin's death a number of supplementary volumes were issued, vol. 36 consisting largely of articles previously omitted. The article was suppressed so long for two reasons: 1) it reveals Lenin's admiration for the German Social Democracy and its stand on war; 2) it reveals his total incapacity as a prophet, since he ridiculed the very idea that Austria and Germany might go to war with Russia. Lenin believed that the Tsar would not risk a major war after his experience in 1905 with defeat and near revolution, and that the interests of the German and Austro-Hungarian Kaisers and the Russian Tsar as reactionary emperors coincided.

8. Ibid., 37:401 and 402.

9. So completely have the Bolsheviks disseminated their black legend concerning Tsarism (which was black enough in all conscience) that it is hard for us to remember that after the Tsar granted a constitution, even the revolutionary parties were allowed

to nominate candidates for the Duma and publish legal journals. State ownership of the only permitted party and of all journals was to be an invention of Lenin.

10. Lenin claimed that this attempt to develop a legal labor movement was aimed at liquidating the underground parties, and he dubbed all its advocates "Liquidators." When the underground Mensheviks refused to expel them he called the underground Mensheviks "Liquidators" too.

11. *V. I. Lenin i A. M. Gorkii: Pis'ma, vospominaniya, documenty* (Moscow, 1958), p. 8. The Poles referred to were, of course, the Austrian Poles who possessed considerable autonomy and directed their antagonism not at the Austro-Hungarian, but at the Russian government. His prophecy that there would "probably not be a war" was written when the First Balkan War was at its height, but this was a little war beneath his notice.

12. N. K. Krupskaia, *Vospominaniya o Lenine* (Moscow, 1957), pp. 187–88 and 191.

13. Ya. Ganetskii (Hanecki), *Vospominaniya o Lenine* (Moscow, 1933), p. 8.

14. Krupskaya, *Vospominaniya*, 187–223 *passim*.

15. See the chapter entitled "The Case of Roman Malinovsky" in *Three Who Made a Revolution*.

16. Including three Social Democratic factions, Social Revolutionaries, Poles, Latvians, etc.

17. Lenin, *Collected Works*, 36:175.

18. Yu. Kamenev, "Na bazelskom kongresse," in *Sotsial-Demokrat*, no. 30 (January 25, 1913): 3–4.

19. Gerard Walter, *Lenine* (Paris, 1950), p. 201. I have retranslated from the French.

20. The phrase in quotes is that of Klara Zetkin, Lenin's friend and admirer and one of the founders of the Communist International.

21. In the end Lenin succeeded in getting hold of the trust fund.

22. *Vorwärts*, December 18, 1913. English text in Gankin and Fisher, *The Bolsheviks and the World War* (Stanford, 1940), p. 94; Russian in *Proletarskaya pravda*, December 21(8), 1913.

23. *Three Who Made a Revolution*, pp. 540–50; testimony of Police Director Beletsky in *Padenie tsarskogo rezhima* (Leningrad, 1924–1927), 3:281 and 286.

24. Lenin, *Collected Works*, 3rd Russian ed., 17:349 and 681. The paper was then called *Put' pravdy*. For the frequent changes of name of *Pravda* between 1912 and 1914, see *Three Who Made a Revolution*, pp. 564–66.

25. In 1913, to celebrate the three-hundredth anniversay of the Romanov dynasty, the Tsar granted a general political amnesty. Martov, Dan, and Kamenev, among others, returned to Russia to live openly and legally there. Lenin might have done so, too. Only his penchant for conspiracy and his distrust of the growing liberties (and perhaps his awareness of how he himself would act toward oppositions if he held power) prevented him from doing the same.

26. *Pis'ma P. B. Akselroda i Yu. O. Martova* (Berlin, 1924), 1:291.

27. Krupskaya, *Vospominaniya*, pp. 221–22; and *Pamyati Inessy Armand, Sbornik pod redaktsiei N. K. Krupskoi* (Moscow-Leningrad, 1926), p. 15.

28. The police reports were published in part by the police itself in 1916, and in part by the Soviet government in 1918, i.e., under Lenin. The relevant passages are cited from the English translation in Gankin and Fisher, *The Bolsheviks and the World War*, pp. 105–6. The latter work also contains the report and instructions prepared for Inessa Armand by Lenin and much additional material throwing light on the matter discussed in this essay. The entire first chapter (129 pages) of Gankin and Fisher is devoted to "The Bolsheviks, the Mensheviks and the Second International."

29. Lenin, *Collected Works*, 37:433–34.

30. Ibid., pp. 245, 247, 605.

31. Gankin and Fisher, *The Bolsheviks and the World War*, p. 132.

5

LENIN–TROTSKY
HOW TWO BECAME ONE

THREE FORMULAE

There were three more or less clearly defined competing outlooks among Russian Marxists [before 1905] as to the nature and prospects of the coming revolution:

1. That of the Mensheviks. The coming revolution is a bourgeois democratic revolution. It will abolish feudalism and absolutism, clear the ground for the free growth of capitalism, establish a progressive democratic republic, bring the bourgeoisie to power. Under this republic, there would be freedom to propagate socialist ideas, to orgnaize the working class politically and economically, and develop in it the culture, self-consciousness, experience and power necessary to prepare, at some future date, a second revolution: its own. But the proletariat in its present condition in this economically, culturally and organizationally backward land, could not dream of taking power. If the Social Democratic Party should permit the power "to be thrust into its hands," it could only compromise itself, since it could not introduce socialism. If it entered into a coalition government with the bourgeoisie, it would become responsible for the actions of a bourgeois government. To be revolutionary in backward Russia meant to fight Tsarism but to avoid power. The Socialists must support the bourgeoisie in its struggle for power, encourage it, push it, force it onto its own revolutionary path, exact from it the promise of a maximum of freedom for the working class, then act towards the new government as a critical opposition.

2. The view of Trotsky, Parvus and Luxemburg. The first tasks facing the revolution are bourgeois democratic tasks such as were accomplished by the Western bourgoisie in their revolution. But the Russian Revolution was taking place much later in history. The proletariat was already on the stage as an independent force. There was already a body of socialist theory for it to utilize. Western Europe was ripe for a socialist revolution. The two

revolutions would tend to be telescoped in Russia, to run into each other, to be combined into one. If the proletariat was backward and unorganized, the bourgeoisie was more so, and cowardly and afraid of mass action and revolution to boot. The proletariat, equipped with the theory and experience of Western socialism and supported by the simultaneously developing peasant rebellion, would have to do the job which the bourgeoisie was incapable of doing.

> Once the revolution is victorious—wrote Trotsky—political power passes necessarily into the hands of the class that has played the leading role in the struggle, the working class.

And once in power? They would have to act like representatives of the class they professed to speak for. The line between their minimum democratic demands and their maximum socialist demands would dissolve. Even the most modest measures, the eight-hour day for instance, might lead to the closing of the factories by the employers. Then a workers' government would have to take over the factories, and lo and behold, you have jumped from bourgeois democratic measures to measures of socialism. In short, "the political supremacy of the proletariat is incompatible with its economic slavery."

In rural areas, the proletariat in power would soon have to go beyond bourgeois democracy, too. It would first win the support of the peasantry by distributing the land, thus consolidating its power. But soon it would be forced to take further measures, leading towards the collectivization of agriculture. Everywhere there would be resistance, from the enraged owners of industry in the city, from the great mass of property-minded peasants, perhaps also from foreign intervention. But to offset this, was not the West already ripe and overripe for a socialist revolution? It needed only the stirring example of revolution in Russia and assurance that it would no longer be threatened, as in 1848, by Tsarist intervention. Thus, the revolution might spread to the West and be kept going "in permanence" in Russia, transforming itself into a whole epoch of revolution at home and abroad.

3. Lenin's position fluctuated between these two poles. In formula, it sounded much like the Menshevik doctrine; in spirit, it was irresistibly attracted to the Trotskyist view. With the Mensheviks, Lenin held that economically and culturally, Russia was ripe only for a bourgeois democratic revolution; with Trotsky, that the bourgeoisie was too weak and cowardly to accomplish its own revolution. With Trotsky, too—and here we come to the real dividing line in practical conduct—*Lenin held that the Social Democratic Party must strive for power.* He doubted that it could take power alone, as Trotsky thought, but in any case, it would have to be prepared to enter a coalition government. This provisional revolutionary

government would have to safeguard the revolution until a new order—what new order?—had been set up.

What new order? Here Lenin hesitated. Sometimes he answered with the Mensheviks, "a bourgeois democratic order." Could the Socialists then stay in the government? Lenin thought not, yet he hesitated. Perhaps, a revolution in Russia would spread to the West and help to keep the Russian Revolution going "in permanence." Here he approached Trotsky once more.

But the core of Lenin's strong will and the focus of his powerful mind were concentrated on something which separated him irretrievably from the Mensheviks and would link him irretrievably with Trotsky and Parvus: the taking of power.

If the proletariat should take power, how then could the revolution be kept democratic and prevented from degenerating into a minority dictatorship? His answer was to reject Trotsky's formula of a "labor government" or a "social democratic government" or a "dictatorship of the proletariat," in favor of a two-class government, a government of two (or more) parties, a dictatorship of the vast majority, "the democratic dictatorship of the proletariat and peasantry.*

TROTSKY IN THE REVOLUTION OF 1905

The great year 1905 subjected all revolutionary theories to the test of life. In the autumn of that year, the Petersburg workingmen formed a delegate council to conduct a general strike. That was the famous Petersburg Soviet. (*Soviet* is merely the Russian word for "council.") It was not the invention of any party, but the spontaneous invention of the workers themselves. The Mensheviks welcomed the Soviet because it seemed to represent the things they had been advocating: self-activity of the masses, for the masses, and by the masses. They hoped that it would put an end to the narrow conspiratorial party of professional revolutionaries speaking and acting for the masses and would lay the basis for a broad party of the masses.

The Leninists, however, were suspicious of the Soviet. Even Lenin himself wavered for a moment. He was suspicious because of the lack of party

---

* "The proletariat constitutes a minority," wrote Lenin in 1905 in criticism of Trotsky's views. "It can only command a mighty overwhelming majority if it unites with the mass of the semi-proletarians, the semi-property owners . . . Such a composition will naturally reflect itself in the composition of the revolutionary government . . . It would be extremely harmful to yield to any illusions in this regard . . . Anyone who attempts to achieve socialism by any other route will inevitably arrive at the most absurd and reactionary conclusions, both economic and political." Prophetic words! Like Trotsky's critique of Lenin's organization plan, they were forgotten in 1917 when Lenin and Trotsky made common cause.

control of this broad body, because he feared what the Mensheviks hoped, that this new workingmen's council might become the basis for a broad, amorphous substitute for his party, something more elementary in consciousness, less "scientific" in program, less subject to socialist leadership and control. He had been hammering on the theory that the workers, left to themselves, could not possibly attain to Socialist consciousness and a Socialist program. They needed to be led, and guided and controlled, and injected with the consciousness which he thought was the peculiar possession of his self-constituted "vanguard" of professional revolutionaries. Burdened by such preconceptions and training, his followers thought of rejecting the Soviet, boycotting it, presenting ultimatums to it demanding that it should adopt Socialist programs and acknowledge Socialist leadership, or disband.

Lenin was abroad at the time. But even from a distance, his practical understanding was superior to his dogmas. He sensed that this was a powerful driving force for revolution and a field in which his party could operate. Always swift to comprehend actual events, he adopted an attitude which suggested that of 1917. But a year later, when the Soviet had dissolved, he retreated to his earlier sectarian approach. "The Party," he wrote in 1906,

> has never renounced its intention of making use of certain non-party organizations like the Soviets in order to extend the influence of the Social Democrats in the working class. At the same time the Social Democratic organizations must bear in mind that if social democratic work among the masses is properly and widely organized, such institutions may actually become superfluous . . .

This is not the language of 1917, which would see in the Soviet a broader, more democratic workers' parliament, superior to parties, because more inclusive and more representative than parties. This is rather the language of 1919 and after, in which the Soviets were slowly drained of power and content, become "superfluous," and are replaced by one-party government.

But in 1905, Trotsky never wavered for an instant. The Soviet was a broader arena for action, a stage on which he would feel at home. This was the germ of a workers' parliament, the embryo of a labor government. He rose rapidly in its councils, stirred it with his resplendent oratory, swiftly composed some of its most dramatic resolutions and manifestos, became, before its fifty days of existence were over, its outstanding leader and spokesman and acting chairman.

When the leaders of the Soviet were arrested, Trotsky distinguished himself once more by the brilliance of his defense of its activities at his trial. In prison he wrote a memorable book, *The Year 1905*. If he had written nothing else in his life, this masterful interpretation of history-on-the-wing by an eyewitness and participant would have assured him a place in history as a prophet of our time. Strangely enough, his worshipful followers have permitted it to go out of print, though it is undoubtedly one of the most significant of his works.

At the very moment when Lenin was writing the estimate of the Soviet I have just quoted, Trotsky was writing in his prison cell:

> The Soviet was in reality *an embryo of a revolutionary government* . . . Prior to the Soviet, there had been revolutionary organizations *among* the workingmen . . . But they were organizations *in* the proletariat; their immediate aim was to *influence the masses.* The Soviet, however, is an organization *of* the proletariat; its aim is to fight for revolutionary power. At the same time, the Soviet was *an organized expression of the will of the proletariat as a class* . . . The Soviet is the first democratic power in modern Russian history . . . the organized power of the masses themselves over their component parts. This is true unadulterated democracy, without a two-chamber system, without a professional bureaucracy, with the right of the voters to recall their deputy at any moment and to substitute another for him . . . There is no doubt that *the first new wave of the revolution will lead to the creation of Soviets all over the country.*

In this remarkable passage, and not in anything Lenin was writing at the time, is the germ of both Lenin's and Trotsky's appreciation of the Soviet in November 1917. Because Trotsky had broken with Lenin on the organization question and rejected his conception of the narrow, conspiratorial, professional party and the tight control of the masses by the party, Trotsky was free to elaborate his conception of the Soviet. Together with the Mensheviks he could welcome this "autonomous local revolutionary self-expression." (The language is Axelrod's.) With the Mensheviks again, he could contrast the party as an organization *in* the proletariat to the Soviet as an organization *of* the proletariat, and find the latter superior to the former. But with Lenin he could see eye to eye against the Mensheviks on the question of *power.* The Soviet was not merely a broad parliament, a place for self-activity and self-education, it was also an embryonic organ of power.

Fatality and will! In fatality, Lenin appeared to be with the Mensheviks against Parvus, Luxemburg and Trotsky. In will, Parvus, Luxemburg and Trotsky were with Lenin against the Mensheviks. If the taking of power should be put on the immediate order of business, then the theoretical links between Lenin and the Mensheviks would surely snap, and the practical concentration of Trotsky and Lenin on power would tend to coalesce. But until that moment, because he had no party of his own, Trotsky and not Lenin would appear to be suspended between two opposing poles. In theory, Lenin would go over to Trotsky's doctrine of "permanent revolution" and soviet-as-organ-of-power. In practice, Trotsky, having no party, would have to go over to Lenin. According to the accepted gravitational theory, when a falling body is pulled toward the earth, the earth is also pulled toward the falling body. But the appearance is that of the earth alone exerting the attracting force and the body falling to rest on the apparently immovable earth.

In the period between the revolution of 1905 and the revolution of 1917, Trotsky showed himself incapable of building a faction. When he went over to Lenin's organization, he accepted Lenin's methods and Lenin's organizational plan without reservations. On the other hand, Lenin was convinced by the war that had been raging since 1914, that a general European revolution was about to begin. Under such circumstances, a bourgeois democratic revolution in Russia could easily spread to "world revolution" and thus become, in Russia itself, the "permanent revolution" that Trotsky had envisaged. As Trotsky dropped his reservations to Lenin's organization plan, Lenin dropped his reservations to Trotsky's estimate of the possibility of an immediate proletarian dictatorship in Russia. That was the *quid pro quo* that produced the duality-unity of which the world became aware in 1917.

FOURTH STAGE: "LENIN–TROTSKY"

When the American Communist leader C. E. Ruthenberg first went to Russia after the formation of the Comintern, he came back singing in Yiddish what purported to be a religious litany of the Russian Orthodox Church. Not the mystery of the Trinity but the mystery of the duality-in-unity of which I have just spoken. A free translation would be:

Karl Marx is one; besides him is none.
Two is Lenin-Trotsky; one is Karl Marx;
Karl Marx is one; besides him is none.
Two is Lenin-Trotsky; two who are one.

That was a general conception, not only outside of Russia but inside Russia as well, from the summer of 1917 until the beginning of the year 1924, when Lenin was laid in his tomb.

6

LENIN–STALIN:
THE PARTY MACHINE

STALIN'S PLACE IN THE PICTURE

What had Stalin to say concerning all that I have described in the way of earnest theoretical debate on the part of the leaders of the Social Democratic movement? The answer is as brief as it is simple: nothing at all. Stalin developed no original theories on these questions prior to his attainment of power. That is to say: we find nothing original on these questions from the pen of Stalin until after 1924. During all the period of which we have so far been speaking, he made real contributions to the movement in the form of activities such as countless other lieutenants of Lenin engaged in. But to this earnest, intensive, soul-searching and subtle questioning as to the path and nature of the Russian Revolution, he did not contribute a single word. When he touched on it in the Georgian press, it was to translate into Georgian, to simplify, even vulgarize, some article or speech of Lenin's on the subject. Being theoretically weak and politically unsure at the time, some of his articles were a mixture of conflicting phrases of Lenin and the Mensheviks. It was not by agreement with Lenin on these matters that he was first attracted to discipleship. His admiration and devotion for Lenin sprang from other sources.

The driving force of Lenin's will (so different in degree, in firmness and in kind from the usual mood of Russian intellectuals) had early made Lenin the leader of what was known in Russia as the "hards." Stalin, too, was by nature a "hard" and gravitated towards Lenin on the basis of common elements of temperament.

Moreover, Stalin was profoundly impressed by Lenin's organization plan. He saw that organization plan, no doubt, in terms much narrower than Lenin's own. But he did recognize that the plan exalted the organization as organization; exalted the role and the power and authority of the leading committees; exalted the control of the party committees over the party members and of the party machine as a whole over the working class. In short, what he saw in Lenin's organization plan was something inherent in that plan if never the whole of it: namely, a tight, efficient, centralized machine.

The machine thus created by Lenin's organization methods and theories, Lenin himself had to fight at three critical junctures: in 1905 when he found that his most devoted followers were holding dogmatically onto his old machine formula in the face of a mass uprising too great to be embraced within its narrow confines; in 1917 when he had to fight his machine to a standstill and whip it into line for a struggle for power; and during the last two years or so of his life when his slow sinking towards death was overshadowed and embittered by the awareness that another fight was necessary with the machine which was even then being taken over by Stalin; a fight, moreover, which he no longer had the strength to carry through.

If the machine implicit in Lenin's organization plans should be disconnected from the drive of Lenin's ideals, if the ruthlessness and autocracy of Lenin's machine methods should be disconnected from the undoubted idealism and socialist devotion which characterized him all his life; if his amoralism concerning the means employed is disconnected from the fact that, in Lenin, all means were subordinated to a sanctifying end—in short, if you disconnect Lenin's machine from the other things that were Lenin and put a man of lesser idealism, humaneness and intellectual horizon in the driver's seat, then you have the juggernaut that rolled over the party and over Russia after Lenin's death: the Stalin machine. In Lenin's concept of the party organization, there were the rudiments of the future Stalin machine. And that is why, inherently, Stalin was attracted to Lenin.

He was further attracted by Lenin's iron will and absorption with the question of power. Here, too, we must observe that Lenin's absorption with power was always connected, as was his organization plan, with the idea of using power as a lever for the realization of socialism. The early Comintern, fashioned in Lenin's image, had the same concentration on the taking of power for the sake of the speedy realization of socialism. But in its later days of degeneration, the Comintern became concentrated on taking power for its own sake, willing to advance any slogans, espouse any principles, however contrary to the basic principles of socialism, in order to promote the conquest of power in a particular organization, a particular country or moment of history. And the power it sought in a given country was not power for its own working class or its own local party, but power for the machine to which it had become completely subordinated, Stalin's own power machine in Russia. Thus the power machine created by Lenin was disconnected from the principles he meant it to serve, and we have lived to witness the machine that was meant to realize socialism, stripped bare of whole sections of socialist principle for the sake of maintaining power.

Finally, Stalin was attracted to Lenin by Lenin's inclination toward the use of physical force as a lever of revolution. During the rising tide of 1905, Lenin was the most outspoken and consistent advocate among the Social Democrats of the necessity for armed bands. And during 1906 and 1907, while the revolutionary tide was ebbing but Lenin was not yet willing to admit it to himself, he continued to encourage the formation of such armed bands, thereby attracting to his standard many who had been outlawed and who found it impossible to return to peaceful, civilian life. As the general support for the revolutionary movement began to decline, armed bands turned to financing the ebbing movement and their own necessities by a series of revolutionary robberies, known as "expropriations," or, for short, simply as "exes." It was in connection with these "expropriations," encouraged by Lenin and utilized by him to finance his own movement, that he and Stalin first came to know and value each other. The main centers of this revolutionary banditry were the Caucasus, the Urals and other border lands of Russia. In the Caucasus Stalin's hand became manifest in organizing *exes* in such a way that he himself did not seem to be involved and that great hauls of funds were made with comparatively small loss of revolutionary lives.

LENIN AND TROTSKY PAVE THE WAY FOR STALIN

In the question of the state, there were two Lenins, as there were two Marxes. Anyone who has thoughtfully examined all the writings of Marx will recognize that for much of his life he was predominantly a centralist and authoritarian socialist. But, as a result of his experiences with the Paris Commune and in his writings thereon, he became more of a decentralist and democratic socialist.

Lenin, a devout and extremely orthodox disciple of Marx, who took all his writings as alike inspired, seems to have been unaware of that duality in his master. He sought to correlate all the writings of Marx and Engels on the state into a single systematic and self-consistent whole. As is inevitable when you take a given body of writings as sacred and regard your own thoughts as mere exegesis, it was possible for Lenin to find now one text of Marx and now another to serve his varying moods and needs. Thus, quite unconsciously I should say, as long as Lenin was not in power he leaned upon the decentralist democratic Marx of the Paris Commune. But as soon as Lenin found himself at the head of the state, he turned to the centralist, authoritarian Marx of an earlier day. All of Lenin's writings from April to November 1917 aimed at the disintegration of the state machine of the provisional government. In them Lenin emphasized control from below, decentralization of power, abolition of police and standing armies, control of production by the trade unions, control of affairs of state by the man in the factory and the man on the street, seizure of the land by the local initiative of the peasantry, arrest or execution of officers by the soldiers and election of their own officers. The state must be dismantled. The whole people must take upon themselves the use of arms in the defense of its conquest. Army, police and secret service must disappear and the masses keep order by virtue of their own conscience and direct action and summary judgment of offenders. Officials, where they might still be necessary for a brief transition period, should be freely elected, subject to definite instructions by their constituents, subject to free and immediate recall, given the same wage as ordinary workers so that they would not get separated from the common outlook and way of life. "Every cook" should become master of the intricacies of statecraft; the state machine should be dismantled and made to "wither away" as swiftly as possible; the need for specially qualified officials should be overcome as rapidly as could be (very rapidly indeed, for the revolution would be a great educator and arouser of the initiative of the masses), and the masses should become qualified to defend itself, direct itself, control its public servants, steadily reduce their autonomy and authority, become the arbiter of its own destiny, run its industries and organize its own life.

One illustration of Lenin's earlier conceptions of a freer, more democratic soviet state is the following: On the eve of the October Revolution, Lenin stated that the coming Bolshevik uprising would install the following system of freedom of the press:

> Freedom of the press means that the opinions of all citizens are given wide publicity. The State power, in the person of the Soviets, takes over *all* the printing shops, *all* the papers, and distributes them *justly*. [All the underlinings are Lenin's.] In the first place comes the State; in the second place come the big parties; and then any group of citizens enrolling a certain number of people and showing a certain number of signatures to that effect. This would be real freedom for *all*, and not for rich people only.

We could find scores of such quotations covering every field of life, but one must serve for all.

After Lenin attained power in the autumn of 1917, often reluctantly and unconsciously, often imperceptibly and gradually, sometimes sweepingly and swiftly, these democratic, decentralist, anti-authoritarian views suffered a complete transformation. The manner in which the Bolsheviks took power, against the other working-class parties and trade unions; the opposition they encountered and the chaos they inherited; the nature of Lenin's temperament and the kind of party machine he had formed; the objective factors of continued war and civil war and general breakdown; the subjective factors of self-confident temperament, conviction of rightness, sureness that he and his self-denominated "vanguard" knew what was good for the masses and must drive them to it, if necessary; the corrupting influence of power upon its possessors except where it is jealously limited and guarded by control from below; the fact that power, unchecked, begets its own habitual enlargement; the general trend to the swelling of statism in time of war and civil war—all these things (and others like them) combined to reinforce the new view of the state which came to Lenin from looking down from above in place of looking up from below.

It is impossible for us to know how much of this was avoidable and how much inevitable. At any rate it unfolded with a tragic fatality beginning with the very moment of taking power.

PROPOSED COALITION GOVERNMENT

The organized labor movement was opposed to the Bolsheviks' taking power. The real strength of the drive for power lay not in the working class, still less in its most advanced and organized sectors, but in the peasants, and what proved decisive, the peasants-in-arms. the Bolsheviks took power with the active support of great sections of the armed forces in the key places and the passive support of other sections.

The day Petrograd was taken, even before Moscow had fallen into Bolshevik hands, the railway unions came to the new government in process of formation and proposed that it should be a coalition government of labor parties and labor unions based upon the Soviets as the democratic and representative parliament of the masses. This proposal for a coalition government awoke a response inside the Bolshevik Party. It was supported by some sections of the Menshevik Party, by the left Wing of the Social Revolutionary Party, and a number of additional trade unions. Lenin was adamant against it. When he found a large section of his leadership for it, he temporized, maneuvered, and worked to prevent its realization by indirection. Trotsky stood with Lenin. When Lenin won his way in his party, the following people resigned from the new government in protest: Nogin, Rykov, Miliutin, Teodorovich, Ryazanov, Derbishev and Shliapnikov. From the Central Committee of the Bolshevik Party Zinoviev, Kamenev, Rykov, Nogin and Miliutin resigned. These men were persuaded to reconsider and remain in the leadership. But the day the proposal of the railwaymen for a coalition labor government was rejected, the first big step was taken which would lead in time to the outlawing of all working-class parties but one, and the reduction of the Soviets from a parliament of many parties and organizations of labor to a mere transmission belt in the mechanics whereby a one-party government would exercise its will.

In due course came the outlawing of the labor press. Some modicum of freedom for the non-Bolshevik parties and unions remained for a longer time than is generally imagined. But one by one the press was shut down. The outlawing of the independent press put an end to all criticism of the government, except such criticism as the officials would choose to permit or order. Criticism narrowed down in time to "self-criticism" and finally to a peculiar mystical performance in which people in disgrace were ordered, often against their own convictions, to denounce and criticize themselves. But free criticism of public "servants" by those they are supposed to serve is the first prerequisite of freedom. The right to oppose the action of officials and "leaders," to denounce and expose them, the right to advance rival proposals, platforms, lists of candidates, in short the right to disagree and to give organized expression to disagreement and attempt to convert the majority to your view—these are the first prerequisites of freedom and of that control from below to which we give the name of democracy. When these rights are gone, freedom has ceased to exist.

For a time there was still a two-party government, of the Left Social Revolutionaries and the Bolsheviks. But objective events and subjectively determined errors combined to put an end to its existence and reduce it in a short time to a one-party government. Ten days after the seizure of power, Vladimir Ilyich Lenin, in his capacity as Chairman of the Council of People's Commissars, received an interpellation from the Left Social Revolutionary Party that was his ally in the government. This is the question sent up to him:

> A number of decrees have been published in the name of the government. These decrees were not discussed in the Central Committee (of the Soviets), nor were they sanctioned by it. The same procedure has been characteristic of certain governmental acts which, in fact, have abrogated the principles of civil liberty.
>
> We therefore present the following questions to the Chairman of the People's Commissars:
> 1. On what grounds were the drafts of the decrees and other governmental acts kept from being submitted to the Central Executive Committee for regular discussions?
> 2. Does the government intend to give up the arbitrary and inadmissable procedure of decreeing laws?

That was only ten days after the two parties had formed a government together!

On January 11, 1918, Lenin said of his partner in coalition:

The Party of the Left Social Revolutionaries is the only party which expresses the aspirations and interests of the peasants.

Thus the coalition of two parties was in intention at least the realization of Lenin's old slogan of the "Democratic Dictatorship of the Proletariat (Bolsheviks) and the Peasantry (Left Social Revolutionaries)." But friction grew, errors on one side or the other contributed, and finally there came the parting of the ways at Brest Litovsk. The Social Revolutionary Party rejected the decision to sign the Treaty, then resorted to assassination and attempted uprising when it could no longer make its will prevail by other methods. It was outlawed, and the Bolsheviks settled down to one-party government.

7

V. I. LENIN AND MAXIM GORKY: A STUDY OF A STORMY FRIENDSHIP

THE POET AND THE POLITICIAN

Between Lenin and Gorky yawned an abyss. Over it was thrown a bridge of friendship and admiration—genuine friendship I think on both sides, and genuine admiration. But the bridge was as insecure as a rope bridge over a rain-forest canyon. Since in Lenin's words, "friendship is friendship and duty duty,"[1] and since each held duty higher than friendship, the fragile bridge was constantly breaking and falling into the abyss.

Like the friendship and the admiration, the abyss was genuine too, and so deep that it is hard to exaggerate the differences between these two men: in temperament, in outlook, in conception of man and his fate; in feelings about politics and organization; in attitude towards the autonomy of the artist as against classes, parties, and organs of censorship and control; in their views of the role literature and art should play in the informing and shaping of life; in what, for want of a better term, we may call the religious faiths of the two men.

Gorky had a downright distaste for politics; Lenin was infatuated with it. Despite a weakness for didactic interpolation into his tales and plays, Gorky was all artist. Despite an affectionate memory of the literary classics he had read in his youth, Lenin was all politician. Lenin believed in classes, class struggle, dictatorship, the Party, and himself as the maker and mover of history. Gorky believed in Man, in freedom, in the redeeming power of art and science, and the sacredness of the individual person. When Gorky let his didactic propensities run away with him, Lenin was furious, not

This essay is an unpublished study Wolfe wrote for a book later published by Praeger Publishers under the title *The Bridge and the Abyss: The Troubled Friendship of V. I. Lenin and Maxim Gorky*. Copyright 1967 by Bertram D. Wolfe.

because the moral marred the fable, but because it was usually the wrong moral from Lenin's point of view. The ideas at the core of Gorky's thought and creation were to Lenin more often than not an abomination. He told the author so in reproving talks and explosive letters, condemning him roundly, though rarely publicly. And no one criticized Lenin more sharply than Maxim Gorky, not only in private correspondence, but often, as during the crucial years 1917 and 1918, scathingly, day after day, in the most popular paper in Russia, *Novaya Zhizn*, published by Gorky himself. Then his criticism was so sharp, direct, accurate, and constant, that Lenin finally closed down his paper by force after covert harassment had failed.

The huge propaganda apparatus of the world's most powerful state has so overlaid the true picture with layers of legend that the average educated man, not only in the Soviet Union but in other lands, too, does not know of the existence of these differences. It is the purpose of the present study to scrape off the various layers of over-painting in order to restore something of the true image of Maxim Gorky as artist and passionate thinker and make clear the complex, uneasy nature of the friendship of Gorky and Lenin.

As in all fields of Soviet history, this is first of all an archaeological task in which the historian must dig through the shards and detritus of successive layers of propaganda, as Schliemann and his successors dug through six superimposed towns to find the original Homeric Troy.

Soviet scholars, on order, have suppressed some of the most important and characteristic parts of Gorky's life and work. From 1949 to 1955 they published what purported to be the complete works of Maxim Gorky in 30 volumes, sponsored and edited by the Gorky Institute of World Literature. One looks in vain in these 30 volumes for the striking little book of articles written against Lenin in 1917, then collected from his signed columns in *Novaya Zhizn* and republished by him as a pamphlet in 1920 under the title *Revoliutsiia i Kultura* (Revolution and Culture). Omitted too is the no less striking and characteristic *O Russkom Krestyanstve* (On the Russian Peasantry), published by Gorky in Russian in Berlin in 1922. Like Sinyavsky and Daniel and Yesenin-Volpin, like Zamyatin with his *We* and Pasternak with his *Doctor Zhivago*, Gorky had to publish these works abroad. His publisher was the Russian socialist publishing house in Berlin of I. P. Lad-yshnikov, who had published many of Gorky's works in Russian in Berlin because they could not be published in his own land under Nicholas II and now was called upon by Gorky to do the same thing for works which he could not publish in the new Russia ruled by his friend Lenin.[2]

Between 1958 and 1960, the Soviet Academy of Sciences and the Gorky Institute of World Literature jointly published in four solid volumes a "scientific," i.e. scholarly, *Letopis Zhizni i Tvorchestva A. M. Gorkogo* (Chronicle of the Life and Creative Work of A. M. Gorky—hereafter referred to as the *Chronicle*) purporting to set down and briefly characterize day by day every event in Gorky's life from birth to death, every letter sent or received, and every scrap of writing from his pen. Here the articles Gorky wrote against Lenin in 1917 and 1918 and collected in 1920 for the little book against the Bolshevik seizure of power are recorded individually by title and date of first newspaper publication, but with no summary or excerpt, as is the case with other writings, nor any hint that they were directed against Lenin, or that Gorky still felt strongly enough about them to make a book out of them in 1920. The book itself is omitted from the *Chronicle*, as it was from the *Collected Works*. Whereas other titles get a line or two of explanation, quotation, or comment, for these articles only the dry bones of titles are given.

How can one know from the entry for January 9, 1918, which reads: " '9 January–5 January,' *Novaya Zhizn*, no. 6," that this is a devastating comparison of the firing of the Tsar's troops on unarmed workingmen on January 9, 1905 ("Bloody Sunday"), with the firing of Lenin's Red Guard upon unarmed workingmen on January 5, 1918, as they were marching under red banners to greet their elected representatives and honor the Constituent Assembly?

Or how can one tell from the colorless entry of July 16, 1918, "Closing of the Journal, *Novaya Zhizn*," an entry documented in pseudo-research fashion by citing another journal which reported the shutdown the following day—how can one guess that it was not Gorky who perhaps closed his journal for lack of funds or loss of interest, but that the shutdown was ordered by Lenin and enforced by his police?

The more one examines the flood of Gorkyana—*Collected Works* in various editions; volumes of *Gorky Archives; Selected Works* and individual works; *Correspondence* and *Literaturnoe Nasledstvo*—the more such gaps appear.

To take only one example, there is the sensitive matter of Gorky's attitude towards the United States. When he visited New York in 1906 to raise money for revolutionaries, his mission was frustrated and his life made bitter by the Tsar's Ambassador, who let reporters know that the actress, Maria Fedorovna Andreeva, with whom he journeyed to America, his wife in all but legal formalities, was not married to him, and that he had a legal spouse, Ekaterina Pavlovna Peshkova, in Russia (from whom he had long ago amicably separated but never been legally divorced). Since Gorky wrote with his heart rather than his head, the result was a series of bitter attacks upon the United States ending with the striking formula, "I could write a million words about America and not one good one among them." But when America aided generously during the great famine of the early 1920s, Gorky wrote, again as his heart bade him, deeply moving words of praise and gratitude to Herbert Hoover and the American Relief Administration of which he was Chairman. On July 30, 1922, for example, he wrote Hoover a letter telling him how many millions of children's lives he had saved, how many thousands of students, how many hundreds of intellectuals.

> In all the history of human suffering [he concluded] I know of no accomplishment which can be compared in magnitude and generosity with the relief that you have accomplished . . . The generosity of the American people resuscitates the dream of fraternity . . . at a time when mankind greatly needs charity and compassion. It will be inscribed in the pages of history as unique, gigantic, and glorious . . . and will long remain in the memory of the millions . . . whom you have saved from death . . . The recollection of American self-sacrifice will make these same children better, more generous men and women . . .

This is not only good Gorky prose; its publication alongside the *City of the Yellow Devil*, republished so many times in so many languages, is an elementary necessity for a complete picture of Gorky's mind and heart as well as of his views of America. Yet this and a companion letter calling the field workers of the A.R.A. "heroes who so splendidly do their work on the vast fields of death, amidst epidemics, savagery, and cannibalism" have never been published in Russia.[3]

Such is the editing for scholars and by scholars of Gorky's life and work. Nor are the scholars to blame, many of whom are devoted men, dedicated to literature and scholarship. But on every literary collegium there is a representative of the party and the police. On doubtful matters the rule is "one man, one vote," and the one man that has the vote is the representative of the party and police.

For the common reader, matters are made even simpler. Thus, on the ninetieth anniversary of Gorky's birth, *Literaturnaya Gazeta* told us: "Gorky unremittingly upheld the principle of combative, highly ideological (*vysoko-ideinii*), party-spirited (*partiinyi*) literature with all the passion and conviction of an artist who had linked his fate with the Communist Party and put his mighty talent at the service of the Soviet people, the Soviet State."

Still more popular accounts assert that Gorky was "formed as a writer by the revolutionary movement organized by Lenin and Stalin" and was a "lifelong friend and comrade-in-arms" of each of these leaders in turn.[4]

This is the official legend which, by dint of the volume, noise, and persistent power behind it, has prevailed not only in Russia but also abroad,[5] over the more human and complex truth.

OUT OF THE DEPTHS

In the middle nineties of the last century Maxim Gorky shot up on the horizon like a rocket from a submarine. Suddenly, from the lower depths, or as one critic put it from "the dregs of society," came a man who had lived as a part of the underworld and could write about it. Dressed like an Old Believer merchant from Central Russia; his face strongly chiselled; his spirit passionate; a romantic, sentimental, sensitive man, swift to tears, modest and shy in the presence of men of letters, noisily assertive, even rude, when faced by a throng of admirers, here was a being who had lived in the world of vagabonds, tramps, broken-down pilgrims, bums, prostitutes, part-time thieves, beggars, migratory workers, and assorted poor of the slums and riverport jungles of the mighty River Volga. Now, with two or three remarkable short stories and the advice and encouragement of a couple of men of letters, he suddenly broke through from the underworld and migratory life in which he had lived for the preceding five years into the world of books and culture of which he had never ceased to dream. Other writers before him had written of this nether world, but none had seen it from within, nor regarded it with his unflinching curiosity. To the educated Russian, this tramp who suddenly became a man of letters was truly a sensation.

Russian society was in a mood to make a cult of the vagabond writer from the lower depths. The educated world was uneasy about its material well-being and lack of moral passion. The cult of the peasant having petered out, a new object of sympathy was being sought, a new class crying aloud for redemption and possessing the power to redeem. It was not unnatural that men should mistake this artist from the world of tramps and outcasts for a "proletarian writer," and his personages for "proletarians." Lenin was not alone in making this mistake.

But if Lenin was not alone, it was he who canonized Gorky as the "greatest proletarian writer" in a polemical article written in 1910, at a moment when Gorky had lined up with the group of Vperyodist Bolsheviks, Bogdanov, Lunacharsky, "and Company," whom Lenin had just read out of his group. These words became a sacred text on which all Gorky criticism was to be based by Soviet critics, although Lenin had written it not for the purpose of exalting Gorky but rather to denigrate his associates. When Gorky broke with Lenin, "the bourgeois press" (and such Socialist dailies as *Vorwärts*) wrote that Lenin had "expelled Maxim Gorky." In his own journal Lenin wrote in reply:

> Indeed, there is no point in concealing the fact . . . that M. Gorky belongs to the supporters of the new group. Gorky undoubtedly is the greatest representative of *proletarian* art, one who has done much for it and may yet do more. Any faction of the Social Democratic Party may justly be proud of his belonging to it. But on that basis to put into its *platform* "proletarian art" means to give that platform a certificate of poverty, means to reduce its group to a literary circle . . .[6]

But Gorky disbelieved in class art, while the men and women of whom he wrote were not industrial proletarians at all. Nor did they fit into any of the legally or socially defined estates of traditional Russian society. They were outsiders, existing below the world of the official estates, thrust there, some of them, because they had been cast out by a society in rapid transition from cottage handicraft to factory industry, but the majority were there of their own free will because they were men and women who could or would not fit into the workaday world. The characters whom Gorky watched and listened to so intently and whose life he had been sharing included gypsies; gamblers; petty swindlers; beggars, broken-down versions of the *strannik*, or holy wanderer and fool of God; ruined gentry; ex-peasants and bankrupt artisans; self-deceiving dreamers expecting any day to escape from the depths into which they had sunk; fugitives from justice driven into outlawry perhaps by a single, even justifiable crime; feckless wanderers who preferred to work briefly only when hunger or thirst for vodka forced them to; thieves—professional as well as thieves-of-occasion, who stole from each other or, while working on some odd job, carried off with them everything not locked up or nailed down, and traded it for a single vodka binge; wandering ex-students and ex-soldiers who had come down in the world; all the misfits and rebels against tradition, all the flotsam and jetsam of a society which had no use for them and for which they had no use.

Gorky looked on the companions of his wanderings with sympathy, understanding, even admiration. He romanticized their impulsive misdeeds. He thought more highly of them than of the artisans and peasants he had known. As long as they were young and strong and fearless, they were heroes for his tales, embodiments of his cult of the strong-willed, the courageous and the free. "I liked their anger at life," he wrote in retrospect, "their mocking hostility towards everything and everybody, and their carefree attitude towards themselves."

They were men and women who so loved their freedom from the restraints and injustices of the conventional world that they were ready to plunge into the lower depths of life in order to attain its precarious freedom. They bore bravely or indifferently its negative aspects, uncertainty, privation, solitude, triumphing over them and retaining in greater measure than the men of settled life he had known the ability to jest, sing, philosophize, discuss the existence of God and the meaning or meaninglessness of life, dream of better things or of attaining the unattainable. Though they existed as naked, homeless, hungry and thirsty animals, they yet remained *Men*— a word which Gorky used with a special reverence and was prone to spell with a capital *M*.

He was sure that these things were so, for he had lived among them and with them, shared their hazards, listened to their sober and drunken talk, heard from each his life story and how he came thus to the depths, witnessed their thievery and debauchery, marked their quips, jests, obscenities, blasphemies, pieties, illusions, dreams, observed everything with an insatiable curiosity, noting all down indelibly on the tablets of his memory.

All of his best stories, and his one good play, appropriately entitled *Na Dne* (At the Bottom), have as protagonists the actual men and women he had known in this world, their stories as they had told them to him, their views, conversations, feelings—transposed only by being filtered through his poetic, romantic and sentimental imagination, and being subjected to the selection and unification which make raw experience into a work of art.

His tragic figures were from the same company as his heroes: the strong men of yesterday seen in premature old age, sick, apathetic, defeated by life, bereft of illusion, disintegrating amidst the bare and dismal surroundings over which yesterday they had triumphed. How swiftly decay came in this hard world!

It did not occur to Gorky to hold "society" responsible for the vagabonds he had met and put into his stories. Later, when literary-political mentors tried to get him to do so, he did it lifelessly, producing cold, mechanical stories, overloaded with pompous didactic excursions that followed neither from character nor plot.

But the last words of an Orlov, who rises from the airless filth of a cobbler's cellar hole to the exalted post of sanitary worker in a hospital, then suddenly throws it all up for the meaningless, boundless freedom of the tramp, are much closer to Gorky's vision of the vagrants he knew:

> So after all [says Gorky] I never accomplished any heroic deeds. Yet I still long to distinguish myself—to reduce the whole world to dust . . . to beat up all the Jews—it's all the same to me! . . . I was born with unrest in my soul, and my fate is to be a tramp. I have wandered everywhere but find no comfort . . . Vodka quenches the heart. As for towns, villages, people of different sorts, I find them all revolting.[7]

In short, Gorky's protagonists were anything and everything except an organized class or a part of organized society. Far from being that "industrial proletariat" on which Social Democracy based its vision of the future and in which Lenin saw the compact, organized force with the aid of which he would batter his way into power, rather were they part of what Marx had scornfully called the *Lumpenproletariat*.

In 1905, such types were actually recruited by the police to form the drunken hooligan mobs that beat up "Jews and students." If in 1917 and 1918 Lenin was able to use them for his purposes, it was because many of his inflammatory slogans, such as *Grab Nagrablennoe!* (Rob what has been robbed!), or exercise "street justice," were pitched close to the level of hooliganism. But in 1903, when Gorky protested the Kishenev pogroms and raised an accusing voice against police and government, Burenin wrote in *Novoe Vremya* that Gorky could not escape his own share of the blame, since those who carried out the pogroms were Gorky's own favorite heroes, the Chelkashes, Konovalovs, and Orlovs of his stories. Gorky withdrew the phrase about "beating all the Jews" from subsequent editions of *The Orlov Couple,* but the closing speech of Grigory Orlov as originally given shows how vivid and true was Gorky's vision of the "*Lumpenproletarians*" whom he had observed with such romantic intensity.

LIBERTY, CLASSES, MAN AND GOD

During the years of his vagrant young manhood, Gorky seems to have developed all the basic ideas that were to inform his writing. These he would hold to stubbornly for the rest of his days; neither the Narodnik Mikhail Romas nor the experienced writers to whom he apprenticed himself, Korolenko and Chekhov, nor the strong-willed men to each of whom he attached himself in turn in his search for "a man with a true and living faith,"[8] was ever able substantially to alter them.

An examination of these basic ideas makes visible the abyss that separates Gorky from V. I. Lenin.

Love of Liberty

It was this that made the young Alexei Peshkov run away from his various employers to become a wanderer. It was the love of freedom in his vagabond heroes that caused him to romanticize their life. What he glorified in them was their freedom from social and personal responsibility, from binding ties and pursuits, from settled habitation, freedom to wander, strength to act on sudden impulses, even wild and lawless ones, and to defy "philistine and slavish" conventions. These free, strong, and undisciplined characters cannot for a moment be confounded with Lenin's factory-disciplined workingmen, nor with his "professional revolutionaries" drilled in the military discipline of a conspirative army. Rather do they represent, as Alexei Tolstoy was shrewdly to note, "Gorky's ideal of a *Bosyak*, intellectuals dressed up in romantic dirty rags."

Several times, under the pressure of the milieu into which he entered as a successful writer, Gorky tried to portray a class-conscious militant proletarian. Always the result was lifeless and cold. Yet he had no trouble portraying khans, princes, merchant princes, legendary heroes, or Promethean figures of legend like the Danko of his grandmother's tale of the man of vision who tried to lead men out of a dark, swampy forest into a bright clear land, and who, when their courage and faith in him faltered in the darkness, snatched his own burning heart out of his breast to light up their path.[9]

For a few years, Gorky earned his living as a newspaper columnist. His columns make dull reading, yet when he writes of freedom, there is a sudden spark of warmth. Thus in the *Nizhegorodskii Listok* of March 31, 1901:

> Who then among you are real men? Perhaps five out of a thousand are such as believe passionately that man is a creator and master of life, and that his right to think and speak in freedom is a sacred right. Perhaps five out of a thousand fight for that right and are ready fearlessly to perish in the struggle for it. But the majority of you are either the slaves of life or its impudent masters—timid philistines temporarily taking the place of real men.

"The right to think in freedom and to speak in freedom" was in Gorky's mind first of all a right for men of letters, men of the written and spoken word, a right he claimed just as resoundingly under Lenin's dictatorship as under the Tsar's autocracy. To Andreev, Gorky wrote in 1902:

> A Russian writer should never live in friendship with the Russian government. It doesn't matter what kind it may be: autocratic, constitutional, or—even!—republican. . . . In all three forms our [government] will by its very essence be equally trashy.[10]

Contrary to official legend, he was a consistent opponent of party control of literature, detesting the idea that party or government bureaucracy—or officious critics—should tell a writer what to write. He welcomed suggestions from experienced writers concerning his craft, but when advice became peremptory and prescriptive, he felt "hatred of those critics who imagine themselves to be district supervisors in the literary section, and, like all Russian policemen, have lost their respect for individuality and individual freedom."[11]

Gorky's stories were full of anger at life. But his anger and his fellow-feeling for his characters were something quite distinct from the prevailing "social protest" that ignored the deeper roots of tragedy in the nature of man and of life itself and sought to explain all evil as mere by-product of the legal forms of ownership, destined to disappear once these forms were altered.

As a provincial writer in Nizhni Novgorod Gorky had organized charities, provided sleigh rides, warm boots, skates, and other Christmas gifts for children, medicines, food, outings, and festivals. As one Bolshevik wrote to Lenin at the time, "Maxim Gorky now spends less than 30 percent of his earnings on himself."

In the early 1900s the revolutionary political parties acquired sufficient influence over him to divert much of his already large earnings, and the much larger sums he collected from the wealthy, away from his charities and into help for the revolutionary movement. But he never gave up his habit of showing his private generosity to persons "deserving" and "undeserving," and he stubbornly resisted the attempt to enlist him as an exclusive contributor to a single party or faction. He gave freely to all, to anarchists, socialist revolutionaries, Mensheviks, Bolsheviks, revolutionary democrats, and liberals. Gorky has told us that he got Savva Morozov to contribute 2,000 rubles a month to Lenin's "finance minister," Leonid Krassin. Lenin never thought to ask how "class interest" could induce Morozov, Schmidt, Bugrov, and other millionairies to contribute to his fighting funds. For the answer to this question he could have gotten little help from Marx, but perhaps some from Sigmund Freud, who would have called it the *death wish*.[12]

The political-minded critics of the early nineteen hundreds wanted more than money from the "proletarian novelist," pressing him to engage in political activity. He drew up or signed a few protests, wrote non-political tales for literary sections of political journals, suffered some police persecution which deepened his hatred of autocracy, but resisted the pressure to do political-thesis narratives. In 1902, he made one such attempt, a play called *Meshchane* (variously translated as *The Middle Class*, *The Philistines*, *Smug Citizens*). The result makes dismal reading and Gorky was sufficiently self-critical to realize it. To Chekhov he wrote:

> Well, the play has turned out to be clamorous, beastly, empty and dull. I dislike it greatly. . . . This very winter I will without fail write another play. . . . This one will have to be finely proportioned and beautiful as music.

For this second play he returned to the people and the life he knew so well. *Na Dne* (*At the Bottom*, *The Lower Depths*, *Lodging for a Night*) is indeed a play with the thematic structure of a musical composition.[13]

Again in 1907, Gorky tried his hand at a propaganda work, the novel *Mother*, celebrated beyond its merits because Lenin found it "useful" and hence the most valuable of Gorky's writings. He wrote it, not on order from Lenin's party, but out of loneliness and impotent vexation as the Tsar's government reestablished itself after the ebbing of the storm of 1905–1906 and he was forced to leave his native land.

> If a tooth could feel after being knocked out [he wrote] it would probably feel as lonely as I. . . . Everything is lost . . . they had crushed, annihilated, exiled, imprisoned everybody. . . . I felt as if a pestilential dust were blowing from Russia.

On Lenin's say-so, Soviet critics treat *Mother* as "the first proletarian novel" and the progenitor of the grim school of "socialist realism." After he read it, Lenin sought a private encounter with Gorky to persuade him to accept the idea of *partiinost* and to limit both his financial aid and his literary contributions exclusively to Lenin's own Bolshevik faction. Gorky helped generously but refused to yield to the demand for factional exclusiveness. In *Novaya Zhizn* in 1917, he could still write:

> For seventeen years I have considered myself a Social Democrat and have served as well as I could the purposes of that Party. But I have never denied my services to other parties, for I am unwilling to spurn any vital cause. I have no sympathy for people who become fossilized and petrified under the pressure of the faith they confess. I go further: In every party and group I regard myself as a heretic. In my political views there are quite likely a number of contradictions which I cannot and do not want to reconcile with each other . . . I should have to kill utterly that part of my soul which loves most passionately the aching, live, sinful, and—if you please—wretchedly pitiful Russian man.

One of Gorky's oldest friends, Ekaterina Kuskova, in her memoir on the writer written on his death, has left us an admirable picture of his "Marxism" and his ambivalent admiration for Lenin. In 1893, when Maxim Gorky had just published his first tales, Kuskova took the young man, so hungry to "learn everything" into her home, well-stocked with books, and into the circle of Nizhni Novgorod intellectuals. The learned woman and the ardent tramp writer found that they had much in common: both were from the Volga, born in Kazan and resident in Nizhni. Both loved books and revered learning. She guided his reading, helping him to understand what he read. But in one thing she was unsuccessful—admirer of Marx though she was, she could not persuade him to take Marx's *Capital*. Many years later, when she learned of his newfound admiration for Lenin, she asked:

> What has brought you to the Bolsheviks? Do you remember how I began to read Marx with you in Nizhni, and you proposed to throw the 'German philistine' into the fire and go out to the garden wall to listen, free from bookishness, to the singing of the nightingale . . . ?"
>
> Oh, he cried out, smiling—"Now, too, I prefer nightingales to Marxist rubbish. I can't take it, by God, even on an empty stomach. But . . . as people they are excellent. Most excellent people, I tell you. They will knock the autocracy's head off, just like that . . . Excellent people . . . And Lenin, by God, sings like a nightingale . . ."
>
> I looked at him. In his eyes were sparks of laughter. Is he mocking? Or has he been taken in somehow? In any case, after this moment of attraction as before, he continued warmly to support every other "activism" aiming at "smashing the ugly mug" of the autocracy. . . .

And, after October [1917], when these "most excellent people" were victorious, nobody attacked them with such definite sharpness as Gorky whose ideal of "man" suffered from the "usurpers of freedom."[14]

As with so much in Soviet historiography, there are different and contradictory versions of the date and nature of Gorky's first face-to-face meeting with Lenin. At least as early as 1903, when there was a great to-do about Lenin's splitting of the *Iskra* group and the Second Party Congress into Bolsheviks and Mensheviks, his name must have been well known to Maxim Gorky. Given Gorky's interest and keen powers of observation, he would undoubtedly have made precise mental notes on this strong-willed man whenever he should meet him for the first time, as he did on all other "strong" characters he had observed from tramps to Tolstoy. If we are to trust Gorky's always vivid powers of observation, and the express words of his remarkable description of Lenin in his *Days with Lenin*, the two did not meet until the London Congress of the Social Democratic Party in 1907.

> I had never met Lenin before this [Gorky writes]. I did not expect Lenin to be like that. There was something lacking in him. . . . He was somehow too ordinary, did not give the impression of being a leader. As a literary man I am obliged to take note of such details. . . .[15]

It is such "little details," of course, that make Gorky's literary profiles so vivid, whether he is dealing with a tramp or with Lenin or Tolstoy.

In 1934, however, when Stalin's great "Operation Rewrite" was in high gear, one of its objectives was to enlarge the role of Lenin in the revolution of 1905. As early as 1931, Stalin attacked an honest writer on an obscure problem of Party history, namely the date on which Lenin first lost his admiration for Kautsky. In an ominous letter *Proletarskaya Revoliutsiya* Stalin charged its editors with "rotten liberalism" for having printed the historian's findings as a "discussion article." The historian disappeared, and "rotten liberalism," "bourgeois objectivism," and "exaggerated attachment to facts," as well as various "archive rats," disappeared with him. Immediately pliant memorialists appeared, ready to "remember" whatever "past" Stalin wished to have remembered.[16]

Among these memorialists was K. P. Pyatnitsky, onetime business manager of Gorky's publishing house, Znanie, who now remembered that Lenin had planned the Moscow uprising of December 1905 from an apartment in Saint Petersburg, and that Gorky had gone from Moscow to Petrograd on November 16, 1905, "to report to Lenin on the mood of the Moscow workingmen." Thereupon, the Stalinist historian Sorin, head of the Lenin Section of the Marx-Engels-Lenin Institute, wrote Gorky asking him to confirm this meeting and his report to Lenin in 1905. The author of *Days with Lenin* was living in Stalin's Russia in 1934 when "histories were succeeding each other as if they were being consumed by a giant chain smoker who lights the first volume of the new work with the last volume of the old," and "historians were appearing and disappearing . . . and vanishing without a trace."

Gorky did the best he could, explaining uncomfortably that he must have gone to report to Lenin "with a high fever, as the result of which my memory of what took place was so confused that I even did not make up my mind to say anything about it in my memories of Vl. Ilyich." And Gorky's wife, the actress Andreeva, obligingly remembered how long the two men had held each other's hands in their first handclasp, how joyously they had smiled at each other, and how Gorky could not get over the pleasure of the meeting for many hours, but she says nothing about a deliberate journey to meet Lenin nor about a "report on the mood of the Moscow workingmen."[17]

Whether we are to accept the idea that a high fever in 1905 confused Gorky into saying that "I met Lenin for the first time in London in 1907," or that the first meeting and "report" were so casual that Lenin made no impression upon him, or, as seems most likely, that no meeting between them took place in 1905, the fact remains that Gorky's first awareness of Lenin as a human being whom he was meeting face to face and observing with enormous interest and with his remarkable writer's attention to details was the result of an invitation to attend the London Party Congress of 1907 as an "honorary guest." He had just finished the novel *Mother*. Lenin, after reading it, introduced into the Central Committee, then consisting of both Mensheviks and Bolsheviks, the motion to invite Gorky to the London Congress. The motion was adopted unanimously. As soon as Gorky registered at a London hotel, Lenin put in an appearance to make his acquaintance. Barely stopping to shake hands, Vladimir Ilyich rushed past his host to the bed in the middle of the room, thrust his hand into the bedclothes, and began moving it between the sheets.

> I stood like a dolt [Gorky told Valentinov afterwards] unable to understand what he was up to. Had he lost his mind! But praise be to Allah, my bewilderment ceased when he returned to my side and explained: "In London the climate is raw and we must see to it that the bedding isn't damp. And," says he, "we must be particularly careful in your case since you have just written *Mother*, a thing useful for the Russian workingman which summons him to battle against the autocracy." Of course, I thanked him for his compliment, but I must admit I was a bit annoyed. . . . To treat my work as if it were a kind of committee manifesto calling for the storming of the autocracy . . . was after all quite unfitting. You see, in this work I tried to treat some very large and very, very difficult problems. The justifying of terror, assassination, and executions during a revolution—you see, that's a big moral problem. You see

it's not possible so lightly to get around the thought that perhaps such killings sully a sacred cause.[18]

Gorky's artistic instincts told him that *Mother* was a poor work. When a Soviet theater manager wanted to have it dramatized, he refused consent, yielding only when the director touched his heart by the promise that half the proceeds would be given to the *besprizornyi*, waifs made fatherless and homeless by the ravages of war and famine. In 1927, when Gladkov wrote him apologetically that he found *Mother* artistically weak and dull and was unable to finish it, Gorky replied: "You are wrong to think that your critical—and quite just—attitude towards my *Mother* might offend me. . . . *Mother* is a really bad book, written under the spell of bad temper and irritation after the events of 1906. . . ."

Three years before his death, Gorky pronounced his final judgment on the novel to his biographer and friend, V. A. Desnitsky: "*Mother* [he wrote] is long drawn out, boringly and carelessly written."[19]

On the subject of party orders and freedom for the writer, we can give the last word to an utterance of Gorky to Konstantin Fedin, which the latter did not dare include in his *Gorky in Our Midst*, but repeated privately to Victor Serge:

> The party commissar is at one and the same time policeman, censor, and archbishop: he grabs hold of you, blue-pencils your writings, and then wants to sink his claws into your soul.[20]

Worker and Peasant

His "congenital disgust with politics," Lenin could forgive in an artist. But not his infuriating refusal to rule out opposition Bolsheviks, Mensheviks, Anarchists, Social-Revolutionaries as worthy of support. Nor the fact that Gorky could never bring himself to accept Lenin's simplistic division of men into classes or his condemnation of whole categories of men to extermination.

Only the peasants he sometimes treated as an impersonal category. He had seen and experienced so many bitter things in peasant life. At twenty he watched his first intellectual mentor and employer, the Narodnik Mikhail Romas, found a general store in the village of Krasnovidovo, where the peasants might gather of a winter evening around the stove, buy goods at low prices, and fill their heads gratis with noble ideas. Gunpowder was put into the store, both he and his employer were ambushed at night, then the store was burned down and they had to flee for their lives into the flickering darkness before a pursuing band. At twenty-three he had been beaten into unconsciousness when he tried to save a naked woman who was being horsewhipped publicly through a village street by her husband followed by a howling mob, because she had been taken in adultery. These experiences of his young manhood made him fear the peasant and hate him.

In 1922, in his O *Russkom Krestyanstve*, he sought to rationalize this hatred. Lumping them then with the workers of the cities, whom he sometimes grudgingly idealized, but more often regarded with gloomy clarity, he wrote:

> In its essence every people is spontaneously anarchic; the folk wants as far as possible to eat more and work less, have all rights and no duties. The atmosphere of rightlessness in which . . . the folk is accustomed to live convinces it of the lawfulness of lawlessness, the zoological naturalness of anarchism. . . . The Russian peasant has been dreaming for centuries of some sort of state without any right to influence his personal will or his liberty of action—a state with no power over man.

He recognized the peasant's love for the land as a "mystic love," and quoted a fine old bearded *muzhik* as saying to him:

> Yes, we have learned to fly like sparrows, and to swim like sprats, but we don't know how to live on earth. We must first settle well on earth and let the air come afterwards. . . . If we peasants had made the revolution ourselves everything would long ago be quiet on earth and orderly. The peasant knows how to work—only give him land. He doesn't organize strikes—the earth won't let him. . . .

After citing such peasants with approval, Gorky returns to his fear:

> Cruelty—that is what has tormented me all my life, and torments me now . . . In Russian cruelty one finds a diabolical refinement, something subtle and cultivated . . . This inventive cruelty was influenced by the reading of the lives of the martyred and tortured saints. . . .

Follows a list of well-nigh unprintable tortures he witnessed during the Civil War. One of the gentler examples will suffice:

> Undressing an officer naked, they tore bits of skin in the shape of epaulettes from his shoulders, and in place of the little stars hammered in nails; they cut strips of skin along the line of the trouser strips and sword belt—this they called "dressing him up in uniform." It took no little time and considerable art. . . . Who was the crueler: the Whites or the Reds? Probably they were both alike. You see, both one side and the other—were Russians. . . .

Gorky was convinced that Lenin's seizure of power and his demagogic calls for terror from below would give free rein to peasant cruelty until it wiped out the cities which to him were the focus of culture and humaneness. In the end this judgment was to prove wrong, for it was from the city that the more ferocious forms of cruelty (forced collectivization, millions of families at slave labor, the great blood purges, inquisitorial torture to fabricate "confessions," the regimentation and atomization of society and of the intellect) were to come. Yet there can be no doubt that it was this justified if one-sided hatred and fear of the peasants that caused Gorky to misread for a time the brutal meaning of forced collectivization and find palatable the massive concentration camps and forced labor armies semantically disguised as "re-education centers" under Joseph Stalin.[21]

On the subject of the workingman, Gorky's mind was a confused whirlpool driven round and round by the conflicting forces of his own clear-eyed observation and the idealizing indoctrination to which he was subjected by the socialist intellectual milieu that accepted him as the celebrator of the lives of the men of the lower depths. Both in his letters and in *Na Dne*, he expressed dislike of the habit of certain "class-conscious workingmen" who boast, "I'm a worker," as a member of the gentry boasts, "I'm a nobleman." He has Peppel quote the locksmith Kletsch ironically:

"I am a workingman" [he says]—and everybody's below him, he'll have you believe. Well, work if you like it—what's there to be proud of? If we're supposed to judge people by their work, then the horse is better than any man—you drive it—and it doesn't talk back.

At times Gorky expressed the hope that the workingman, as a city dweller, would not prove immune to the enlightenment offered by the intellectual, that he might be illumined by the light of culture, science, "Europe" (by which Gorky means European civilization), and joy in heroic and creative work. Sometimes, as in the Stalin years, he tried to persuade himself that the worker was actually rejoicing at the speedup and privations of forced industrialization and had become an ancient Russian Bogatyr, a titan engaged in heroic, legendary feats of labor. But the illusion did not last. The whirlpool made a turn, and he saw the workingman as yesterday's peasant with the same limited horizon, anarchic cruelty, and laziness, with not even a redeeming attachment to his work to match the peasant's mystic attachment to his piece of land. What if, on getting power, he asks, the worker should repeat the age-old saying, "All one needs is a quiet corner and a woman"?

What if indeed the millions of Russia suffer the bitter pains of the revolution only because in the depths of their souls they cherish the hope of liberation from work? A minimum of labor and a maximum of satisfaction—that is quite as unobtainable as any other [utopia].

Knowing well this whirlpool in his own mind, Gorky wrote in his memoir on Lenin at the latter's death:

I am a very dubious Marxist. . . . I do not have any faith in the intelligence of the masses in general.

Man, the Creator of Life

In the main, Gorky's writings deal not with classes but with man. The very word stirred such feeling in him that, as we have seen, he found it difficult to write the word *Man* without a capital. At the very outset of his career he voiced the hope that what he wrote might express "eternal truths" with "imperishable beauty" so that his work might live and serve man. In a dialogue between Writer and Reader (1898), *The Writer* declares that the aim of his art is to

help man understand himself, raise his faith in himself, wage war against vulgarity in men, arouse in their minds, shame, wrath, courage . . . make them noble and strong, make them capable of suffusing their life with the holy spirit of beauty.

It is a confession of faith. But a sense of the difficulty of this high resolve makes him give to *The Reader* the last word consisting of a mocking song concerning the blind leading the blind, and a troubling question—one that was to trouble Gorky always: "How can you be a guide when you yourself do not know the road?"

To Tolstoy, when the two were convalescing in the Crimea, Gorky said: "Even a great book is no more than a dead, dark shadow of the Word. It only hints at the Truth, whereas man is a depository of the living God . . . I deeply believe that there is nothing better on earth than man. Only man exists, the rest is no more than a point of view. . . . I have always been a Man-worshipper, only I have not been able to express it with sufficient force."

Two major themes are interwoven in the play *Na Dne*. One is the theme of Man. The cunning old wanderer Luka, Gorky's principal mouthpiece, rings its changes, now echoed, now called in question, by each of the other characters in turn. Luka has no sooner entered the "cavelike basement" than he rebukes the declassed Baron for taking pride in his vanished estate. "All of you are just human beings. Put on as much as you like, wriggle as much as you will, but just as you are born a man, a man you will die." By way of counterpoint, he assures the broken-down Actor: "Man can do everything . . . if he only wants to."

To each of these creatures that once were men, the pilgrim Luka gives sympathy, instills courage, encourages a forlorn hope "to live better"—or at least, to die more easily.

When the other lodgers, long used to the failing health of the slowly dying Anna, speak mockingly of imaginary attendants waiting on her, the old wanderer comforts her in her last hours, rebuking the callous fellow inmates of the cellar:

> How can anybody make a joke of it? How can anybody cast off a human being . . . ? Whatever condition he may be in, he is always worth something. There'll be peace and quiet there [he assures her]. . . . Death quiets everything. Death is kind to us humans. When you die, you'll have rest . . . for where can a human find rest in this world? . . . You have to die with joy, without fear. To us, I tell you, death is like a mother to little children.

Only to the brutal lodging house owner, Kostylov, does Luka deny manhood, telling him in riddles that "some people are mere people while others are truly men." Dispossessed for his defense of Kostylov's victims from the landlord's wrath and brutality, Luka resumes his wandering. The last act seems the poorer for his absence, yet, one by one, the other characters take up his theme of the meaningfulness of man, arguing its truth or falsity, its sense or nonsense, developing it further, until at last the character Satin, who in some ways is Luka's antagonist, assumes the old man's defense in a drunken eulogy from which swell the triumphant notes of the old man's theme:

> What's truth? *Man*—that's the truth! He understood this—you don't. . . . I can't get the old man out of my head. . . . The old man had a head on his shoulders . . . He had the same effect on me as acid on an old dirty coin. . . . Everybody [he said]; everybody lives for something better. That's why we have to be considerate of every man—Who knows what's in him, why he was born, and what he can do? Maybe he was born . . . for our greater good . . . A man is free—he pays for everything himself—for belief and disbelief, for love, for intelligence, and that makes him free. Man—that's the truth. What is man? It's not you, nor I, nor they—No it's you, I, and they . . . all in one. You understand? It's tremendous! In this are all the beginnings and all the ends. Everything in man, everything for man. Only man exists, the rest is the work of his hands and brain. Man! That is splendid! It has a proud sound! . . .

Tolstoy said to Gorky concerning *Na Dne*, "Much of what you say comes out of yourself, and therefore you have no characters, and all your people have the same face." This is true. It deprives *Na Dne* of ordinary theatricality but gives it its poetic, or as Gorky puts it, its "symphonic" development. For this reason the traditional Moscow Art Theater treatment of the play as a realistic drama of life in the lower depths, the endless hours spent by actors and directors slumming in dens and hovels, studying drunkards, vagabonds and prostitutes, the meticulous attention to such matters as to how to roll a *makhorka* cigarette—got the play off to a wrong start. It became tremendously popular as a supposed drama of social protest concerning "a society that compels men to live in such misery," and as such it made Gorky's reputation in many lands. But as one reads it, or sees it performed in another tradition, one becomes aware that *Na Dne* is more than a realistic picture of men at the bottom—more, and quite different. It is Gorky's confession of faith. Its characters do not speak in language appropriate to their lives and their broken-down state. It is a liturgical-poetic drama filled with Gorky's anger and despair at the way life is; Gorky's hope-against-hope for man, and what he may become; Gorky's faltering doubt that this, his dream, can be fulfilled. At the bottom of life as at its every level, he is saying, man is man, with the same hopes, dreams, passions, weaknesses, illusions, the same hopeless condition, the same potentialities for hope. The play is what Gorky promised Chekhov that it would be, a tone poem in dramatic form, with broken-down men and women as the orchestral instruments taking up, developing and interweaving two themes. The first of these is Man. The second leitmotif we must reserve for consideration in the next [section]. It is an interweaving of two themes in a poetic drama that the play must be read, and as poetry it must be played. Indeed, it is the only completely successful poem Gorky ever wrote.

In Quest of God

In 1901, Gorky and Tolstoy talked about God:

"The minority feel the need of God [Gorky records Tolstoy as saying] because they already have everything else, and the majority because they have nothing." But I would put it differently: The majority believe in God out of weakness of spirit, and only a few out of fullness of soul.[22]

This is authentic Gorky and authentic Tolstoy. It infuriated Lenin when he discovered this streak in his "first proletarian novelist." Even in the novel *Mother* this must have been visible to Lenin, had he not chosen to overlook it. The hero, Pavel, permits himself to be persuaded by the peasant Rybin that "God exists in the reason of man, though not in the Church." The problem propounded by the novel, "whether terror, assassinations, and executions do not sully a sacred cause," is a moral and religious one. And Pavel's mother becomes reconciled to her son's consorting with revolutionaries only after she has managed to identify them with the Christian martyrs of her faith. "Errors," Lenin thought, "but I shall explain them when we meet." And so he did, while Gorky seeming not to hear, made no reply. Within a year, they were on the outs again—because of God.

In the author's childhood, one of his few consoling joys was the religion into which his beloved grandmother drew him. Religion gave him his first letters in the form of Old Church Slavonic; its sonorous phrases crept into his writing and colored his thought. Music, incense, tapers, icons, church services, the simple, vivid language in which his grandmother talked to God, formed a corner of light and warmth in his cold and wretched childhood. Later, when learned men and books had shaken his faith, he felt that virtue had gone out of him. As late as 1922, as we have seen, when he was writing of Tolstoy, he said: "I was seeking then, I am still seeking now, and shall continue to seek until I die, for a man with a true and living faith." This quest brought him to Lenin as it had to Tolstoy, but it was a quest which, as Gorky formulated it, aroused Lenin to fits of uncontrollable rage.

In 1906, Gorky wrote a book about an orphan, *The Story of a Man Nobody Needed*, a *roman policier* whose miserable central character is too weak to resist evil, becomes a police spy, and ends by committing suicide. A dialogue between the orphan and his uncle, the village blacksmith, marks the beginning of a new stage in Gorky's search:

> "Why does God let devils into the church?"
> "What's it to him? God isn't the church watchman."
> "Doesn't he live there?"
> "God? What for? His place is everywhere. Churches are for people."
> "But what are people for?"
> "But people—they, so to speak ... in general, for everything! Without people you can't manage anything—isn't that so ... ?"
> "They—are they for God?"
> The smith looked sideways at his nephew and answered hesitatingly: "Of course ..."[23]

The wretched orphan of the novel, Yevsei, is Alexei Maximovich transposed—there, he might say, but for the grace of God, go I. But the voice of the blacksmith is Gorky's too, hesitating to decide whether God is for the people, or the people for God. With his question, the quest is renewed.

Later that year the *Mercure de France* conducted an international *enquête* concerning religion. Gorky answered that he opposed the religions of Moses, Christ and Mahomet because they engendered antagonisms among men and subordinated him to outside forces. He offered instead a religious faith in man, not man as he was but as he might become if he strove to make himself into a "perfect being" through the development of all his faculties and a "happy and proud awareness of a harmonious link that joins him to the universe."[24]

At the end of 1907 Gorky began work on his novel *Ispoved (The Confession)*, destined to take its place alongside of *Na Dne* as a confession of faith. It is a narrative poem in biblical and liturgical prose. It has fared ill with Russian critics because of its very virtues, which to them seem to be its vices. Before Lenin knew what the work was about, he asked for an excerpt to publish in the literary section of *Proletarii*, but when he read the piece, he returned it with a demand that it be revised or something else be sent in its place. With this ultimatum the friendship between the two men cooled for several years.

Gorky's novel is more than a confession of faith; it is in addition a fictional statement of the proposition that the socialist movement is a surrogate religious creed.[25] The hero of the novel is again an orphan, this time called Matvei, who like Alexei Peshkov—Gorky himself—wanders through the world in quest of a "true and living faith." He visits monasteries, talks with holy men, joins pilgrimages, seeks wisdom from a celebrated and prideful religious man who engages in coarse talk about women (modeled on Tolstoy). In the end, he gets light from three workingmen, allegorical representatives of the apostles John and Peter and the Archangel Michael, from whom he learns that God dies when men disagree, and that when the people have fused into one mighty force and freed themselves from all discord and disharmony, they will resurrect God out of their own midst as once before He came out of them as a carpenter in Galilee. At the novel's close, Matvei witnesses a miracle performed by a procession of the people, a procession of which he has become a part: their faith, their emotional exultation, and their collective will take possession of a paralyzed girl, enabling her to arise and walk. Now at last Matvei is indissolubly bound up with the folk and knows that he is joining them in an endless forward march towards an unseen yet certain goal, the apotheosis of the people itself through its toil and wonder-working miracles into a single, unitary, all-knowing, all-powerful god.

That night, alone in the woods yet alone no more, Matvei's certitude opens his lips that his mouth may declare the praise of the God in process of creating himself:

> I saw the earth, my mother, in the space between the stars. . . . And I saw her master—the omnipotent, immortal people. . . . and I prayed:
> Thou art my God and the Creator of all Gods, weaving them out of the beauty of Thine own spirit, in the labor and the turmoil of Thy quest. Let there be no other gods beside Thee, for Thou art the one and only God, the worker of miracles."
> This I believe and do confess![26]

Lenin's rage when he read this knew no bounds. He believed, or professed to believe, that this was not Gorky's thought, and that the naive author was being misled by the more sophisticated Bolsheviks, Bogdanov, Bazarov, and above all, Lunacharsky, three men whom Lenin, at that moment, was expelling from the co-leadership of his group. Indeed, Lunacharsky had been following a similar train of thought in a two-volume work, *Religion and Socialism* (1906–07), where, with far less artistry than Gorky, he mixed the history of religion, sociological analysis, and poetic enthusiasm, all culminating in an apotheosis of Marxism as a "natural, earthly, anti-metaphysical, scientific and human religion" destined to put an end to all "supernatural, transcendent, unscientific, fetishistic, authoritarian, hierarchical faiths," and in their place put the faith of man in his socialized self and in the endless development of his powers. Socialism needed this touch of religious ardor, Lunacharsky maintained, for "religion is enthusiasm, and without enthusiasm you can accomplish nothing."

Publicly, it was a critical review of Gorky's *Ispoved* by Lunacharsky that Lenin chose to attack, for "propagating a current which breaks with the foundations of Marxism . . . and wages war against proletarian, Marxian socialism.[27]

In tactful, persuasive letters, Gorky remonstrated with Lenin, urging him to come to Capri to talk the whole thing over after the fashion of friends and comrades with those against whom he was pronouncing anathema. At this Lenin waxed yet angrier:

> . . . to preach a degenerate agnosticism . . . to teach the workers "religious atheism" and the "deification" of the highest human potentialities (Lunacharsky) . . . no! that is too much. . . .

With Gorky himself he strove to be more indulgent:

> . . . I think that an artist can draw much that is useful for him out of every philosophy. . . . *Even if it be an idealistic philosophy*, you can come to conclusions which will bring to the workers' party enormous usefulness. That's true. But all the same . . . Your present article . . . you must rework. . . . any other conduct on your part, i.e. a refusal to rework the article, or a refusal to collaborate in *Proletarii*, will lead, in my opinion, to a sharpening of our conflict . . . and to the weakening of the . . . cause of the revolutionary Social Democracy in Russia.[28]

On March 16, he again rejected an invitation to Capri:

> to talk with people who permit themselves to preach the unity of scientific socialism with religion, I *can not* and will not. . . . I have already *sent to press* . . . a formal declaration of war. The time for diplomacy has passed.

He added tart greetings to Maria Federovna Andreeva—"she, I hope, is not for God, hah?"[29]

Finally even the tolerant Gorky lost patience and wrote to the editorial board of the publishing house, Znanie, of which he was the leading spirit:

> . . . Concerning the publication of Lenin's book [*Materialism and Empirio-Criticism*]: I'm against it because I know the author. A great wise-man, a

wonderful person, but a fighting-cock, he would only mock at a chivalrous act such as that. Let Znanie publish this book, and he will say: the fools!— and those fools will be Bogdanov, I, Basarov, Lunacharsky.

At the same moment, Lenin was writing his sister, "As to Znanie, I have almost given up hope. . . . We will have to look elsewhere. . . ."[30]

In his letter to Znanie, Gorky made clear that he was breaking with Lenin on philosophical matters too, and joining forces with those Bolsheviks whom Lenin was expelling as heretics:

> . . . The dispute flaring up between Lenin and Plekhanov on the one hand and Bogdanov, Bazarov and Co. on the other is extremely important and profound. The first two, though they differ with each other on tactics, both believe in and preach historical fatalism; the other side preaches philosophical activism. For me it is clear on which side the greater truth lies. . .[31]

Then Gorky's reverence for culture as a redeeming force brought on a new dispute to sharpen the old. From his own earnings and funds gathered from wealthy friends, Gorky started a school to bring culture and enlightenment to Russian revolutionary workingmen and to bring to his home on Capri a bit of Russia. The school would pay the students' way to and from Russia, maintaining them in lovely Capri while they studied. A railway clerk named Vilonov, who had been arrested and escaped many times, had been beaten by the police, and contracted tuberculosis in prison, came to live with Gorky while convalescing. He returned clandestinely to pick worthy students for the school, thirteen of whom finally arrived after all sorts of adventures en route. Bogdanov lectured on political economy, Pokrovsky on Russian history, Lunacharsky on the history of socialism and revolutions, and on the history of art, Gorky on Russian literature, Alexinsky on the labor movement—no mean faculty, for Lenin was to pronounce Bogdanov's book the best text on political economy and Pokrovsky the best Marxist historian, while Gorky was the best proletarian artist, Alexinsky had been Lenin's spokesman in the Second Duma, and Lunacharsky would one day be his Commissar of Education.

With his longing to "unite all constructive elements," Gorky dispatched an invitation to Trotsky, who accepted and took the workingmen on a guided tour of the museums of Vienna, but failed to show up at the school; to Karl Kautsky and Rosa Luxemburg, who declared themselves too busy; to Menshevik leaders like Martov and Axelrod and Plekhanov, who did not appear either.

Of course, Gorky extended a warm invitation to Lenin. Ever a pugnacious factionalist, Lenin decided without investigation that the school was a faction plot against him, hence against the Party, to be disrupted at all costs. In vain did the school council (both students and faculty) invite Lenin to come himself to teach and to bring three other members of his faction with him as teachers; in vain did they offer to accept the "ideological control of the Bolshevik Center in Paris," i.e. of Lenin. Lenin would be content with nothing less than the expulsion from the faculty of those whom he was bent on expelling from his faction, Bogdanov, Bazarov, Alexinsky, Lunacharsky, Pokrovsky, and all "God-builders" (which included the school's very founder), as well as all those who had opposed him recently on tactical matters concerning the Duma deputies. The school must be disbanded on Capri and all its students, without its faculty, must come to him in Paris for their education.

> There are no Bolsheviks among your instructors [he wrote to the bewildered worker-students]. The Island of Capri has already become known even in general Russian literature as the literary center of the God-builders. . . . He who goes to study Social Democratism in Paris goes to study real Social Democratism. He who goes to study on Capri goes to study a *special* factional "science." . . . The school was organized on Capri expressly to *cover up* its factional character, to conceal the school from the Party.

Poor Gorky, who detested politics and factionalism and who had organized the school to solace his loneliness for Russia and to further the culture of Russian workingmen, was forced into party squabbles. Though Lenin avoided using his name as much as possible, every attack on the Island of Capri was a stab in the heart of a man who tried to turn his home—always a sort of Grand Hotel for homeless or needy Russians abroad—into a school for Russian workingmen.

The school ran nearly five months. During the fourth month, Lenin's bombardment of factional attacks, aided by a workingman among the students who was secretly a police agent (the police had standing instructions to "split, and split, and again split," which, for different reasons, was Lenin's motto also), persuaded five students to come to Paris to study. All they got there was a series of lectures by Lenin on "The Present Moment and Our Tasks" and a lecture on "The Agrarian Policy of Stolypin," but Lenin's aim was accomplished. *Proletarii* wrote finis to Gorky's dream in an article entitled "A Shameful Failure."

Immediately Lenin set about wooing Gorky away from the others, apologizing for having "mistakenly" regarded his motives, and those of Vilonov, as "exclusively factional."

> I had all along thought [he wrote] that it would be stupid for me to try to discuss in a friendly manner with you. . . . Today I had a heart-to-heart talk with Vilonov both on party matters and on you, and I saw that I had been terribly mistaken. . . . and I want firmly to press your hand. Through your

talent as an artist you have brought the workers of Russia so much that is useful and will continue to be of such great use that it is not at all permissible for you to surrender to the gloom induced by an episode in the faction struggle of us exiles. . . . I warmly press your hand and Maria Federovna's, for now I have the hope of meeting you again and not as enemies.

Luck was with Lenin. Lunacharsky's wife, who was Bogdanov's sister, quarrelled with Gorky's wife, until the sunny little colony on Capri broke up in personal squabbles. Then Lenin found it possible to go to Capri.[32]

Lenin and Gorky seemed to patch things up. Yet there was pain in Gorky's heart, and smoldering wrath in Lenin's. In November 1913, the storm broke again. This time Gorky's sin was a coy jest in which he told some intellectual "God-seekers" that they would "find no God for the moment" because none had as yet been "created." Lenin thundered:

What is this you're doing? It is simply horrible, really!

You write "But the quest for God must be postponed *for a while* [only for a while?]. There is nothing to seek where you have not put anything. Without sowing you can't reap. You have no God, you have not yet [yet!] created Him. Gods are not sought, *they are created*. . . . "

So it turns out that you are against "the quest for God" only "for a while"! . . . Against God-seeking only in order to replace it with God-building! Now isn't it horrible that such a thing *should come from you*? God-seeking differs from God-building no more than a yellow devil from a blue one. To speak of God-seeking not in order to come out against all devils and gods, against all ideological copulation with a corpse (every bloody little god is copulation with a corpse. . . .)—and to prefer a blue devil to a yellow one is a hundred times as bad as not to say anything at all. . . .

Every religious idea, every idea of any little god, even every bit of co-quettishness with a little god is unutterable vileness. . . . A Catholic priest who violates a young maiden . . . is *much less* dangerous . . . than a priest without a cassock, without a gross religion, a priest full of ideas and democracy who preaches the construction and creation of little gods. For the first kind of priest is *easy* to expose, denounce, get rid of, while the second kind is *impossible* to get rid of so easily, and to expose him a thousand times more difficult. . . .

Really this is horrible. . . . Why do you do this? . . . This is hellishly harmful.[33]

Lenin had argued this all out with Gorky when he visited Capri in 1910, but Gorky had remained stubbornly silent, as he frequently did to avoid argument, a silence which Lenin took for assent. Lenin saw the new article then as a "relapse," which helps to account for his fury. To appease him, Gorky apologized for having "let slip" the words, "postponed *for a while*." But he did not yield in any other respect. Instead, without employing Lenin's angry and abusive tone, he offered a quiet defense of his views:

God is the complex of the ideas worked out by tribes, nations, mankind, which awaken social feelings and give them organized form with the aim of linking the individual personality to society and of taming zoological individualism. . . . God-construction is the process of the further development and enlargement of these social feelings in the individual and in society . . .

At this, Lenin hurled again his anathemata: "reactionary . . . idealistic . . . hocus-pocus . . . Priestly . . . clerical . . . lulling the class struggle to sleep . . . strengthening oppressive class rule . . . simply horrible . . ." But realizing how deeply he had offended, he did not repeat the phrase, *copulation with a corpse*.[34] Gorky did not answer.

On Christmas Eve 1917, with Lenin already in power and incorporating militant atheism into the official religion of the State as previously he had of his party, Gorky wrote in *Novaya Zhizn*:

Today is the day of the birth of Christ, one of the two greatest symbols created by the striving of man for justice and beauty. Christ—the immortal idea of charity and humanity, and Prometheus, enemy of the gods, the first rebel against Fate—mankind has not created anything greater than these two incarnations of his aspirations. The day will come when in the spirits of men the symbols of pride and charity, meekness and unimaginable courage in the attaining of one's goals . . . both these symbols will fuse into one great common feeling, and all mankind will recognize its meaning, the beauty of its strivings, and the single corporeal fusion of all men with one another.

In 1924, the year of Lenin's death, he returned to this theme with the words:

Only when the smithy is the church of the blacksmith, the ship the church of the sailor, the laboratory the church of the chemist, will it be possible for men to live in such fashion as not to disturb the lives of others by one's wickedness, one's whims, and one's habits.[35]

Finally, in 1927, when Lenin's heirs asked him to write an article for the tenth anniversary of the Bolshevik seizure of power, Gorky showed that he was of the same opinion still:

Years ago . . . I called man a God-builder, meaning that man, both within himself and in the external world, creates and incarnates the power to create miracles, justice, beauty, and all the other faculties with which Idealists endow a power alleged to exist outside of man. Man knows that outside himself there are no miracle-working forces. . . . He is certain that "only man exists, everything else being only his point of view and the work of his own hands." . . . It is this man who has undertaken the great task of educating the toiling masses "in his image and likeness."

There was no doctrinaire Lenin now to thunder against "little-god building" as "copulation with a corpse." Under the front-page heading of *Moi Privet ot Maxima Gorkogo* (My Greetings, from Maxim Gorky), the stubborn Gorky's heretical doctrine of God-building got in at last, into the sacrosanct pages of *Pravda* and *Izvestia*.[36]

NOTES TO CHAPTER 7

1. Letter of Lenin to Gorky, January 1913. Lenin, *Sochineniya*, 4th Russian ed., 35:44. Unless otherwise noted all quotations from Lenin are taken from this edition, which will hereafter be referred to as *Lenin*.

2. Gorky's collected works bear the title *Sobranie Sochinenie v 30 Tomakh* (Moscow: Institut Mirovoi Literatury im. Gorkogo, 1949–1955). The reader is given to understand that with vol. 30, *Pis'ma, Telegrammy, Nadpisi* (Letters, Telegrams, Inscriptions), published in 1955, all the last odds and ends are included. There have since been a number of additional letters and archives published but neither *Revolution and Culture* nor *On the Russian Peasantry* has been "rehabilitated."

3. The first of these letters is in the possession of the Hoover Institution, Stanford University, and the second is quoted in the authorized biography of Herbert Hoover written by Eugene Lyons (Garden City, N.Y., 1964, p. 147.) The only reference to the Hoover Commission in the four-volume Gorky *Chronicle* is an entry under the date of July 25, 1921, saying that Hoover telegraphed offering aid and "putting political conditions." It does not suggest that aid was given or accepted, or that Gorky knew gratitude or wrote these letters, but merely adds ironically that part of Hoover's telegram was used in an article in *Krasnaya Gazeta* on August 11 under the heading "The Greek Hoover and His Gifts" (*Danaets Guver i ego dary*—the epithet *Danaets* being derived from Laocoon's warning concerning the Trojan horse, *Timeo Danaos et dona ferentes.*)

4. See the article on Gorky in the *Bolshaya Sovetskaya Entsiklopediia*, 2d ed., sent to press on May 28, 1952, 12:245–55.

5. The *Encylopedia Britannica* in its article on Maxim Gorky (1956, 10:532) says: "In 1917, he gave his support to the Bolsheviks," though 1917 and 1918 were the years of his bitterest opposition to Bolshevism.

6. This was published in Lenin's journal *Proletarii* on March 6, 1910, and is in his *Collected Works*, 4th ed., 16:183–87. Lenin was engaging in a debater's trick, for it was Bogdanov, not Gorky, who had as one of his pet doctrines the possibility of a purely class "proletarian art." Long after this particular squabble was forgotten, as so often happens in Lenin's continuously polemical writings, the pronouncement remained to become an axiom of Soviet critical thought and to be developed by exegesis into a whole body of doctrine on the possibility and the content and style of "proletarian class art."

7. From *The Orlov Couple*, written in 1897.

8. These words come from Gorky's *Vospominaniya o Lve Tolstom*, but are applicable no less to the other "strong-willed men" to whom Gorky attached himself: "I kept studying Tolstoy so intensely because I was seeking then, am still seeking

now, and shall continue to seek until I die for a man with a true and living faith."
(p. 49). The date of publication of these words is 1922.

9. The continuity of Gorky's ideas and even his images is strikingly shown by comparing his characterization of the merchant prince Ignat Gordeyev (1899) and of the Promethean folk hero of his grandmother's tale, Danko (1895), with his characterizations of Lenin.

The merchant princes of the Volga, Ignat Gordeyev and his associates, have Lenin's concentration of power, his insistence on a wide network of organization which must embrace everybody and everything and put each man in his proper place, even Lenin's monolithic dream that "When the state is able to inspire all its citizens with a single opinion, compelling everyone to think alike, this is beauty." (The quoted words are from one of Gorky's merchant princes, not from Lenin.) Of Ignat Gordeyev, he writes: "He was one of those people who are always and in everything accompanied by success—not merely because they are talented and fond of hard work, but more because, possessing enormous reserves of energy, as they make their way they do not ponder, in fact are incapable of pondering over their choice of means. . . ." These sentences from the novel *Foma Gordeyev* were written in 1898 and 1899, before he knew Lenin. They reappear almost verbatim in his hostile characterizations of Lenin in 1918 and in his autobiographical memoir of 1924.

In the latter, Danko reappears too. "For me Lenin is a hero of legend, the man who tears out of his own breast his burning heart in order by its fire to light up for people the road out of the shameful chaos of our time, out of the rotting and bloody swamp of stifling 'statism.' "

10. *Letters of Gorky and Andreev, 1899–1912* (New York, 1958), p. 41.

11. To Andreev, in ibid., p. 104.

12. In 1918, *Pravda* attacked Gorky's *Novaya Zhizn* as being "financed by the bourgeoisie." Gorky answered with a personal accounting, then added: "From 1901 to 1917, hundreds of thousands of rubles passed through my hands for the cause of the Social Democratic Party. Less than ten thousand came from me personally, the major portion from the 'bourgeoisie.' *Iskra* was published with the money of Savva Morozov. . . . Your filthy sallies against *Novaya Zhizn* disgrace not my journal but yourselves."

13. Lenin, Krupskaya tells us cyrptically, "saw Gorky's *Lower Depths* at the [Moscow] Art Theater in 1922 . . . but he disliked the theatricality of the production, the absence of those details of social life which . . . portray the environment in all its concreteness."

14. E. Kuskova, "Na rubezhe dvukh epokh: Pamyati A. M. Gorkovo" ("On the Border Between Two Epochs: In Memory of A. M. Gorky"), in *Posledniya Novosti* (Paris, June 26, 1936).

15. Gorky, *Days with Lenin* (New York: International Publishers, 1932), pp. 4–5.

16. For an analysis of this phenomenon, see the writer's "Operation Rewrite: The Agony of the Soviet Historian," in *Foreign Affairs*, October 1952, reprinted in Wolfe, *Communist Totalitarianism* (Boston, 1961), and the writer's paper presented at a historiography symposium in Geneva under the auspices of the Institut Uni-

versitaire de Hautes Etudes Internationales in 1961, reprinted in John Keep and Liliana Brisby, eds., *Contemporary History in the Soviet Mirror* (London, 1964). The paper is entitled "Party Histories from Lenin to Khrushchev."

17. See *Letopis*, 4:386; *V. I. Lenin i Maksim Gorkii*, pp. 291 and 234; *V. I. Lenin o Literature i Iskusstve* (V. I. Lenin on Literature and Art) (Moscow, 1957), pp. 568, 575–76. This last work, strangely, dates Gorky's letter to Sorin in the Marx-Engels-Lenin Institute as June 12, 1928, while the *Letopis* and the volume on *V. I. Lenin and Maxim Gorky* put the exchange of letters, correctly, in 1934.

18. N. Valentinov, "Vstrechi s M. Gorkim" (Meetings with M. Gorky), *Novyi Zhurnal* (New York), no. 78 (1965):138–39.

19. For the exchange of letters with Gladkov, see *Literaturnoye Nasledstvo*, (Moscow, 1963), 17:63 and 95. For his opposition to the dramatization of the novel, see ibid., p. 230, letter 6 and note 1. His letter to Desnitsky is cited by David Shub, "Maksim Gorkii i Kommunisticheskaya Diktatura," in *Mosty* (Munich), no. 1 (1958):249.

20. Victor Serge, "Recollections of Maxim Gorky," from *Pages from the Diary of Victor Serge*, cited in *The New International* (New York), July–August 1950, p. 249. Fedin was writing in the bleakest period of Stalin's rule so that Gorky's words on freedom from party censorship is not the only omission. There is nothing about Gorky's attempt to save the life of the poet Gumilev, nothing on Trotsky, or Gorky's protest at the suppression of the Kronstadt sailors, nothing on Gorky's opposition to the Red Terror, nothing on Boris Pilniak, whose life Gorky saved, and there are other eloquent silences.

21. Gorky said of the peasant writer Podyachev: "Thanks to him we now have a better idea of the beast in the shape of a man that lives in the Russian village" (Valentinov, "Vstrechi," p. 132).

22. *Vospominaniya o Lve Tolstom*, p. 11.

23. M. Gorkii, *Zhizn Nenuzhnogo Cheloveka*, in *Sobranie Sochinenii* (Moscow, 1961), 5:11.

24. *Mercure de France*, April 15, 1907 (April 2, Old Style), reproduced in Russian in *Nov*, April 5 (O.S.) 1907. Works about Gorky in Russian tend to be silent about this interview, as if it were a shameful thing. Neither in *V. I. Lenin i A. M. Gorkii: Pis'ma, vospominaniya, dokumenty*, published by the Marxism-Leninism Institute of the CC, CPSU, and the Gorky Institute of World Literature of the Academy of Sciences in 1958, nor in the enlarged German version published in East Berlin in 1964 is there any mention of it. The four-volume *Letopis* says merely that "he sent to *Mercure de France* an article, 'Answer to a Questionnaire on the Fate of Religion.' " But, as with all embarrassing matters, it gives no hint of the nature of the answer. (*Letopis*, 1:653).

25. On this see Wolfe, *Marxism: One Hundred Years in the Life of a Doctrine* (New York, 1965), pp. 369–70 and 375–77.

26. M. Gorkii, *Ispoved*, in *Sobranie Sochinenii* (Moscow, 1961), 5:304–5.

27. From a resolution adopted by a conference of the Bolshevik Center, with Bogdanov and his comrades excluded, held in Paris in 1909. Lunacharsky's review urged that not "the people," which would make Gorky a "narodnik," but a collective

man born amidst the smokestacks and the machines would be the core of Gorky's God and would "perform the real work of transforming men into mankind." Thus he thought to salvage Gorky's "Marxism." When the State Publishing House in 1957 published A. Lunacharsky, *Articles on Gorky*, it omitted that article of Lunacharsky completely.

28. *V. I. Lenin i A. M. Gorkii*, letter of February 25, 1908, pp. 29–31.

29. Ibid., p. 38.

30. Ibid., pp. 42 and 43.

31. Ibid.

32. The account of the school and the faction struggle around it is to be found in *Lenin*, 15:431, 432, 436, 437, 438, 440, 463; *Letopis*, 2:99–101; *Lenin*, 34:353–54; *Otchet pervoi vysshoi shkoly dlya rabochikh* (Report on the First Higher School for Workers) (Paris, 1910).

33. *Lenin*, 25:89–91. Except in the words *bogostroitelstvo* (god-creation) and *bogoiskatelstvo* (god-seeking), which were technical terms of contemporary intellectual discussion, Lenin refused to use the word *bog* (god), substituting throughout the letter a belittling diminutive, *bozhenka*, which defies translation by any English term which would convey his contempt. The nearest I could come to it in the most insulting sentence Lenin ever wrote to Gorky is to render it in English rather than American fashion: "Every *bloody little god* is copulation with a corpse."

34. *Lenin*, 35:92–94.

35. M. Gorkii, *Zametki iz dnevnika: Vospominaniya* (Notes from My Diary: Memories) (Berlin, 1924), p. 57.

36. *Izvestia*, October 23, 1927; *Pravda*, November 6, 1927.

8

TO THE FINLAND STATION

By 1916 all strata of "public opinion," from Grand Dukes and Duchesses to leaders of the patriotic Duma parties and members of the General Staff, had become convinced that Nicholas II must go if Russia were to continue to wage successful war.

Nicholas would have made an amiable head of a private family, happily henpecked, a good husband and father, devoted to the service of church and state. He would have been kind to the servants and liked by the neighbors and the servants. But for a sovereign with well-nigh absolute powers he was too weak and irresolute, too uncomprehending of public affairs, too completely dominated by his strong-willed, fanatical, credulous, devoted spouse. A German princess wrongly suspected of pro-Germanism, she conceived the new convert's enthusiasm for Orthodoxy and Autocracy. Her intense will was dedicated to making her husband "strong" and preserving his autocratic power undiminished for transmission to their son, a lad who at any moment might bleed to death because of his congenital hemophilia. To keep the Crown Prince alive, she surrounded herself with quacks and clairvoyants. To keep the Autocracy strong, she made up a court of sycophants. Increasingly she had come under the influence of the dissolute, shrewd, corrupt, holy man, Rasputin, whom she credited with supernatural powers by means of which he kept her son from death and saw deep into the future. He was loyal to his Sovereigns, to the peasantry and to Russia, but carried on scandalous sexual affairs with devout ladies of the Court, babbled state secrets when in his cups, and was not above accepting bribes to use his clairvoyant powers for the advantage of a proper benefactor. Rasputin guided the Tsarina, and the Tsarina the Tsar.

In August 1915, when the war was one year old, Alexandra persuaded her husband to take personal responsibility for blunders and defeats by personally assuming command of the army, while she took control of things in Petrograd during his absences at the front.

"I long to poke my nose into everything," she wrote to "my hero" in September 1915, "to wake people up, to put all in order, and unite all forces." And her hero answered gratefully that she would "be his eyes and ears . . . keep peace and harmony among the Ministers . . . I am so glad that you have at last found a worthy occupation."

Under her "unifying" hand, the last remaining competent and devoted men among the Ministers were driven away, to be replaced by the corrupt rabble of adventurers that paid court and tribute to Rasputin and his circle. Some of her appointees were rumored to be pro-German, or to favor a separate peace with Germany. B. V. Stuermer, a contemptible bureaucrat of German name and descent, was made President of the Council of Ministers; A. D. Protopopov, half insane and apt to decide important questions by casting horoscopes, became Minister of the Interior, which heads the police; a "grotesque and sinister procession of nonentities and adventurers" engaged in a demoralizing game of "ministerial leapfrog"—while Russia struggled with the natural winter shortages of fuel and bread afflicting all warring lands that third winter of the war. Only in Russia they were made worse by bureaucratic blunders (such as fixing the same price for grain in the capital as in the grain areas, thus destroying all incentive to move it to market), and by the vastness and backwardness of the Russian land.

Patriots were repulsed and frustrated in their ardent desire to help. Rumors of the Tsarina's supposed pro-Germanism, of Rasputin's, of Stuermer's, filled the country. When, in response to the War Minister's incautious "I may be a fool but I am not a traitor," the Duma spokesman, Miliukov (leader of the Constitutional Democratic Party), pronounced his famous indictment, each article of which ended with the words: "Is this folly, or is it treason?"—there were many who were ready to believe that it was treason.

Later, each man's responsibility would be examined in solemn hearings under the future Provisional Government. There was no evidence of treason, unless corruption and incompetence are treason, but the winged word, suppressed from the published report of Miliukov's speech, flew over the land.[1]

In the upper circles of society, all the blame was heaped upon Rasputin. At the year's end of 1916 (the night of December 30) Prince Yussupov got the holy man drunk, and with the help of Grand Duke Dmitri, and the conservative monarchist leader of the Duma, General Purishkevich, tried to poison, then shot, him to death. On New Year's Day, 1917, first day of the fateful year, all the members of the royal family, including Grand Dukes and Duchesses, united in a petition to the Emperor asking for clemency for the murderers. But Rasputin's death only increased the stubbornness at Court and the isolation surrounding it.

The General Staff had become involved, too. General Alexeev, Chief of Staff to the Tsar and one of Russia's great military men, entered into an agreement with the Duma leaders, Prince Lvov and Guchkov, to arrest the Empress the next time she should visit the front and immure her in a nunnery where she could no longer meddle with affairs of state. Grand Duke Nicholas was privy to this plot.

Generals Krymov, Polivanov and Gurko were in close touch with Guchkov in a related plot to surround the Tsar's train and force his abdication in favor of another Prince of the Blood. In January, 1917, when he visited Petrograd, General Krymov conferred with Duma leaders at the home of Duma Chairman Rodzyanko on the need of a change of sovereigns:

> The news of a coup d'état—he informed them—would be welcomed with joy . . . we will support you. Clearly there is no other way . . . no time to lose.

Rumor carried the hints of treason and conspiracy all over the land—to the anonymous mass of peasants in gray greatcoats troubled by shortage of munitions; to their families in a countryside stripped of all able-bodied men and frustrated by bureaucratic price-fixing of grain; to workers whose rising wages lagged behind the skyrocketing cost of living and whose factories closed down at critical moments for lack of power and fuel.

All that autumn of 1916 and winter of 1917, the police kept sending reports of increasing discontent in the queues in front of bakeries and butcher stores. "Either give us food," people were saying, "or stop the war." "End the war, since you do not know how to fight." "The army in the rear," warned one report, "may refuse to participate in punitive measures . . ."

The enfeebled revolutionary parties with their leaders squabbling in isolated exile abroad, or cut off in the lonely wastes of Siberia and the Arctic region, had no inkling of this crisis affecting all ruling circles and spreading downward into society as a whole. Lenin spent his days in Zurich libraries and self-righteous quarrels with his fellow Zimmerwaldists and even with the Zimmerwald Left, oblivious of the great ferment. His weird slogan, "Defeat of your own government," never reached the Russian soldiers or workers or peasants: if it had they would not have understood it, or understanding, would have rejected it. He himself had to put it under wraps when he got back to Russia. "The masses of the people," the police reported truthfully along with their other grim warnings, "respond only feebly to the Social Democratic propaganda; and it is only hunger and the high cost of living that may drive them toward an open demonstration."[2]

But Minister of the Interior Protopopov ignored the reports himself or greeted them with pleasure as anticipations of a chance to "put down the mob." They never reached the Tsar.

The plots and rumors of plots for a palace revolution gradually spread. "The sparrows on every rooftop chirped of revolution—even on those roofs on which the last tsarist Minister put the last policemen with machine guns."[3] Only some allied diplomats urged "patience, in order that there should be no great disturbance in Russia until after the war."[4] While the plans for a revolution from above multiplied, while General Staff, Duma circles and members of the Royal Family debated the when, the how, and the where, the spring thaws closed the roads and disorganized river transport; Petrograd ran short of bread, fuel and electric power.

Demonstrations of women in front of bakeries began like so many other demonstrations; factory shutdowns and strikes added to the crowds in the streets; the demented Minister of the Interior sent around provocateurs, one of them disguised as Miliukov,[5] calling upon other workers to strike, so that he might suppress them all with a greater flourish.

"The mass moved of itself." This time the soldiers refused to fire on the crowds, permitted themselves to be disarmed, blended into the mobs. Generals at the front were reluctant to respond to the Tsar's call for punitive expeditions. The Duma, dissolved by imperial edict, adjourned, but refused to go home, transforming its meetings into "unofficial sessions." In the apt words of Duma Deputy Shulgin: "They [the revolutionaries, both those at Court and in public life, and those underground] were not ready, but all the rest was ready." The Tsar fell.[6]

Here ambiguity arose. On the banners of the leaders at Court, in the Duma, and in the General Staff, was inscribed: "Patriotism and the War." But on the banners, or in the cries, of the bakery queues and street demonstrations, and among the soldiers who mingled with them, the slogan was more apt to be: "Peace and Bread." Patriots thought that revolution would sweep away the treason or inefficiency in high places that was disgracing Russia and preventing the proper equipment of her armies and the prosecution of the war. Republicans and socialists who had devoted a lifetime to fighting against the Tsar felt that now the new free Russia would be something to defend, until it could use its influence to bring about a decent, speedy, general peace. Up to the moment of Lenin's return this new "revolutionary defensism" prevailed in the Bolshevik high command in Petrograd, too.

Some revolutionaries, living with the memories of the Great French Revolution as their guide, recalled how in 1793 the armies of revolutionary France had defeated the invader, spread the Revolution, overthrown sovereigns and old regimes, marched all over Europe. Why should not this revolution turn new, overpowering energies into a revolutionary war to defend free Russia?

On the other hand, the old regime of tradition, habitual obedience, and coercion which had kept men working submissively in factory and farm and fighting at the front, now completely disintegrated. What would keep the masses, with their rudimentary or non-existent sense of nationality and lack of comprehension of the country's war aims, still at war? Would the revolution kill the war, or would the war kill the revolution? "Patriotism and the War" or "Peace and Bread"— in these antithetical slogans was the ambiguity the new government would inherit, as it issued out of the most general, universal, all-class revolution in modern history, with its virtually painless and bloodless end to a three-hundred-year-old dynasty.

Despite all his polemics against the peace slogan, "Peace and Bread" were the words which Lenin picked up from the streets and inscribed on the banners of his demonstrations, when the unprecedented freedom permitted his return to Russia. Power was in the streets; the slogans were in the streets. To take power, he would have to revise his attitude towards peace—his attitude, or at least under the pressure of the popular will, his utterances.

Actually, this would-be leader of the masses and tribune of the people had never faced the masses before, never felt the pressure of their "spontaneous" desires, never so much as addressed a single hostile or friendly or indifferent mass meeting of ordinary workingmen, or peasants, or soldiers, until the famous sealed train provided by the German General Staff carried him across Germany, Sweden and Finland to the Finland Station in Petrograd, where a great mass of workingmen and soldiers awaited his coming.

His audiences had always been little conclaves of handpicked supporters, committee members, delegates to underground conventions. His isolation from the workingmen in whose name he insisted he was speaking had been even greater than that of the other underground leaders of his generation. Even Plekhanov had once addressed an illegal May Day meeting on Kazan Cathedral Square. All his contemporaries had more than once risked their persons to address illegal mass meetings. But with that selfless egoism that enabled him to identify his person and leadership with "the cause," Lenin had always carefully preserved "the leadership" from the hazards of such public appearances. Even in the émigré squabbles abroad, where Lenin's speeches had been among the most provocative, he was swift to disappear from a meeting in which it came to blows—"for the good of his health," as he himself once put it.[7]

Many of Lenin's admirers have taken note of this trait. Some have justified it, more or less as Trotsky does in the following passage:

> Karl Liebknecht was a revolutionary of unlimited courage. Thoughts of personal safety were completely alien to him. But Lenin on the contrary was *in*

the highest degree concerned for the *inviolability* of the leadership. He was the chief of the general staff, and always remembered that in time of war he must protect the high command.

In 1904, when the youthful working-class leader N. V. Volsky (later to write memoirs concerning Lenin under the name of Valentinov, and brilliant essays on ideological questions under the name of Yurevsky) went to pay homage to Lenin in Geneva, the latter questioned him enviously about the mass meeting Volsky had been addressing when the police arrested him.

"Ah, so that's how it was! That's fine! Did you really manage to talk to two thousand workers? And how long?"

"Fifteen minutes or so, and not two thousand, but perhaps two thousand five hundred."

"What luck!" said Lenin with some envy ... "Gusev, too, managed to speak to thousands in Rostov. In all my life in Petersburg I never had a chance to talk to as many as fifteen workers. I don't even know whether my voice would be strong enough ..."

Even in the year of the Great Rebellion of 1905, when the Tsar's police system weakened and most of the Russian socialist leaders of Lenin's generation hurried back from exile to go about all day long with cracked voices from addressing great assemblages, Lenin with characteristic caution remained abroad from January to November, till the Tsar issued his amnesty manifesto. When he did get to Russia, he was so cautious in preserving the safety of "the leadership" under pseudonyms and physical concealment that he never got to address a mass meeting of his own, or the great Petersburg Soviet, or any other public body. It is possible that he participated briefly, under the name of Karpov, in one single debate on a political resolution before as many delegates or spectators as could crowd into the spacious hall of the home of Count Panin. But that is all. Then he fled once more, first to Finland, then to Geneva, without ever having addressed a large body of ordinary workingmen.

His wife writes in her memoirs that she herself "never dared to make a speech even at a small meeting," until she got to Russia in 1917. About her husband she is not so explicit, yet unconscious touches reveal the isolation of this would-be leader of the masses.

Thus while in Zurich in 1916 they arranged to board at a house whose clientele turned out to be from the city's underworld—a boarder whose skull was cracked in some adventure, a prostitute, a lodger of a "semi-criminal" type. They stayed on because these middle-class "proletarian revolutionaries" felt closer there to the lower-class life towards which they were yearning.

Ilyich liked the simplicity of the service, the fact that coffee was served in a cup with a broken handle, that we ate in the kitchen, that the conversation was simple . . . about matters of interest to the boarders . . . the prostitute spoke quite openly about matters of her profession . . . it must be said that in the conversations of these people there was more of the "human," the living element, than in what was heard in prim hotel dining rooms . . .

When fear that an unexpected police raid on some fellow boarder might spell trouble for him led Lenin to move, they landed in a nearby alley dwelling, where the stench from a sausage factory was so intolerable that they could only open their window at night. "For the same rent, we could have found a better room," Krupskaya reports, but the family was "a workers' family," and when Lenin heard the landlady say that the soldiers ought to turn their weapons on their governments, "Ilyich would no longer listen to any suggestions about moving." Actually, their landlady must have been playing back Lenin's own recording, for her husband, interviewed years later, reported that his wife had not wanted to take the lodgers because Mrs. Lenin "looked like a Russian and her skirt was too short." And when the Ulyanovs said they were leaving to go back to Russia, she expressed concern about their going into "that insecure country at such an uncertain time." This "working-class family" had no Bolshevik iron in its soul.

During more than a decade abroad, Lenin had been strangely uninterested in the socialist movements of the lands he lived in. But in 1916 some Swiss Zimmerwald Left adherents plus a couple of pro-Bolshevik Poles and some Russian Bolshevik workingmen working in Zurich factories combined forces to give Lenin a chance to meet with local Swiss socialists.

They began meeting in a small café . . . The first meeting was attended by about forty. Ilyich spoke sharply on current matters and posed the problems very sharply . . . The Swiss were quite embarrassed by the sharpness . . . Our meetings began to melt away. To the fourth meeting only the Russians and Poles came, and, after exchanging some banter, they went home.

Thus Lenin lost his first "mass" audience, for he took no account of the real feelings of ordinary workingmen on peace and war and did not know how to talk to them.

That summer, at a sanitarium where his wife was taking the milk cure, he found a solitary Swiss soldier sent by his Government to cure his weak lungs.

Vladimir Ilyich hovered around him like a cat after lard, tried several times to engage him in talk about the predatory character of the war; the fellow would not contradict him, but was clearly not interested.[8]

How far would this "mass leader" have gotten with his dream of a New International free of patriots, pacifists, and orthodox Marxists who were not at the same time "defeatists"—if the fall of the Tsar had not given him the sounding board of a vast land in revolution, the absolute freedom to urge and plan the seizure of power, and then the prestige that came with success?

On March 15, 1917, Lenin went to the library as usual, probably to "consult" with Hegel. At noon, when he was finishing his midday meal at home, Bronsky (the admiring Polish Socialist whom Stalin would one day kill as a retroactive spy of the Polish Government) burst in with the cry: "Haven't you heard the news? There's a revolution in Russia." That afternoon Lenin neglected Hegel to hurry down to the lakeshore where all the latest newspapers were posted. The dispatches, filtering through censorships and through unprepared reportorial minds, were fragmentary, confused, confusing.

But not for Lenin! All his life he had waited for this hour, and all his certitudes were ready. First, there were directives to send to the shapeless group of his followers, whom, he knew by experience, only he could whip into shape. Second, he must figure how to get back to Russia through the flaming frontiers of war. Third, he must start at once organizing a new revolution against the government that had just succeeded the Tsar.

About the new government he did not waver, nor wait to see what it looked like or what it did. He was certain that its democracy and freedom would not be "genuine," that a free Russia without his program and rule would not be worth defending, that it would not give *his* party freedom. Since what is "worth defending" is a question of values, it is not subject to empirical proof. But on all the other counts Lenin could not possibly have been more wrong.

To Alexandra Kollontai in Stockholm he wrote next day for her transmission to his followers in Russia:

We of course retain our opposition to the defense of the Fatherland . . . All our slogans remain the same . . . The Kadets will allow nobody to form a legal party [except supporters of the war] . . . Even if they do, we must combine illegal and legal work . . . a war against imperialism . . . an *international* proletarian revolution . . . conquest of power by the Soviets . . . The Tsar is evidently making ready for counter-revolution . . . The main thing is not to let ourselves get caught in stupid attempts at "unity" with social patriots, or still more dangerous . . . with vacillators like Trotsky & Co . . . *not a trace* of trust or support to the new government . . . but *armed waiting, armed preparation* of a wider basis for a *higher* stage. . . .[9]

Yet another day and Lenin and Zinoviev had prepared "theses" for the faithful, without waiting for the facts. Lenin did not try to consult his followers who were in Russia, but began a series of directive *Letters from Afar* full of misstatements and absurd conjectures, but strikingly clear on certain formulae for action which no amount of empirical information would cause him to re-examine or alter.

As usual, he warned about peace. The Tsar, "it was clear," was plotting a counter-revolution through the announcement of "an immediate separate peace with Germany." (Actually, the Tsarina, who shared Lenin's view that history was a conspiracy, believed that the Tsar would go back on his abdication, though she would not for the world have consented to a separate peace. As for Nicholas, once he was convinced that his abdication was necessary for the further defense of Russia, he abdicated without reservations. His farewell to the army showed that he preferred death to the dishonor of a separate peace.)

Under no circumstances, Lenin insisted, should the new government be looked upon as a possible instrument for bringing about a democratic peace. To suggest it was "equivalent to approaching the keepers of a house of ill fame with a sermon on virtue." The Soviets should be made into "organs of insurrection" for a second revolution to overthrow the new democracy and set up armed Soviets at the head of the armed people.

> Only such a government . . . will be able to solve the most important problem of the moment, the problem of peace . . . a true, permanent, democratic peace, which cannot be attained without a proletarian revolution in a number of countries . . .
>
> It would declare that it expected no good from bourgeois governments, and proposes to the workers of all lands to overthrow them and transfer all power to Soviets . . .
>
> And *for such* peace terms, in my opinion, the Soviet Workers' Deputies would be ready to *wage war* against *any* bourgeois government and against *all* the bourgeois governments of the world, because that would be a really just war and *all* workers and toilers of *all* lands would *help it* to succeed.[10]

Thus Lenin's already familiar "coexistence" program had not been altered in the slightest by the fall of Tsarism, merely turned into an instrument intended to encompass the fall of the new Democracy.

But the first problem was to get home; to end the era of good feeling, the honeymoon with liberty that was taking possession even of his "rock-hard" followers; to use the peace slogan, the bread slogan, the land slogan, to overthrow the government which had succeeded the Tsar; to use the slogan of "All power to the Soviets" as a cover for all power to his party and his program.

But how to get home? Switzerland was an island of peace in a world at war. To the West lay Russia's ally France; to the South, her ally Italy; to the East, her enemy Austria-Hungary; to the North, her enemy Germany; her ally England, controlled the seas.

The Allies, Lenin felt sure, would not let a self-proclaimed "defeatist" through their lines to add to the Russian chaos. Nor would the Provisional Government, "sold to the Entente," press its allies for his right to return. (The Provisional Government did use successful pressure to free Trotsky from a Canadian prison, opponent of the war though he was, and ensure his safe journey home.)

Lenin hatched one fantastic plan after another. He would get an airplane. He would put on a wig, be photographed in it, paste the picture onto a Swedish passport, and travel as a "neutral" Swede. But he knew not a word of Swedish, and history called too urgently for him to take time to learn. He would be a deaf-mute then, not speaking a word on the whole trip. "You will see Mensheviks in your dreams and start cursing them and shouting, scoundrels! scoundrels!" his wife told him, "and give the scheme away."

He inquired of Hanecki, whom he knew to be working for the Russian émigré Parvus, who in turn had connections with the German government and war machine, whether there was not some way he could be smuggled through Germany. If not "friendly" territory, "enemy" territory then—in terms of his own war it was all one to him.

At this point the upright Menshevik Internationalist Martov, impatient at the delay all internationalists were experiencing, tentatively proposed negotiations with Germany for an exchange of blockaded Russian émigrés for German war prisoners held in Russia. Lenin jumped at the idea. Martov's uprightness would provide a cover for his amoral indifference to means. Martov toyed with the plan and waited for actual prisoner exchange negotiations, but "Lenin snatched at it at once." He negotiated through the Swiss State Councillor Grimm, Chairman of the Zimmerwald anti-war movement, whom he had been denouncing, and would soon denounce again, as a "centrist," a "pacifist," a "concealed Kautskyan," and a traitor to the cause of revolutionary defeatism; through Platten, a young Swiss adherent of the Zimmerwald Left; through Hanecki, who negotiated in turn with Parvus, thus bringing in the German General Staff. Grimm, and Martov, wished to wait for the approval of the Petrograd Soviet, but Lenin and a little group of his close followers decided not to wait. (A month later Martov, too, followed the same route in a German sealed train.)

General Ludendorff says in his memoirs: "From a military point of view his [Lenin's] journey was justified, for it was imperative that Russia should fall." General Hoffman writes: "Some man at home who had connections with the Russian revolutionaries exiled in Switzerland came upon the idea of employing some of them to hasten the undermining and poisoning of morale of the Russian Army . . . In the same way as I send shells into the enemy trenches, discharge poison gas at him . . . I have the right to employ the expedient of propaganda against his garrisons." The "man who had connections with the Russian revolutionaries in Switzerland" was Parvus. The German Ambassador to Switzerland got such urgent instructions to assent to Lenin's wishes that he left on two hours notice; Krupskaya did not even have time to return their library books.[11]

Before leaving, and more than once on the journey, Lenin asked: "Will they not arrest us when we arrive and take us straight to prison?" At Beloostrov, a little distance from Petrograd, Shlyapnikov and some other Bolsheviks got on the train to welcome them. "Ilyich asked the comrades who sat with us if we would be arrested on our arrival," writes Krupskaya. "But they only smiled."

When it was reported at the Executive Committee of the Soviet that Lenin was arriving that evening (April 3), the Executive, made up of men whom Lenin had denounced and in whom he had urged "not a shadow of confidence," voted "to cover the sealed train with its authority" and to "arrange an honorable welcome for the honored exile." True, Tseretelli, who was first chosen to represent the Soviet, refused the repugnant task, so "the Presidium, Skobelev and Chkheidze, had to go the station." The Soviet also sent "troops with bands and armored cars." The Bolsheviks always knew how to get up a show, so they appeared with delegations of workers from factories, with red banners embroidered with gold legends.

It was late at night. A mounted searchlight swept the great square in front of the Finland Station. A thunderous *Marseillaise* boomed out on the platform, as Shlyapnikov brought Lenin straight to the Tsar's special waiting room. In a round cap, his face looking strained or frozen, Lenin, awkwardly carrying a magnificent bouquet, stopped in front of the welcoming Chkheidze "as though colliding with an unexpected obstacle." Chkheidze, still glum, pronounced reluctant words of welcome "in the name of the whole revolution . . . But—we think the principal task of the revolutionary democracy is now the defense of the revolution . . . We hope you will pursue these goals with us."

Lenin did not even look at the spokesman of the Soviet to which he had urged the granting of all power. Turning his back on Chkheidze he addressed the "Comrade soldiers, sailors, and workers":

> The piratical imperialist war is the beginning of civil war throughout Europe . . . The hour is not far distant when . . . the peoples will turn their arms against their own capitalist exploiters . . . Any day now the whole of European capitalism may crash. The Russian Revolution achieved by you has prepared

the way, and opened a new epoch. Long live the world-wide Socialist revolution!

Everyone present, Bolsheviks included, was too startled by this "voice from outside" to make any reply. Lenin was hurried in an armored car to the palace of Ksheshinskaya, a ballerina favored by the Tsar, whose home had been "expropriated by the Bolsheviks." From the dancer's balcony, he made another speech about "the capitalist pirates . . . the extirpation of the peoples of Europe for the sake of profits of a handful of exploiters . . . the defense of the fatherland means the defense of one set of capitalists against another . . ."

"Ought to stick our bayonets into a fellow like that," one of the "welcoming" soldiers suddenly shouted. "Must be a German . . ."

And even Sukhanov, a dyed-in-the-wool internationalist and opponent of the war, felt that Lenin's words were "devoid of the most elementary 'diplomacy,' any calculation of the concrete background and the soldiers' mentality . . . their nakedness and clumsiness . . . might do great harm . . . were risky . . ."

> After he got his bearings—Sukhanov continues—Lenin grasped this very quickly, adapted himself, and took a "diplomatic" line ("We never said we had to stick our bayonets into the ground when the enemy was ready for battle," etc.).[12]

Lenin was to learn a more complicated approach to the problem of peace. After all, it was his first contact with soldiers and workingmen in the mass.

NOTES TO CHAPTER 8

1. Few phenomena have been as well studied as the fall of the Romanov Dynasty. A good short account is in Michael T. Florinsky, *Russia: A History and an Interpretation* (New York, 1953), 2:1361–179; another in Bernard Pares, *A History of Russia* (New York, 1953), pp. 477–89. The best full account is Sir Bernard's *The Fall of the Russian Monarchy*, where the student can find verification for all the assertions in the above.

2. The Tsarist police reports are to be found in *Krasnyi Arkhiv* (Moscow), 17 (1926): 1–35.

3. Gregory Aronson reminiscing forty years later in *Sotsialisticheskii vestnik* (New York), 36, no. 5, p. 87.

4. Pares, *Fall*, p. 431.

5. According to others, including Miliukov himself, it was German agents who conceived and acted the comedy of the false Miliukov.

6. Pares, *Fall*, pp. 431–32.

7. The above quotation and the account that follows is taken from N. Valentinov, *Vstrechi s Leninym (Meetings with Lenin)* (New York, 1953), pp. 47–48.

8. Krupskaya, *Memoirs*, 2:176, 177, 182, 183, 187, 188, 226.

9. Lenin, *Collected Works*, 35:238–41.

10. Ibid., 23:282–86, 291–333.

11. The story of the negotiations and the sealed train is told by Krupskaya, *Memoirs*, 2:200–2, 204–11. Further details may be found in David Shub, *Lenin* (New York, 1948), pp. 180–85. The fullest review of the evidence so far is in S. P. Melgunov, *Zolotoi nemetskii klyuch Bolshevikov* (Paris, 1940). Evidence continues to accumulate that Lenin did receive substantial sums from the German government through the agency of Parvus-Helphand, and his Bolshevik employee, Hanecki-Fuerstenburg, and perhaps through other channels. The latest pieces of evidence are two documents seized from the files of the German Ministry of Foreign Affairs during the occupation of Berlin. The originals are in the possession of the British Government and have been published in English translation with comment by George Katkov in *International Affairs* (Quarterly of the Royal Institute), 32, no. 2 (April 1956): 181–89. It is not my intention to discuss this matter here, but in another work in progress. In any case, I should like to make it clear that I reject the idea, advanced by Kerensky, Miliukov and others, that Lenin was a "German agent" or permitted the German Government or General Staff to influence or determine his activities, either in the demoralizing of the Russian Army or in the eventual negotiation and signature of a separate peace with Germany at Brest Litovsk. Ludendorff, Hoffman and Erzberger wanted to use Lenin for their war, as he wanted to use them, or their facilities and funds, for his. At a crucial moment in history their two sets of aims coincided for a little space, and their two wars seemed to reinforce each other. As in all Lenin's attempts to use others, from German generals to naive fellow-travelers and leaders of other lands or movements, the central problem, as Lenin succinctly put it, was: *Kto kogo?* Who uses whom? (Pronounced *Kto kovó*; in literal translation, *Who whom?*) The political graveyards of the "Popular Front," the "United Front," and the "People's Democracies" are full of the corpses of those who thought they could use the Bolsheviks. Nor are new candidates for the same end lacking now in Near and Far East and even in the West.

12. Krupskaya, *Memoirs*, 2:211–12; N. N. Sukhanov, *The Russian Revolution, 1917* (New York, 1955), pp. 270–77. Except where expressly ascribed to Krupskaya, the words given in quotation marks are from Sukhanov.

9

1921: LENIN'S
CHANGE OF COURSE

Master of revolutionary strategy and tactics, with an almost infallible instinct for knowing exactly when to take the offensive and administer the coup de grâce, Lenin also knew when to pull in his horns and make temporary concessions. In either case, whether on offensive or defensive, the game essentially was the same. First an idea would take shape in his mind, his alone, not that of the Bolshevik Party leadership. Then he would polish it up and present it to the other Bolshevik leaders and Party militants, many of whom initially would oppose it. But in the end it would triumph within the Party and subsequently be "proved right" by events.

This had happened at three decisive moments in the history of the Russian Revolution when the Bolsheviks suddenly seized the offensive. The first was April 1917, when Lenin put forward his famous "April theses" over strong opposition within the Party. The next was October–November of that year, when he committed the Party to seizing power in Petrograd, again over opposition within the Central Committee both before and after November 7. The third was January 1918, when he forced immediate dissolution of the Constituent Assembly, i.e., as soon as it convened. A witness recalls:

> During the intermission that followed the opening speech by Chernov, Assembly president, our group was rather incoherently debating the Assembly's fate. Lenin broke in and with a few biting phrases, proved the need for abolishing this counter-revolutionary institution, which he proposed to do as follows: When the meeting adjourned, all the delegates would be allowed to leave the Taurida Palace, but the next day only the communists and Left-Socialist Revolutionaries would be let back in. The proposal was adopted and executed.[1]

On the other hand, the initiative was also Lenin's when it came to switching to the defensive. Typical examples were the peace of Brest Litovsk and the change of course in 1921. The Brest Litovsk issue had split the Party and led to open formation of a leftist faction within it, with Lenin even finding himself in a minority on the Central Committee. Similarly, the first hints of the change of course in 1921 also stirred up currents of resistance. The Soviet Government had published its decree about the concessions to foreigners on November 23, 1920, and less than a month later, in his speech of December 21, Lenin had to admit: "According to our information, the concessions that we have granted have caused widespread concern and unrest, not only in Party circles and among the working masses but among many of the peasants too."[2] In the debate on the trade-union question, which was raging during that same month, he was again outvoted in the Central Committee (for the last time in his life), the committee dividing temporarily into two groups of almost equal number. On one side were Lenin, Zinoviev, Kamenev and Stalin, on the other Trotsky, Bukharin and several others, including the committee's three secretaries, Krestinskii, Preobrazhenskii and Serebriakov. But again Lenin won out, and with regard both to the concessions and trade unions his were the policies adopted.

The change of course in 1921 differed from the preceding ones in its unparalleled scope. Whereas the switches in tactics of April and October 1917 (before the seizure of power) affected only the Bolshevik Party, and those after November 7 (e.g., the peace of Brest Litovsk) involved the Bolshevik Party and Soviet State, the change of course in 1921 had profound effects on three fronts: Bolshevik Party, Soviet State and Comintern. The consequences for the latter were further-reaching than for Soviet Russia, for the following reasons. In deciding to switch from offensive to defensive inside Russia and replace militant communism with the NEP, Lenin was seeking of course to gain time in the face of an obviously receding revolutionary wave, for, as he was fond of saying, to win time is to win all. In implementing this maneuver, he was prepared to yield a little in the economic sphere while surrendering nothing in the political. He could afford to fall back to his strong defensive position, his absolute power within Russia, and wait for a new revolutionary surge, whether in Soviet Russia or the capitalist world. But when in 1921 he imposed this new defensive tactic on the Comintern, the communist parties in the capitalist countries had no similar stronghold to retreat to. In power nowhere, they did not even represent a majority of the working class.

Since in Lenin's eyes a switch to the defensive was necessitated by objective circumstances, the new policy would inevitably bring to the fore a basic contradiction inherent in the very being of the Comintern, a contradiction that was to haunt it to the end of its days. First, the Russian Bolshevik Party, the Comintern's acknowledged pilot and steersman, acting through the same single group of leaders—technically the Politburo in the Kremlin, but actually only Lenin (and later Stalin)—governed Soviet Russia on the one hand and ran the Comintern on the other, functioning in the first instance as the party in power in one country, in the second as the driving spirit behind a world revolution. This dichotomy dated, of course, from the Comintern's birth in Moscow, but its effect was felt less in 1919 and 1920 than in 1921 and after. Lenin had acted initially on the assumption of imminent revolution in Europe; later he would act under an exactly reversed assumption, having lost faith in the advent of that revolution. At first, Soviet Russia's position as Europe's only communist country and ruler of the Comintern was seen as only temporary; later it was accepted as final and permanent, and the Comintern had to tailor its policies to fit events in Russia (the NEP, famine, re-establishment of relations with capitalist countries and, a little later, the bitter struggle among Lenin's would-be successors). The relationship between Soviet Russia and the Comintern changed. Instead of Soviet Russia's being at the disposal of the international communist movement, as was Lenin's idea in 1919 and 1920, it was the international communist movement that thenceforward would have to shape its deeds and policies to serve the interests of Russia. Though officially Soviet Russia remained the avant-garde of communist world revolution, in truth the international communist movement became the tail of the Russian dog, wagged at will by its owner. From then on, as in any war, the subordinate Comintern would be under the orders of the Russian general staff, which would always take care not to endanger its best troops (the Russian Bolshevik Party and Soviet power) in wasteful attempts to rescue any expendable divisions of the Comintern threatened with annihilation. After 1921, unqualified support of Soviet Russia became the number-one public and official duty of all foreign communist parties—with no reciprocal obligation on the part of Russia, however. This one-sidedness was made explicit at the third Comintern congress, held in June–July 1921, where it was proclaimed in the theses on the Comintern tactics: "Unqualified support of Soviet Russia remains, as before, the prime duty of communists in all countries."[3] This was a complete reversal from the position which Lenin had formulated himself at the second Comintern congress, when he advanced the thesis that the country in which the revolution had already triumphed (Russia) had to accept the greatest sacrifices in supporting without reserve the international communist movement. He wrote at that time: "Proletarian internationalism requires, first, the subordination of the interests of the proletarian struggle in one country to the interests of that struggle on a universal scale; second, the capacity and the readiness of nations which are in the process to defeat the bourgeoisie to accept the greatest sacrifices in order to overthrow international capital."[4]

When after 1921 the probability of revolution in Europe grew smaller every day, while the Soviet regime continued to strengthen its hold on Russia, two irreversible processes began in the Comintern. On the one hand, all the non-Russian sections became increasingly dependent on the policies and decisions of the dominant Russians. On the other, the incompatibility of Soviet Russia's national interests with the global interests of the international communist movement deepened. As long as a wave of revolution seemed to be sweeping over Europe, this incompatibility was not felt to exist, not even by so lucid a European communist leader as Paul Levi, who at a closed meeting of the German Communist Party's Central Committee on August 25, 1920, after his return from the second World Congress, rejected the very thought of any conflict of interest between the Comintern and Soviet Government: "That danger, conceivable in theory, I cannot imagine ever actually materializing. My own feeling is that it cannot possibly exist in practice, because the identity of interests between the Communist International and Russian Soviet Republic . . . is so great that no such clash can develop."[5] Barely six months later, when this same Paul Levi was engaged in public battle with Moscow, the underlying cause of his break with the Russian leaders was that the "impossible" had happened after all. The interests of the German communists had collided with the Kremlin's.

The general conflict of interest between the Soviet Government and Comintern was to be augmented after 1921 by a set of individual conflicts involving each of the national sections. Most of the big communist parties had come into being after the second World Congress in 1920, whose decisions were predicated upon the assumed inevitability of international civil war. Not only had these parties failed in the attempt to foment revolution but, with two or three exceptions, had now ceased even trying. Organized to operate as revolutionary movements—with secret networks, professional revolutionaries, iron discipline, insurrectionary techniques, etc.—they were condemned to function henceforth, to vegetate, without recourse to any major revolutionary act. Thus after 1921 the Western communist parties were to exist in a kind of vacuum, without hope or prospect of revolution or civil war. In a sense they would then partly resemble what they had reproached the pre-1914 Socialist parties with being: revolutionary in word, reformist in deed. But the communist parties would not lapse into the "opportunism" of the Socialist parties, for two reasons. First, unlike the old Socialist International, whose structure and organization were democratic, the national sections of the Communist International became gradually patterned after the Bolshevik model. Secondly, the Comintern's growing dependence, after 1921, on both Soviet Russia, the first and only communist state, and its Bolshevik Party, whose leadership had to be followed by all the foreign parties, would restrain the latter from wallowing in the sins that Lenin laid at the door of the Second International: reformism, pacifism, parliamentary cretinism, ministerialism, class collaboration, etc. After 1921, Moscow would steer the foreign parties more and more toward a Bolshevik-type organization, and this produced another paradox. As the prospects of revolution diminished, and the foundations of the Western communist parties contracted, their administrative apparatuses grew and grew.

REASONS FOR THE CHANGE OF COURSE

The change of course in 1921 did not occur all at once or simultaneously in all areas of Bolshevik policy. In the foreign policy of Soviet Russia it began after the Red Army's defeat in Poland, starting with such measures as the decree of November 23, 1920, regarding the foreign concessions, and continued into early 1921 with the signing of the first treaties of friendship with countries in the Middle East (Iran, Afghanistan and Turkey), and conclusion of the first commercial treaty with a Western, so-called imperialist power (Great Britain) on March 16. The new direction was evidenced economically through introduction of the NEP, inaugurated at the Bolshevik Party's tenth congress in March 1921. Within the party it was first reflected, again at the tenth congress, in the forbidding of intra-party factions and a massive purge of the membership.

It was in the policies of the Comintern that the change occurred last and most slowly, because of the priority that Lenin gave to internal Russian affairs, and also because the Kremlin did not yet have the Comintern firmly in hand. In internal Soviet affairs there was a lag, generally, of only a few weeks between final recognition that the situation now called for a defensive strategy and actual implementation of the new policy, while in the Comintern the process took an entire year and was completed in four phases. The first was November–December 1920, when Lenin at last realized that revolution in Europe was less imminent than had been supposed, which he began acknowledging in his public speeches. The second came after the collapse of the uprising in Germany, in March 1921, when Lenin criticized that action directly, if not publicly, to a number of those responsible. The third started when he had the "theory of the offensive" openly condemned at the third Comintern congress, in June–July 1921, over the opposition of several important European communist parties. The fourth began in November– December of that year, when he cooked up, and had adopted by the Comintern leadership, his United Front ploy, though he himself did not take part in the meetings of the top-level Comintern agencies, leaving it to Zinoviev, Radek, Bukharin and Trotsky to defend the new policy.

A prime political talent of Lenin's was his ability to take the pulse of a political environment that he had just stepped into, which explains why he would draw different conclusions with regard to the same problem, depending on whether he was a political refugee in Zurich or the Bolshevik leader back again in Petrograd, whether he was in hiding across the Finnish frontier or presiding as chairman over the Council of People's Commissars. In 1914, as a refugee in Switzerland out of touch with Russia, he called for transforming the imperialist war into a civil war, but by April 1917, newly returned to Petrograd, he realized that that would harm the Bolshevik cause. Also, while still a refugee in Switzerland when the so-called bourgeois revolution broke out in February–March 1917, he did not at the time believe that it could be converted directly into what he called a Socialist proletarian revolution, yet after his arrival in Petrograd he proclaimed that very thing as his party's objective. As he knew how to read the signs in Russia's revolutionary atmosphere of 1917, he was later able to read them too in another environment, one entirely new to him, i.e., the domain of Soviet power, where again he matured rapidly, as illustrated by his handling of the peace of Brest Litovsk. A man who knew Lenin well, but was not specially predisposed in his favor, Leo Jogiches, noting how power had matured him, remarked to Clara Zetkin after the first year and a half of his reign:

> The revolution has educated Lenin. He has learned much, indeed an enormous amount. Look what he has become! Who among us would have dreamed it?! The revolution has forged out of the Bolsheviks that leadership-giving party that it needed. We can well believe that this party has experienced some powerful inner process. The Mensheviks and SRs put great faith in formulae and slogans, but behind it all they lost touch with the lifeblood of the revolution. ... The Bolsheviks have grasped what the present situation requires.[6]

Thus, generally, Lenin could size a political situation up immediately and correctly gauge the strengths of the opposing forces, so long as he was there and could observe it in person. But if it was far off, he needed time to study and digest it. This explains why he was able, during 1918–1920, to make realistic decisons about Russian affairs while being so wrong in his analyses of events in the West. Cut off from Europe's labor movement, he could not personally take its pulse, hence his diagnoses were poor. He was not wrong, of course, in judging it impossible for Soviet Russia to guarantee the survival of Soviet Finland in 1918 and Soviet Hungary in 1919, but he certainly was badly overestimating the chances of revolution in Europe, particularly Germany. He was right in ceasing, by the summer of 1920, to regard it as a function of the Soviet Government to make revolutionary propaganda, a task which he had expressly assigned it in 1918. When Kamenev, chosen to head the Soviet delegation in political negotiations with the British Government, told Lenin that he intended to conduct the affair "in the spirit of the broadest possible agitation," Lenin immediately advised against it: "In this situation any unmasking [of British imperialists] could be harmful. This is not 1918. We have the Comintern for such purposes."[7] But Lenin was not right in believing that the Red Army advance into Poland would trigger a communist revolution first in that country, then in Germany.

Though he did analyze most situations in the light of his own revolution-oriented preconceptions, when conflicting facts or developments intervened, he did not try to brush them aside but faced squarely up to them, amending his schemes and tactics as seemed necessary.[8]

The second Comintern congress had finished its work on August 7, 1920, in the general atmosphere of euphoria generated by the Red Army advance on Warsaw. Hanging on the outcome of the battle in Poland, Lenin was busy with many things, all pertaining to that revolutionary struggle, as evidenced by his notes and telegrams, not published until much later. On August 3, for instance, he telegraphed the military commanders, Smilga and Tukhachevskii, to "do everything possible to broadcast throughout Poland the Polish Revolutionary Committee's manifesto, using our aircraft for the purpose."[9] In a telegram on August 9 he admonished the heads of the Polish Revolutionary Committee, Dzerzhinskii and Marchlevsky: "Your reports are too laconic. We very urgently need detailed information on the mood of the farm laborers and Warsaw workers, also on the political outlook in general. Please reply today if possible."[10] Despite the scarcity of news from the front, on August 14 as the Soviet advance was about to be halted in the commencing battle for Warsaw, which lasted from the 14th through the 17th, Lenin cabled Kamenev in London his certainty of victory: "We have almost no news from Poland. What news there is supports our conclusion, shared by the entire Central Committee: a little extra vigilance and victory should be ours!"[11]

To the Polish affair Lenin had assigned top priority, sent the Red Army's best troops, ablest commanders, even his War Commissar, Trotsky, and had gathered some trusted veterans from the Polish pro-Soviet movement (e.g., Dzerzhinskii) and some of the Comintern representatives (Radek) to put together a Polish Revolutionary Committee that was to serve as a provisional communist Polish government. As late as August 19, the day after the Red Army had begun its retreat (the extent of which Lenin did not yet realize), he sent Radek a telegram demanding a firm policy of liquidation of the big estates and kulaks, and effective aid to the poor peasants.[12] The first brigade of Germans was then being formed at Minsk, to be commanded by Melcher, an Austrian communist who had taken part in the Russian Revolution. Arvid, a Baltic communist, was to be its political commissar.[13]

His hand strengthened by his policy's having received the approval of the Bolshevik Central Committee's full membership, Lenin entrusted its implementation to persons unconvinced of its correctness, in this case Trotsky, who was put in charge of the military operations, and Radek, who was to run the political show. Later, behind closed doors, the latter described to the leaders of the German Communist Party the hopes cherished in Moscow at the time:

During the war in Poland the Executive Committee believed that the movements in Western Europe were coming to a head, and that the Red Army's westward thrust would have the effect not of introducing Bolshevism there by force but merely of breaking through the crust of the ruling class's military power, the assumption being that sufficient internal forces had been unleashed in Germany to sustain the initiative . . . . The Executive Committee thought that the situation in Germany was reaching a point at which it would be possible to seize political power. Their belief was that, once we got to Warsaw, there would be no further need for us to march on Germany. . . . [14]

The hopes, alas, came to naught. Defeated before Warsaw, on August 17 the Red Army started to fall back. Brest Litovsk was abandoned on the 21st, and the eastward retreat became general along the entire front. Peace talks at Riga followed, starting on September 11. Lenin had to recognize that he had been wrong about Poland. He did not say so publicly, though he did in private, in a conversation with Clara Zetkin on October 12: "Radek told us in advance what would happen. He warned us. I was angry with him, called him a defeatist, but he was right. He knows the situation outside Russia, especially in the West, better than we do, and he is clever. I recently made up with him."[15] In that conversation Lenin also acknowledged that the Polish workers had behaved as anything but allies of the Red Army:

And these [Polish peasants and lower middle-class elements] looked upon the Red Army not as brothers and liberators but as enemies. They felt, thought and acted not at all like socially conscious revolutionaries but like nationalistic imperialists. The revolution in Poland, on which we were counting, failed to materialize. The peasants and workers, the wool pulled over their eyes by the Pilsudski and Daszynski people, defended their class enemies; they let our Red Army soldiers starve, and lured them into traps and slaughtered them.[16]

Though admitting that he had been wrong about Poland, he was not yet revising his outlook regarding the overall prospects for revolution. The setback in Poland he viewed initially as more of an episode than a turning point, an episode in the sense that the forward march of the revolution was bound to have its ups and downs, as he had often written (particularly and most recently in *Left-Wing Communism* . . .). But there would be no turning point in the sense that any single event would terminate one phase of the revolution (the offensive) and inaugurate another (the defensive). In late August, on the eve of the peace talks between Soviet Russia and Poland in Riga, he summarized in a communist journal the prospects opened up by the second world congress: "The revolution of the proletariat, the throwing off of Capitalism's yoke, is coming and will come in all countries of the world."[17]

On September 22, he reaffirmed his conviction that the war against Poland had nearly toppled imperialism and had profoundly influenced Germany: "Poland, the last bulwark against the Bolsheviks, being entirely in the hands of the Entente, is so much of a keystone in their system that, when the Red Army threatened it, the whole structure began to totter. . . . The advance of our troops on Warsaw threw all Germany into an uproar. The scene there resembled the one in our country in 1905. . . ."[18] A few days later, on October 15, the preliminary peace treaty with Poland having been signed on the 12th, he again reiterated that article of faith which he had been enouncing since the October Revolution: "We see it confirmed that our Russian Revolution is but one link in the chain of international revolution, and that our cause stands firm and invincible, for the cause of revolution is on the march throughout the world, and the economic situation is so evolving as to weaken our enemies and make us stronger every day. That this is no exaggeration, idle boast or wishful thinking has now been proved to you again by the Polish War."[19]

That he had not immediately seen the handwriting on the wall and recognized that the revolutionary wave in Europe was starting to ebb after the Soviet setback in Poland, was partly due to the fact that, two weeks after the defeat before Warsaw, revolution seemed to be brewing in another major country: Italy. The seizing of factories by workers, which had started in Milan on August 31 and was spreading to many other places, not only came at just the right moment to distract attention from Poland, but it appeared to confirm Kremlin expectations of an early revolution in Italy. Even during the Polish campaign there were those on the Executive Committee who, according to Radek, kept insisting that the main revolutionary thrust should be directed against Italy:

> Another view held by some Executive-Committee members, i.e., those favoring the so-called southeastern gambit, was that the main stab should be aimed not at Germany but along an entirely different front, namely through the countries sitting on an agrarian powder keg (Eastern Galicia, Rumania, Hungary), the idea being that, once we reached Trogir and the Sava, this would speed up revolution in the Balkans, thereby creating the necessary agrarian hinterland for revolution in Italy.[20]

It was at this juncture that the Bolshevik leaders drafted an appeal to the Italian Socialist Party and to Italy's "revolutionary proletariat." Written by Bukharin, expanded by Zinoviev, and co-signed by Lenin on August 27, its aim was to produce an immediate break with the Turati "right." When several days later the mentioned disorders erupted in Italy, they seemed to confirm the correctness of the Lenin diagnosis that Italy was ripe for revolution. But when the wave of strikes subsequently subsided, Lenin saw that as confirming another of his axioms, namely the inevitable treachery of the Right-Socialists and Centrists. On September 24 he wrote in the Bolshevik party newspaper: "Events in Italy should open the eyes of even the most stubborn of those maintaining that there is no harm in 'unity' and 'peace' with the Crispiens and Dittmanns. Italy's Crispiens and Dittmanns (Turati, Prampolini, d'Aragona) began to *thwart* the revolution there the very instant it showed promise of becoming *real*. And real revolution, sooner or later, is what there is going to be, all over Europe, all over the world—whatever the cost in agony and suffering."[21] On November 4 he wrote a long article on the problems facing the Italian Socialist Party. Having nobody who could explain to him the situation in Italy, as Radek was able to do for Germany, and knowing even less about the movement in Italy than the one in Poland or Germany, he stuck to his delusions about "the impending decisive battle of Italy's working class against the bourgeoisie for control of the State."[22] Again the only danger that he could see was the one allegedly posed by the reformist leaders: "If vacillating leaders desert the field at a time like this, it will not weaken but actually strengthen the party, labor movement and revolution. In Italy now such a time is at hand. That the revolutionary crisis there is engulfing the entire nation, is seen and acknowledged by all."[23]

He published this article on November 7, the birthday of the Bolshevik Revolution, perhaps intending it as a symbol of the devotion to the revolutionary cause in Europe, where militant actions by workers were being reported nearly every week from all corners. But, like the one in Italy, these too ended in failure. On October 23 a general strike began in Rumania, and led to repressive measures by the government; by October 28 it had been crushed. On November 2 the miners in Belgium walked off their jobs, staying out until the 15th, when they finally capitulated to the government. On December 1 Norway's railway workers struck, but that strike too collapsed. On December 8 another strike was called, at the Czech industrial center of Kladno, and threatened to sweep the country when most Bohemian and Moravian workers went out on December 13. On the 14th the Czech government struck back, smashing the strike and arresting many of the leaders. On December 30 a general strike was proclaimed in Yugoslavia. Again the authorities responded vigorously, snuffing out the strike by January 3, and using the pretext to crack down on the communists.

When the score was added up, the list of countries in which the offensive-minded labor movement had been crushed, plus those in which it had not dared to be offensive, was long. It included the five nations deemed by Lenin most essential to Europe's revolutionary cause. In two of them, Italy and Czechoslovakia, the radical spirit of the labor movement had been flattened. In the other three, no spontaneous mass action had occurred. Poland had not wavered under the Soviet onslaught, nor had Germany been swayed.

The militancy in France was nipped in the bud with the breaking of the strike of May 1920, following which the communist and syndicalist leaders were arrested, even before the SFIO was split.

His brain flashing, at computer speed, any and all changes in the relative strengths of the revolutionary and counter-revolutionary movements, Lenin could not fail to react to this avalanche of disappointments and defeats, all within less than five months after the end of the second congress. It is interesting to note at exactly what point the share of attention devoted to world revolution in his writings and speeches, that hitherto overriding theme, suddenly started to get smaller around the end of 1920. From 1918 until then, his speeches, reports, articles, pamphlets, etc., referred often and emphatically to the imminent or inevitable world revolution. But once he realized and admitted to himself that it was perhaps not so imminent, his assertions of its inevitability (in even the more distant future) grew rarer.

On November 6, 1920, in celebration of the Bolshevik Revolution's third anniversary, Lenin spoke—possibly for the last time—of the coming international revolution in Europe, of which, he said, the one in Russia was but a part, only the beginning. In the speech he admitted that the Bolsheviks would never have dared to seize power in Russia, had they not been firmly convinced that a world revolution would follow: "We knew at the time [in 1917] that our victory would be secure only if our cause triumphed throughout the world, and we went ahead with our part of the show only because we expected the rest of the world to follow suit."[24] He saw the Russian Revolution as merely the prelude to revolution in the more developed countries: "We have always known and must never forget that our cause is an international one. Until the old order has been toppled in all countries, including the richest and most civilized ones, we have only won half the game, perhaps less than half."[25] But anyway revolution was "due" in Europe, notwithstanding its temporary setbacks in a few small countries:

> You probably already have a fair idea of what is happening in one of the countries [German] now readiest and ripest for revolution. But the same is going on in all countries. Communism has developed, gained strength, forged itself into a party in all the advanced nations. During this time of course, the international revolutionary cause has suffered minor defeats in a few small countries where robber-barons have moved in and helped crush the movement, as Germany, for instance, helped smash the Finnish revolution, and those colossi of Capitalism—England, France and Austria—snuffed out the revolution in Hungary. But, in so doing, they just strengthened a thousandfold the forces of revolution in their own lands.[26]

Two weeks later Lenin was retreating from this position. Though still clinging to the thesis that the Russian Revolution was inconceivable without a subsequent revolution in the highly developed countries ("For our victory to be secure and lasting, we must achieve victory for the proletarian revolution in all, or at least a few, of the main capitalist countries."[27]), he acknowledged that his earlier predictions of imminent revolution in the West had not come true. But now the Bolshevik victory in Russia, which two weeks before he had called winning only half the game (or less), suddenly emerged as the dominant fact: "We have seen that neither side has yet really won or lost, neither the Soviet Russian Republic nor the capitalist rest of the world. And we have seen that, even though not all of our predictions have been literally and quickly fulfilled, enough of them have to give us the important thing, the chance and ability to keep the proletariat in power and the Soviet Republic alive, even if Socialist revolution has been delayed in the rest of the world."[28]

By the end of 1920 Lenin had abandoned his hope of seeing the revolution engulf the capitalist world. He replaced it with the more modest aim of securing Soviet Russia's coexistence with the capitalist countries, as he confessed a little farther along in his speech of November 21: "Though we have not yet won a world victory (the only kind that can be secure and lasting for us), we have fought our way into a position where we can coexist with the capitalist powers, who now are forced to have trade relations with us."[29] On December 6 he explained to the Bolshevik militants of Moscow the intended direction of his change of course, initiated with the concessions just granted, freely admitting that Soviet policy would no longer be based on an expected imminent international revolution: "But the speed, the tempo, at which revolution is developing in the capitalist countries is far slower than it was in our country . . . which is why we cannot keep relying on guesses about the future, or count at present on that tempo's speeding up."[30] A fortnight later, on December 21, at the eighth All-Russian Congress of Soviets he brought the subject up again, still in connection with the concessions, but this time omitted any mention at all of world revolution or the presumed speed of its approach. In his second report, the following day, he gave birth to another distinction, thereafter to be *de rigueur* in Soviet land. Speaking of the activities of the Council of People's Commissars, he pointedly no longer lumped together the policies of the Soviet Government (whose aspects he was reviewing) and the doings of the Communist International, concerning which he again said not a word about the prospects for revolution abroad.

Thenceforward, if he spoke of world revolution at all, it was merely to say that it would not occur in the near future. On March 15, 1921, at the tenth Bolshevik Party congress, after he had just completed the change of course in domestic policy and introduced the NEP, he was discussing the payment of taxes in kind, when he suddenly threw in, in passing, as an axiom apparently requiring no further elaboration, the statement that: "So long as there is no revolution in other countries, it would take us decades to extricate ourselves ... Basically the situation is this: we must satisfy the middle peasantry economically and go over to free exchange; otherwise it will be impossible ... in view of the delay in the world revolution, to preserve the rule of the proletariat in Russia."[31] In his closing speech, on March 16, he did mention at the end "our party as the focus of world revolution," promising that, once certain differences were overcome, the Party would "march on to ever more decisive international victories." But the promise was perfunctory and vague. A month later, on April 25, he again referred to world revolution, saying only that it had been postponed, which in turn had compelled the Bolshevik Party to make some concessions within Russia: "... for, if the workers' revolution has been delayed in other countries, then we shall have to make certain sacrifices, if only to bring about a rapid, even immediate, improvement in the situation of our own workers and peasants."[32]

Lenin's loss of hope for revolution in the West later became firmly rooted in his mind. In the 1921 celebration of the fourth anniversary of November 7, 1917, he exactly reversed the respective relative amounts of space devoted to world revolution and the Russian Revolution as compared with the year before, when the first two-thirds of his speech had dealt with world revolution, only the final third with the Russian Revolution. In 1921 his brief remarks pertained solely to problems of the Russian Revolution; world revolution received no mention at all. Similarly, in an article that he wrote at the time, there was only one reference to international revolution: "We began the job. Exactly when the proletarians of this or that nation will finish it is unimportant. The important thing is that the ice has been broken, the way opened, the path marked."[33]

In abandoning his hope of revolution in the West in the near, not to say immediate, future, Lenin was not only sacrificing a key element of his revolutionary credo since November 7, 1917, but was reaching a conclusion held by his worst enemies, Kautsky and Hilferding. When in August 1918 Karl Kautsky wrote his critique of Bolshevism, *Die Diktatur des Proletariats*, he did not fail to comment upon this aspect of Lenin's revolutionary creed:

The Bolshevik revolution was founded upon the assumption that it would serve as the trigger for a general European revolution, that Russia's bold initiative would inspire the proletarians of all Europe to rise up. ... All very logical and learnedly sustained, provided one accepted the premise that the Russian revolution indeed would spark a European revolution. But what if it didn't? So far it hasn't.[34]

In his reply to Kautsky, written in October–November 1918, Lenin rejected this line or argument, accusing Kautsky of bad faith and betraying Marxism:

Kautsky has switched cards on us, loading the deck with a tactic predicated upon European revolution at or within a specific time *instead* of one predicated upon the revolution's occurring within the reasonably near future, not at any given instant. A neat little trick, very neat!

The former premise would be stupid. The latter is a *must* for Marxists, for any revolutionary proletarian and internationalist, a *must* because only it is consistent with Marxist theory in making proper allowance for the objective situation in all Europe's war-torn countries; only it does justice to the international tasks facing the proletariat. . . . This Kautsky, a renegade in politics, when it comes to theory, does not even know how to phrase the question about the objective premises of a revolutionary tactic. . . .

For a Marxist, relying on European revolution is a must, provided of course a *revolutionary situation* is present.[35]

Zinoviev, reproducer of Lenin's ideas, was fond of repeating the latter's revolutionary credo, right up to the minute that he revised it. At the Halle congress, on October 14, 1920, Zinoviev drew a basic line of division between Germany's Independent-Socialist leaders (like Rudolph Hilferding) and the communist leaders, accusing the former of not believing in world revolution and extolling the latter for being so firmly convinced of it, and he urged the former to confess their heresy publicly: ". . . of course it is no crime for you to be persuaded that world revolution is impossible at present, but in that case you should clearly and honestly say so."[36] On November 13, after returning from Halle, he again made the same accusation: "[This Hilferding] is a skeptic through and through. He is convinced that the revolutionary movement has passed its peak and that today Germany and all Europe are merely experiencing the death throes of an ebbing revolutionary wave."[37] Yet a month later Lenin himself, though hardly a "skeptic through and through," was to say virtually the same thing—in his own way, to be sure.

Arriving in December 1920 at the same observation that Kautsky and Hilferding had made long before, Lenin, needless to say, did not draw the same conclusion from it. While he was forced to abandon hope for revolution in Europe, he did not cease hoping for revolution in general. At the end of June 1919, with a wave of revolution rolling over Europe, with Russia living under wartime communism, he wrote a piece in support of the "Communist Saturdays,"[38] which contained the following simile: "If, to help mankind conquer syphilis, a Japanese scientist has had the patience to test 605 preparations before finally hitting upon the 606th, which met all the key requirements, then those of us working on the much harder problem of defeating capitalism ought to have the perseverance to test, if necessary, hundreds and thousands of ways, means and devices for use in the good fight, so that we may perfect the best of them."[39] And once he realized that revolution in Europe was not imminent or even visible on the far horizon, he started looking around for some of these "ways, means and devices for use in the good fight" of which he had spoken. He came up with two. He found the one, the United Front tactic, the year after initiating his change of course, and at the end of 1921 he imposed it on the communist parties in the capitalist world. He found the other at the outset of his change of course, when he commenced shifting his hopes for revolution from the industrialized capitalist West to the underdeveloped colonial Near and Far East. In so doing, he was simultaneously revising both classical Marxist theory and the Bolshevik version of it as formulated at the beginning of the November revolution. In the sphere of revolutionary action, he helped open up a vast fertile field for the revolutionary movements to come.

During the first two years of the victorious revolution in Russia, from November 1917 to November 1919, Lenin's speeches and writings contained little or no mention of any role to be played by revolutionary movements in the Orient. He had pinned his hopes entirely on the West. It was Stalin, then People's Commissar for Ethnic Minorities, who in his editorials published in the journal *Zhizn natsionalnostei* in December 1918, under such characteristic titles as "Don't Forget the East" and *"Ex Oriente Lux,"* first stressed the importance of this non-European region. According to the manifesto promulgated at the Comintern's founding congress in March 1919, liberation of the colonial and semicolonial countries was directly dependent on a Socialist revolution in the so-called imperialist countries: "The freeing of the colonies is inconceivable except as accomplished simultaneously with the liberation of the working class in the parent countries. The workers and peasants not only of Annam, Algeria and Bengal but also of Persia and Armenia cannot enjoy an independent existence until the day when the workers of England and France, after overthrowing Lloyd George and Clemenceau, take power into their own hands."[40] When Lenin finally did take notice of the revolutionary movement in the East, it was for internal consumption only. He happened to be addressing (on November 22, 1919) the second Russian congress of Communist Organizations of Eastern Peoples. He did not even have the speech published (it did not appear in print until 1932). In it he said that the Socialist revolution was not merely or even mainly a struggle of the revolutionary proletariat of each country against its own bourgeoisie but of all countries oppressed by imperialism. He concluded by defining three different roles, to which he assigned different degrees of historical importance. One was that played by the Russians, who had been first to undertake a revolution. Another, obviously the most important, was that of the Western proletariat, who would assure ultimate victory for the Socialist cause. The third, and least significant, was the function of the colonial peoples, whose job it was to aid in the general assault upon the capitalist-imperialist world: "It goes without saying that only the proletariat of all the world's advanced countries can win final victory. We Russians have started a job that the British, French and German proletariat will finish. But they cannot triumph without the help of the toiling masses of all the oppressed colonial peoples, especially those of the East."[41] At the second Comintern congress the last paragraph of the supplementary theses on the colonial question was given a similar phrasing, the capitalist countries getting top priority in the grand design for world revolution: "In this way the masses in the backward countries, led by the awakened proletariat of the developed capitalist countries, will reach communism without having to pass through the preliminary stages of capitalist development."[42] In his speech to that congress on July 30, Lenin stated as a self-evident truth: "Speaking generally, in the world-historic sense, it is fair to say that a Chinese coolie in a backward country cannot by himself wage a revolution. . . ."[43] Four days earlier at the same congress he had condemned the idea, already expressed by some communists (and which he himself would come to accept) ". . . that the fate [of the revolution] in the West would depend entirely on the progress and strength of the revolutionary movement in the Eastern countries."[44]

Once his hopes for imminent revolution in the West began to fade, the view that he expressed in July 1920 had inevitably to be revised. It was no coincidence that in his speech of December 6 that year, to the members of the Moscow section of the Bolshevik Party, he acknowledged for the first time that the "revolutionary tempo" in capitalist countries was different from that in the Russia of 1917, and that the basic Marxist watchword had had to be amended accordingly: "The Communist International has published and addressed to the peoples of the East the slogan 'Proletarians of all countries and ye oppressed peoples, unite!' One comrade has asked me 'But when did the Executive Committee order the wording of the slogans to be changed?' To tell you the truth, I don't remember. Of course this new slogan doesn't entirely stick to the letter of the 'Communist Manifesto,' but that document was written under very different circumstances. In the context of today's political situation, this new slogan is the right one."[45] But that was merely one step in the evolving of Lenin's strategic and tactical thinking, and it was not his habit to go only halfway. A few months later, in his speech closing the Bolshevik Party's tenth national congress on May 28, 1921, he spoke of the decay of capitalism, stressing not the revolutionary doings of the industrial proletariat in the West but the stirrings of the oppressed colonial peoples:

> Of course, when we set out to fashion a policy that we intended to have last for years, we must not for a minute forget that the international revolution, the speed and circumstances of its coming, may change everything. For the

moment a kind of temporary, unstable, yet functioning equilibrium has been established, one in which the imperialist powers, despite their hatred of the Soviet Union and desire to strangle it, have given up the idea because the capitalist world is progressively decaying and increasingly disunited, and the pressures exerted on it by the oppressed colonial peoples, whose numbers total more than a billion souls, grow greater every year, every month, every week."[46]

Finally, when Lenin presented his report on Russian Communist Party tactics to the Third World Congress on July 5, 1921, he told that areopagus of world communism that the role of the colonial peoples in the coming revolutionary struggle would be greater than previously supposed (i.e., before his change of course): "And it is clear that the movement of the majority of the earth's population, aimed orginally at national liberation, may play a much larger role in the coming decisive battles of the world revolution against capitalism and imperialism than we all had expected."[47]

DIRECTION AND EFFECTS OF THE CHANGE OF COURSE

The two changes of course, one in the policies of Soviet Russia, the other in the tactics of the Comintern, were so closely interwoven that it is difficult to separate them, either in time or substance. As it gradually dawned on Lenin that there would be no revolution in Poland, Germany, Italy or anywhere else, the need to change course, in both Soviet Russia and the Comintern, began to haunt his thoughts. But, in early 1921, the dangers that he saw menacing Russia's Soviet regime from within required that top priority go to domestic affairs. Revision of Comintern policies could wait. A short time later, at the third Comintern congress, where his main contribution was to have been a report on the tactics of the Russian Communist Party, he found that this subject was no longer controversial. The number-one problem had become the tactics of the Comintern, so he had to deal with that instead.

Lenin saw his dual change of course as a single integrated fallback executed on two different battlefields in the same war. Once embarked on the new course, which included granting concessions to foreigners and engaging in trade negotiations with capitalists, he was at pains to emphasize that the new tactic constituted neither opportunistic desertion of communist principle nor any peace treaty with the capitalist world. In that same speech on December 6 he denied any resemblance between his tactics and those of the opportunistic Socialists, reminding his listeners of Brest Litovsk: "One hears talk, among other things, of opportunism. Opportunism is sacrificing one's fundamental interests for paltry short-term gains. That is the essence of its theoretical definition. And that is where many have gone astray. In the negotiations at Brest Litovsk, for instance, we did sacrifice some Russian interests, as one defines 'interests' from the standpoint of patriotism, but from the Socialist standpoint they were minor interests. So, yes, we did sacrifice a great deal, but everything we sacrificed was minor."[48] On December 21 he rejected the allegation that having contacts with capitalists meant making peace with capitalism: "It would be a big mistake to assume that just making a peace treaty granting concessions [to capitalists] means making peace with capitalism. The treaty was about a war; it was the lesser evil for us, and for the workers and peasants, less evil than being pulverized by tanks and artillery. . . ."[49] On April 11, 1921, in his closing speech on the foreign concessions (kept secret until 1932) he redrew for the Bolshevik members of the Soviet trade unions his favorite analogy comparing the concessions of 1921 to the 1918 Brest Litovsk negotiations, vigorously insisting that both were mere ruses of war intended solely to trick the enemy:

> Remember the treaty of Brest Litovsk. Why was the job so ticklish? Why the result so hard to defend? When I was asked [at the time] whether I was hoping or planning to trick the Germans, officially I had to say no. But now the treaty is history. . . . As we know, Comrade Ioffe, our ambassador to the German Government, was expelled from Germany on the eve of the revolution there. So who can say who was tricking whom. We cannot tell the exact number of days that will elapse between the signing of an initial treaty of concessions and the outbreak of the first major European revolution.[50]

Finally, in his speech of October 17, devoted to the NEP, he returned to the theme, but this time the key word was not *trick* but *beat*: "That is what this whole war boils down to: who is going to win; who will get to the trough first. . . . In short, who will beat whom? If the capitalists get organized first, they will drive out the communists, and that will be that. One must look at these things soberly: who will crush whom?"[51]

Lenin was repeatedly to argue that his change of course meant neither opportunism (abandoning the ideology and goals of communism) nor the end of the communist war against capitalism. Yet it would have important consequences, one of which would survive him and become a permanent feature of Bolshevik practice on both the domestic and international fronts: the disappearance of candor, a quality which, until then, Lenin had liberally displayed. If his doctrinal and political thinking did not change, what he said publicly most distinctly did. He had been in the habit of expressing openly, not to say brutally, not only his formal thoughts but even his informal ulterior motives, sometimes to the consternation of foreign communists, as when in the spring of 1920 he wrote in *Left-Wing Communism* . . . that one should freely lie, tell whatever falsehoods might be necessary, to worm one's way into the reformist trade unions, also that the British communists should support the Labour Party "as a rope supports a hanged man."

But after the change of course, while perhaps retaining his candor in private, his ulterior motives were no longer paraded in public. If occasionally he did lapse into his old brutal openness, it was only in reference to Russian affairs, which were firmly under the Party's control, not to international matters affecting the interests of capitalist governments with which he was seeking to establish contacts. On December 6 he made a second speech to Moscow's Bolshevik militants, devoted to the foreign concessions, second chronologically but first in political importance. It was published in an abridged form in *Krasnaia gazeta*. Not until three years later, in 1923, was it exhumed from the Party archives and republished, but again not in full, as explained in the accompanying editor's note in Lenin's *Collected Works*, first edition: "The editors have deleted several passages whose publication would be inappropriate today."[52] Lenin's next and still more important speech on the subject was delivered on December 21 to the Bolsheviks attending the eighth All-Russian Congress of Soviets (the few Socialist opponents attending were excluded). It was given behind closed doors and not published until 1930, with no indication of whatever deletions may have been made. (By 1930 the concern for textual accuracy, even where Lenin's writings were concerned, had fallen far below that of 1923.) Another example of the new policy of not divulging what was said in inner Bolshevik circles was the decision of the tenth Party congress, in March 1921, not to publish point 7 of the Resolution on Party Unity, written by Lenin personally, which spelled out the methods of ejecting from the Party any and all members found guilty of sowing dissent and/or violating discipline. Yet another Lenin speech, delivered and recorded on April 25, 1921, on those same concessions to foreign capitalists in Russia, was not published until 1924, after his death. Some statements that he made to Bolshevik members of the Central Trade-Union Council on April 11, 1921, did not appear in print until 1932. He himself had warned on that occasion against publishing everything that communists said in confidence to one another: "Here, the trade-union people and Party leaders must exercise some discretion about what can and should be told to the press, for the Russian press is read by many capitalists. At the time of the Brest Litovsk negotiations, for instance, we did tip off the world about what instructions we were giving to Comrade Ioffe."[53]

The Bolshevik Party leaders did not permit publication of everything that Lenin said and wrote in 1921, which would have thrown more light on the true direction of his change of course.[54] But certain texts, though never published in the USSR, were nevertheless filed away in the Party archives. One was a note that Lenin wrote in March 1921, which later, in February 1924, shortly after his death, happened to be copied by Yuri P. Annenkov, an artist officially appointed to look over the photographs of Lenin, as well as his printed articles and manuscripts, in the collection of the V. I. Lenin

Institute. Annenkov's job was to prepare artistic material for books being written about Lenin. The note that he copied said:

> From my own observations during my years as an émigré, I must say that the so-called educated strata in Western Europe and America are incapable of comprehending the present state of affairs, the real balance of power. Those elements should be regarded as deaf-mutes and treated accordingly. .... A revolution never develops in a straight line, in a process of uninterrupted growth, but in a zigzag of ups and downs, forward thrusts and temporary lulls, during which the forces of revolution wax gradually stronger, in preparation for the day of final victory.
>
> This being so, and in view of the time needed for the Socialist world revolution to mature, we must take special steps to speed our victory over the capitalist countries.
> a) To soothe the fears of the deaf-mutes, we must proclaim a separation (fictional though it be) of our government and its agencies (the Council of People's Commissars, etc.) from the Party and Politburo and especially from the Comintern. We must declare with a straight face that the latter entities are independent political organizations merely tolerated on Soviet soil. Mark my word, the deaf-mutes will swallow it.
> b) We must declare our wish for immediate resumption of diplomatic relations with the capitalist countries—on a basis of complete noninterference in their internal affairs. The deaf-mutes will swallow this too (hook, line and sinker). In fact, they will be beside themselves with joy, will throw open their doors to us—and in will march our Comintern agents and Party spies to infiltrate their countries, dressed up as diplomatic, cultural and trade representatives.[55]

In any case, after the change of course the Soviet Government and particularly its diplomats did start behaving as Lenin had recommended in his private memos of 1921. On August 31 and September 1 of that year, for instance, he wrote two notes to Eugen Varga (not published until 1965) about setting up a Berlin-based institute for collecting intelligence on the international labor movement. To implement the project, Varga stayed in touch with Lenin and Zinoviev, and Moscow agreed to supply the necessaries (money, personnel, etc.), but from the outset Lenin admonished Varga to avoid any contact whatever with official Soviet agencies in Berlin: "The Institute must not communicate at all with Russian embassies."[56] Its link to the Comintern was, of course, to be kept secret. On September 6, at Lenin's behest, the Executive Committee Presidium formally did establish the institute, but the official minutes of the meeting made no mention of the matter.[57] A few weeks later, on September 27, in response to charges by Lord Curzon, British Minister of Foreign Affairs, that the Soviet Union was violating the Russo-British treaty by disseminating communist and Soviet propaganda in Britain's Asian territories, Assistant Commissar for Foreign Affairs Litvinov drafted a denial directed at the gullibility so confidently assumed by Lenin in his disquisition on "deaf-mutes":

> The Russian government wishes to take this opportunity to stress once again, as it has many times before, that merely because the Third International has for obvious reasons chosen Russia as the seat of its Executive Committee— Russia being the only country that permits completely free dissemination of communist ideas and grants communists personal freedom—and merely because some members of the Russian government belong to that Executive Committee in their capacity as private citizens, this does not warrant identifying the Third International with the Russian government any more than equating the Second International (which is based in Brussels and includes among the members of its Executive Committee men like Monsieur Vandervelde, Belgian government minister, and Mr. Henderson, British cabinet officer) with the Belgian or British government. Moreover, the Executive Committee of the Third International has thirty-one members, only five of whom are Russian, and only two of those five hold positions in the Russian government.[58]

After the change of course in 1921 all official and/or public contact between the Soviet government, and especially its Commissariat of Foreign Affairs, and the Communist International was to be scrupulously avoided. Until then no effort had been made to conceal the ties between them. One instance of this was the contacts maintained by Chicherin and his ambassadors with the foreign communist leaders, which did not thenceforth cease to exist but did have to become sub-rosa. Lenin himself set the example, on May 7, 1921, when he sent a telegram to V. Kopp, the Soviet government's official representative in Berlin, requesting him to "pass along quickly and secretly to Thomas [the Comintern agent] my letter to Levi and Zetkin. . . ."[59] In their confidential reports, Soviet diplomats sometimes complained of shortcomings in the foreign communist organizations. A secret letter sent by Boris Souvarine, French Communist Party representative in Moscow, to the French Communist Party headquarters in Paris, tells of the following initiative by a Soviet diplomat: "Several months ago Comrade Karakhan made a suggestion that Vaillant-Couturier forwarded to Paris. . . . I have just received another letter from Karakhan, who is now Soviet government representative in Warsaw, asking me to expedite action on his suggestion. . . . He wants an *Humanité* correspondent sent to Warsaw, someone who would be in close touch with the Soviet representative and from whom he would receive information and documents. . . ."[60] (The letter went on to discuss whether the Party would authorize the correspondent's remuneration by the Soviet embassy.) Conversely, confidential complaints were also registered about the slowness and other failings of the Soviet diplomatic service, as when the head of the Czechoslovak Communist Party, B. Jilek, told the Presidium of the Comintern's Executive Committee in June 1922:

> ... The Russian diplomats in Prague are not very reliable. . . . For example, a packet of documents addressed to the Executive Committee of the Communist International, to be used for drawing up a careful report, though delivered in Prague on the 15th, has not reached Moscow yet. This is the quality of the Comintern Executive Committee's link with Prague. It is an intolerable state of affairs, one which in a ticklish situation could have very disagreeable consequences for us.[61]

All of which was in perfect conformity with the first point in Lenin's memo, i.e., on the newly-to-be-feigned separateness of the Comintern from the Soviet government. But then there was point two: the promise not to meddle in the internal affairs of other countries. Thus the diplomatic note sent by Chicherin on January 15, 1921, to the Minister of Foreign Affairs of Rumania, concerning pending negotiations aimed at establishing formal relations between the two countries, contained the official assurance: "May I assure you that, for its part, the Russian republic has no intention whatever of interfering in Rumanian affairs or engaging in any action hostile to Rumania. The Russian republic is firmly determined not to permit the peaceful relations now existing between Russia and Rumania to be disturbed."[62]

The switch in policy in 1921 produced changes in the outward behavior of both the Soviet government and Communist International. Thenceforth the Comintern's publicly visible activities started to diminish, but its secret operations burgeoned. Its official texts and releases (press, *agitprop*, speeches and writings of its top leaders) became rich in formulae, arguments, watchwords, etc., designed to throw sand in the world's eyes, to conceal rather than reveal what was actually going on. When the Comintern launched any major initiative, such as the conjuring of the "United Front" in December 1921, elaborate care was taken to keep Comintern involvement a deep secret. Its financial dependence on the Russians was denied flatly and vehemently. The fact that it maintained webs of emissaries in the foreign communist parties was shrouded in silence. The upshot was that it simply became more difficult for contemporary observers and future historians to see the Comintern's true face.

From the start of his career as a revolutionary, Lenin held to the basic belief that economics always did and always must take a backseat in politics, that voluntarism would triumph over determinism, and he saw his change of course as primarily a political act. Political too, in his view, was his purely economic NEP. He based all his decisions on political considerations, from the start of the switch in November 1920 (decree on the concessions to foreigners) to its last act a year later (birth of the United Front in December

1921). On December 6, 1920, in explaining to Moscow's Bolshevik militants the purpose of his concessions to the foreign capitalists, he used mainly political, not economic arguments, for, as he said on that occasion, "The political factor outweights all others." On December 21, in his report to the Bolshevik members of the Soviets about those same concessions, he again stressed the overriding importance of the political: "So, in negotiating the concessions, our own primary interests were political. . . . The economic aspect was secondary. The meat of the matter is political."[63] In explaining to the tenth Bolshevik Party congress the new "tax in kind," the NEP's crown jewel, he declared in the first sentence: "Replacing the assessment with a tax is first and foremost a political act. . . ."[64] His attitude was the same regarding Comintern affairs. On August 31, 1921, he wrote out for E. Varga his "theses" on the founding of an institute which should bear, Lenin said, the official name "Institute for Research on the Forms of Social Movements," and which must devote no more than 20 percent of its energies to the study of economic and social questions, 80 percent to political questions.[65] Finally, after the Soviet regime had surmounted the internal crisis of 1921, in reappraising that event at the fourth Comintern congress, he called it a purely political crisis, not an economic one, depsite the famine and other economic scourges it had brought: ". . . But in 1921, having just come through the crucial civil war, which we won, we found ourselves confronted with a new crisis, in fact the biggest internal political crisis that Soviet Russia has ever faced."[66]

Lenin's essentially political motives for his change of course had an internationalist dimension. True, the objective world situation, which saw no revolution in the West and the survival of Soviet Russia as the only communist power, had profoundly influenced the new policies, yet he continued to behave not merely as a Russian communist but as an internationalist Russian communist. Compelled to base his policies on the facts as they were, he devoted himself thenceforward more to the continuing revolution in Russia than to the nonexistent ones elsewhere. The line that he laid down during the change of course, and which he preached to the communists, was largely adopted in both the Bolshevik Party and Communist International.

Insisting that this new policy flowed inexorably from the objective situation in Russia and the world, he had the courage to admit the errors in judgment and mistaken predictions made by him and the other Bolshevik leaders. On February 28, 1921, in his remarks to the Moscow Soviet about the terrible famine, he confessed: ". . . It was all our mistake—there's no use trying to hide the fact—just as we didn't try to hide our error in the matter of the Polish war. . . ."[67] On July 5, addressing the third Comintern congress, he again acknowledged: "We know for sure that we made some big mistakes."[68] The errors admitted, the important thing was to learn from them, to reshape Soviet policy and Comintern activities accordingly. Which was what Lenin was busy doing throughout 1921.

Unable to fan or any longer even dream of revolution in the West, he fell back on a device which he was convinced had helped save the life of the Soviet regime immediately after November 7, 1917, and again in the Brest Litovsk negotiations: exploiting the contradictions in the capitalist camp while at the same time dredging up new allies for Soviet Russia and the international communist movement. Setting out to explain the slowdown in world revolution and his resulting provisional economic agreements with "the capitalist sharks," he kept emphatically asserting, as in his speech of November 26, 1920: "So far we are winning out over the world bourgeoisie because they are unable to unite."[69] Ten days later, in an address to Moscow's Bolshevik militants, he expounded from end to end his entire theory about exploiting contradictions in the capitalist world:

> The main thing about the concessions, from the political standpoint—and both political and economic factors are involved here—but the main thing to remember about them from the political standpoint is that well-known rule of thumb which we have not only mastered in theory but effectively put into practice, and which for a long time to come (until Socialism finally triumphs throughout the world) will be our golden rule: to exploit the antitheses and contradictions between the two imperialisms, between the two groups of capitalist states, pitting the one against the other. Until we have conquered the entire world, we shall be economically and militarily weaker than the capitalist rest of the world. So until then we must stick to our golden rule; we must learn to exploit the contradictions and antitheses between and among imperialists. Had we not stuck to this rule in the past, we would all have been hanged long ago, each from a separate tree, and the capitalists would have cheered and celebrated.[70]

A logical corollary of this new policy became the quest for new allies, which was pursued in three domains. The first was inside Russia. Though as late as December 23, 1920, in his closing speech to the eighth Congress of Soviets, he was threatening to step up the social revolution and civil war in the countryside, to eradicate the last traces of private capitalist agriculture, scarcely three months later he was in full retreat, diligently introducing the opposite policy. To the third Comintern congress he explained: "We have made an alliance with the peasants. . . . We had to show them that we can and will change our policy quickly so as to ease their suffering at once."[71] Too, Soviet Russia's foreign policy would now be directed toward rapprochement with countries disadvantaged by the Treaty of Versailles. The purpose was to heat up their dispute with the powers that benefited from that treaty. Then, when it came to the Comintern, Lenin imposed on its

Western sections a policy of seeking political alliances with non-revolutionary forces, particularly the Social-Democrats and reformist Syndicalists, just as in Russia he had switched horses and allied himself with the non-(if not anti-)Socialist peasants.

Another tactical lesson that he taught the leaders of Soviet Russia and the Comintern was about the many ways in which the class enemy could be attacked. Though he had already dealt with this problem at length in the spring of 1920, in *Left-Wing Communism* . . . , then he was merely teaching the rudiments, applicable to the situation at that uncomplicated time, when the revolutionary wave was still rising. But by the end of 1920 and after, having introduced his change of course, he had to go much further. He applied his same old rules of tactics, but now to the new phase of revolutionary ebb. Again, what he said and did in 1921 about domestic policies in Russia were soon mirror-imaged in the doings and mouthings of the Comintern.

In October that year he told a conference of the Moscow Bolshevik Party: "We are in the position of people who have to keep retreating in order, in the end, to seize the offensive."[72] This was a rehash of the idea he had expressed to proponents of the "offensive theory" three months earlier at the third World Congress. Citing the example of the Japanese capture of Port Arthur in their surprise attack of February 1904, he pointed out the two alternating tactics used, direct assault and siege, and drew a parallel with the new situation of the Bolshevik Party and Communist International: "By the spring of 1921 it was clear that we had been defeated in our attempt to achieve 'by storm' our intended conversion to a Socialist system of production and distribution, i.e., to bring it about by the shortest, quickest, most direct method. The political situation then prevailing made us see the wisdom of retreating to state capitalism in many sectors of the economy, in other words, of switching from a strategy of assault to one of a siege."[73] He also preached that, in addition to assault and siege, there was a third tactic, namely exchanges and contacts of every kind between communists and non-communists, a process from which the communists, he said, stood to gain much more than their adversaries. In his lectures on the subject to communists of Soviet Russia and in the Comintern, he reasoned: "So how come that, from all our contacts with bourgeois Europe and America, it is always we who have been the gainers and not they? Why always they who have been afraid to send delegations to our country, and not we to send our delegations to theirs? And, from those they have dared to send, we have always managed to lure some of its people (however few) over to our way of thinking, despite the fact that they have mainly been Menshevik elements and individuals who came here for only a short time."[74]

Lenin's change of course after the dual defeat in the late summer of 1920 (in August at Warsaw, in September in Italy) injected into the political war against capitalism an important new element: active opposition to the Treaty of Versailles. It was new in that it represented a radical departure from the Soviet position until then, important because it was to influence Soviet-Russian foreign policy and Comintern tactics for many years to come—long after Lenin's death.

So long as the Kremlin expected capitalist Europe, both the countries that had won the war and those that had lost it, to be soon engulfed by communist revolution, the Treaty of Versailles was regarded as an unimportant symbol of imperialistic capitalist injustice. Attaching little significance to it, the Bolshevik chieftains at first dismissed it as a diplomatic farce being acted out by two camps of "imperialist brigands." It went without saying that the Treaty of Versailles and all its works would inevitably collapse in the revolution to come, just as the fall of Imperial Germany had erased the Treaty of Brest Litovsk. The manifesto of the second World Congress, written by Trotsky and signed by Lenin, Trotsky, Zinoviev and Bukharin, equated the vanquished imperialism of the Central Powers with the triumphant imperialism of the Entente: "The design for Europe concocted by German imperialism in the flush of its great military victories has been taken over by its vanquishers, the Entente. If the rulers of the Entente now put the defeated bandits of the German Reich in the dock, it will merely be a case of criminals trying criminals."[75]

But once the prospect of European revolution began to fade in victor and vanquished countries alike, and had to be replaced by Moscow's new policy of exploiting contradictions within the capitalist camp, the Bolshevik attitude toward the Treaty of Versailles changed. The goal thenceforward—if not exactly common action against the victors—became at least parallel or mutually supporting moves by Soviet Russia and the countries disadvantaged by the treaty. After his defeat in Poland, Lenin promptly proclaimed the interests of Soviet Russia to be compatible with those of vengeance-seeking Germany. By September 22, 1920, in his address to the ninth Bolshevik Party conference, convened shortly after the Polish debacle, he was already announcing an identity of Russian and German interests in opposition to the Treaty of Versailles: "Our army's advance on Warsaw demonstrated beyond question that somewhere in that region lies the center of world imperialism's whole system, which is based on the Treaty of Versailles. . . . And in Germany we have witnessed the creation of the unnatural alliance between the Black Hundred and the Bolsheviks."[76] Three weeks later, on October 15, he again roasted the Treaty of Versailles, in language very similar to that later to be used by Hitler, restressing the Russo-German unity of purpose in opposing it:

What is this Treaty of Versailles anyway? It is an unheard-of covenant, a peace imposed by looters, which reduces to slavery tens of millions of people, including some of the most civilized. It is not a peace at all but a list of demands dictated by brigands, knife in hand, to a defenseless victim. The treaty strips Germany of all its colonies. . . . And at that moment the Red Army was crossing the Polish frontier, heading for the German border. Everybody in Germany, even the Black Hundred and monarchists, was saying that the Bolsheviks will save us; everyone could see that the peace of Versailles was coming apart at the seams, and that here was a Red Army that had declared war on all capitalists.[77]

After another two months his new idea had evolved further. He now no longer spoke of the matter with reference only to the recent past (Russo-Polish war) but as a factor to be reckoned with far into the future:

Not counting America, Germany is the most advanced country. . . . And this is why, fettered by the Treaty of Versailles, it finds itself in an impossible position, one in which it is naturally being pushed into an alliance with Russia. . . . The Treaty of Versailles has created a situation in which Germany has no hope of relief, no hope of not being sacked, looted of its means of livelihood, with nothing left to look forward to but starvation and the extermination of its people. Obviously, the only way it can save itself is by joining hands with Russia, and that is the direction in which it is looking.[78]

When Lenin changed one of his basic political beliefs, this automatically altered his tactics too. So with his abruptly changed course in 1921, the related attack upon the Versailles treaty became a constant theme of both the Russian government and Communist International. But the new direction was reflected first in the government's policies, only later in those of the Comintern. When it came to the latter, getting communists to agitate against the Treaty of Versailles was naturally easier in the defeated countries than in those on the winning side. So, initially the Bolsheviks concentrated their attention on Germany, but now for a new and added reason.

Before their change of course, the Bolsheviks had regarded Germany as the most important foreign country, the key to the expected general communist revolution throughout Europe. After it, they still considered Germany the most important, but now in the new context of the campaign against Versailles. In the first instance they had been banking on the German communist movement; in the second they were compelled to rely on Germany's government, politicians, financiers and military men—all of whom, domestically, were death on communism. So, after the change of course, Moscow pursued a two-faced policy toward Germany, one reflecting a carefully balanced political choice. On the one hand, representatives of the Soviet government, people like Victor Kopp, were negotiating initial agreements with the German authorities. On the other, agents of the Comintern (like Bela Kun) were busily trying to stir up insurrection in Germany. Sometimes one and the same individual was working simultaneously for both. An example was Karl Radek, who quasi-clandestinely stayed on in Germany several months, from early October 1920 to early February 1921, just as the change of course was being initiated.

Needless to say, these parallel activities all originated from the same source, the Politburo, i.e., with Lenin himself, but the targets were different. Target of the one was the bourgeois government of the foreign country in question; target of the other its domestic communist party. In this three-handed game the situation of each player was unique. The Bolshevik Politburo naturally knew all about these two different spheres of foreign activity abroad, since it planned and directed both itself. The bourgeois government of the foreign country, naturally aware of its own official contacts with Moscow, was not unaware of the ties between the Kremlin and the local communist party. The third actor in the play was that local communist party, whose members (with rare exceptions) knew nothing at all of what was going on between Moscow and their country's government. Being kept in the dark severely handicapped them. Moscow negotiated with the government and told the local communist party what to do; the government dealt freely with Moscow and cracked down at will on the communist party. Caught in the middle, the latter could only stand there and take it, unable to say boo in either direction, for fear of being crushed.

After the change of course this two-faced Moscow policy would hamstring the Comintern till the end of its days. And every time when this three-pronged game came a cropper, it was the local communist party that paid the piper, not the bourgeois government, and certainly not Moscow. An early, indeed the first example, which turned out to be typical (if not classical) for the whole history of the Comintern, was the affair in Turkey.

The Bolsheviks had two reasons for wanting to have friendly relations with the regime of Kemal Atatürk. First, as part of the Comintern strategy, the communists were professing solidarity with the anti-imperialist-oriented national-liberation movements, and Atatürk's government fitted nicely into this category. Secondly, the aim of Soviet diplomacy, especially after the change of course, was to exploit contradictions within the capitalist world, with special attention to the defeated countries disadvantaged by the Treaty of Versailles. Turkey fitted into that category too. Not surprisingly, the Soviet and Turkish governments found an area of common interest beyond the ordinary framework of normal diplomatic relations, as stressed in a note sent by Chicherin on June 2, 1920, to Atatürk, in reply to a letter from him, dated April 26, proposing establishment of diplomatic relations between the two nations: "The Soviet Government has the honor to acknowledge receipt of the letter expressing a desire to enter into regular relations with it and to take part in a common struggle against the foreign imperialism menacing our two countries."[79] In November 1920 Atatürk appointed his diplomatic representatives to Moscow and replied that same month to Chicherin's note, using in it language almost identical to that of Zinoviev, Radek and Bela Kun in their speeches at the Baku congress two months before:

> I am deeply convinced, and my conviction is shared by all our citizens, that on the day when the toilers of the West and the oppressed peoples of Asia and Africa realize that international capital is using them in order to enslave and destroy them in the interests of their masters, the capitalists, on the day when the realization of the criminality of the colonial policy reaches the hearts of the toiling masses of the world, the reign of the bourgeoisie will be over.[80]

In this three-handed poker game the third player was the Turkish communist group, founded in Soviet Russia and elevated to the status of a communist party in 1920. Another Turkish communist party, founded in Turkey at the instigation of Atatürk himself and made up of his friends and followers, was refused recognition by Moscow as a Comintern section. The Kremlin-sanctioned Turkish communists were headed by Mustapha Subhi, Turkish Socialist who was in Russia at the time of the Bolshevik Revolution, had joined up with the Bolsheviks and, in 1918, put together a Turkish communist cell. In March 1919 he took part in the Comintern's founding congress as the only Turkish representative in a delegation from the Central Bureau of Eastern Peoples, embryo of the later Comintern organization for the Far and Middle East. He subsequently went to the Crimea, then to Baku, to be nearer Turkey. In September 1920, in Baku, he attended the first congress of Eastern peoples, at which Zinoviev extolled the support given by the Bolsheviks to the Atatürk regime. Having written to Atatürk on June 15, 1920, requesting permission to return to Turkey to make communist propaganda in the Anatolia region, when the Baku congress was over, Subhi and fourteen of his henchmen crossed the frontier and established themselves in Kars, Turkey's most out-of-the-way provincial capital. After a brief stay, they moved on to Trabzon on the Black Sea. Regarding themselves as the provisional leaders of the Turkish Communist Party, they met with a hostile attitude on the part of local authorities, who rounded them up and clapped them on a boat, which on the 28th of January, 1921, capsized at sea. To a man the passengers were drowned.[81]

After this mass elimination of an entire communist-party leadership, probably the first case of its kind in Comintern annals, the Kremlin was reluctant to stir up trouble by openly glorifying the victims or damning their executioners. Yet that same year, when a few communists were temporarily detained in Spain and Yugoslavia, the Comintern's propaganda engines roared into action, bewailing and bemoaning these acts of repression, with a grand display of solicitude. On the other hand, less than a month after the collective assassination of Turkey's communist-party leaders, a Turkish-government delegation was welcomed to Moscow to negotiate a "treaty of friendship and brotherhood," which was duly signed on March 16, 1921. Its preamble proclaimed "the brotherhood of nations," "the solidarity in the struggle against imperialism," "a desire to establish enduring and cordial relations between [the two nations] and a sincere and unbreakable friendship."[82] The Turkish communists were obviously not included in this "sincere and unbreakable friendship," for less than two months later an Ankara court sentenced several communist leaders to up to 15 years in prison. Not long after that, on July 27, 1921, the Turkish Government banned all communict activity. That same month the Comintern held its third world congress, at which the spokesman for the Turkish communists expressed the party's loyal support for the Atatürk regime: "So long as the national movement for Turkish independence continues, we other communists must help it along, because extermination of the Entente and imperialists will be the beginning of the world revolution that will abolish all slavery."[83] This was still the line at the next Comintern congress, in 1922, when one of the leading lights at the time, Karl Radek, made no bones about the matter: "This is why we say to the Turkish communists today, notwithstanding the persecution they are suffering: 'Your job as defenders of the independence of Turkey, which is so very important to the revolution, is not yet finished. Protest against the persecution, by all means . . . but understand, too, that you still have a long road to travel in the company of the bourgeois revolutionaries.' "[84]

As long as the Turkish nationalist and bourgeois government pursued the policy of alliance with the Soviet Government, the latter swallowed the domestic persecution of Turkish communists, and the Comintern as well as the Turkish communists themselves followed suit. It was only when the Turkish government appeared willing to modify its policy vis-à-vis the Soviet Union, that Moscow pressed the alarm button within the Comintern. Thus in an appeal to the communists and the Turkish toiling masses, issued at the end of the fourth Comintern congress, it was said: "The Turkish Communist Party has always supported the bourgeois and nationalist government in the struggle of the toiling masses against imperialism. The Turkish Communist Party has even consented, in the presence of the common enemy, to sacrifice temporarily a part of its program and of its ideal. . . . The nationalist government getting ready to ally itself with imperialism, is striving to destroy your genuine representatives and to separate them from your foreign friends."[85] This appeal was revealing in a twofold sense: it confirmed the subordination of the Turkish communists to the foreign policy of Soviet

Russia, and it showed how precarious an alliance of the Soviet Government with a nationalist-bourgeois regime was. From the "sincere and unbreakable" friendship of March 1921, Moscow had come already in November 1922 to suspect the Turkish government of its willingness to ask accommodation with "imperialism" and to abandon its "foreign friends."

CONSEQUENCES OF THE CHANGE OF COURSE ON THE ORGANIZATIONAL PLAN

To be complete, the change of course had to go beyond mere strategy and tactics and fundamentally reorganize the Bolshevik Party, which was bound in time to affect the Communist International, modeled on and run by the Bolshevik Party. With the advent of his change of course, Lenin had to teach the Bolshevik Party and subsequently the Comintern an important lesson, namely that, whenever the Party softened its external policies, it had to harden its internal discipline—discipline being more necessary in a retreat than in an advance. In this connection he proclaimed and put into practice certain principles not previously vested with the force of "law" in the Bolshevik Party: the forbidding of all internal opposition and/or dissent, and periodic purges of the membership. At the tenth Party congress in March 1921, concluding his report on behalf of the Central Committee, he declared: "What we need now, Comrades, is not 'opposition'! Either we are for or against a thing—and will say so with our guns. But 'opposition'—no! It is the situation itself that requires this; no individual is to blame. And my belief is that this Party congress will have to come to the same conclusion— that we must now have done with opposition, must clamp a lid on all of it. We have had our fill of it!"[86] To settle the hash of what opposition there was ("democratic centralism" and "workers' opposition"), he wrote his Resolution on Party Unity, which was adopted. Strictly forbidding factionalism and ordaining the dissolution of all opposition groups, it demanded liberal use of disciplinary measures (up to and including exclusion from the Party). A vast purge followed and was vigorously prosecuted particularly in August and September 1921. During the next twelve months some 140,000 members were expelled from the Party.

Though opposition and dissent were now forbidden in the Party, in 1921 they still existed in sections of the Comintern. The reason was that the Party had reached, so to speak, its political "adulthood," while the Comintern was still a child. But after the change of course an unfailing pattern became established: Whatever happened in the Bolshevik Party would sooner or later be carbon-copied by the Comintern. To use a formula dear to the Bolsheviks in other contexts, one could say that it was the old "law of unlike development leading to an identical outcome." During the last three years of Lenin's life, for instance, the Comintern leadership was to hold successively three different attitudes toward factionalism and dissent in the foreign sections. At first dissenters were tolerated, sometimes even negotiated with, since there was then no way to get rid of them. Next, in each foreign party Moscow started supporting the group whose current thinking was closest to its own. When that group ultimately (and predictably) prevailed (with an assist from the Kremlin), *it* was proclaimed to be "the Party," and all other groups were expelled and/or damned. In the Comintern, too, the purge gradually became the main tool. In his Resolution on Party Unity, Lenin had spoken of "purging the Party of unreliable nonproletarian elements." Later that year he wrote an article on "the purge," drafted a Central Committee circular letter on it, and wrote a letter on it to the Politburo. These three documents served as the theoretical foundation for the ensuing vast purge. But it happened that at this period the leadership of the communist parties in the West and elsewhere was jam-packed with these so-called nonproletarian elements, who also mainly comprised the opposition groups to emerge after 1921 in many parties. It would fall to the Comintern to lay on the Lenin lash, and purge them one and all.

Another instrument of discipline introduced by Lenin in 1921 that spread from the Bolshevik Party to the Comintern was the refusal to accept a communist leader's resignation. The only way out was to be thrown out; the option of resigning was not available. The Party could force a person to take a job against his will, and then snatch the job away again and even expel the individual out of the Party, all with the most perfect disregard for his wishes. Typical was the incident at the tenth Party congress when Shliapnikov, spokesman for the "Workers' Opposition" who had been elected to the Party's new Central Committee, handed in his resignation. Lenin's response was vehement: "As for the announced resignation, I submit the following resolution for adoption: 'The congress calls upon all members of the disbanded group known as the 'Workers' Opposition' to bow to Party discipline, orders them to remain at their assigned posts, and refuses to accept the resignation of Comrade Shliapnikov and/or anyone else.' "[87] Then, after getting Shliapnikov stripped of any right to resign, as he did on March 16, Lenin waited only until August 9 to demand, again in the name of the Party, that this same Shliapnikov be not only thrown off the Central Committee but hurled out of the Party into the bargain—a motion which fell only three votes short of the two-thirds majority required under the bylaws for that extreme. Several months later, in December 1921, there was a similar case in the French Communist Party. Some members elected to the Directing Committee who supported the official Comintern line, but found themselves in the minority at the Marseilles congress, tendered their resignation. Immediately labeling their action a political mistake, the Comintern did its best to get them reinstated. A few years later it had those same leaders (with the exception of Vaillant-Couturier) ejected from the French Party.

This progressive withering away of any individual will within the Bolshevik Party and later Comintern was accompanied by the gradual introduction and assiduous propagation of the Great Myth—to the effect that the decisions taken were not really those of the actual persons who alone had the power to shape and enforce them but flowed instead from the imaginary brain of two exalted abstractions: the Party, which was always right, and the Comintern, which was infallible. When the change of course began to subject Party members to harsh new restrictions, A. A. Ioffe, an important personage and ex-member of the Central Committee, wrote Lenin a letter on March 15, two days before the tenth congress ended. Though never published, its tenor can be guessed from Lenin's reply: "You are wrong to keep saying (as you have a number of times) that the Central Committee is really just I. A thing like that could be written only by someone in a highly nervous state and under great strain. The old Central Committee (1919–1920) opposed me on one very important matter, as you may remember from the discussion. On questions of organization and personnel, I have been outvoted many times. You often saw examples of this when you were a member of the Central Committee."[88] It was true that Ioffe was in a highly nervous state, and that Lenin sometimes had been outvoted on the Central Committee, but Ioffe was nevertheless right in observing that now, in March 1921, there was an increasing tendency to equate the Party with one man, a trend soon to become more pronounced. It would be even more so in the Comintern, whose foreign members felt inferior to the Russians, hence always knuckled under to the Bolshevik Party.

The change of course in 1921 was to have another consequence for Lenin personally. More and more of his time and attention would be taken up with Russian affairs, less and less with those of the Comintern (which increased the importance of Zinoviev's role by default, so to speak). The shifted emphasis was evident in all Lenin's activities—his speeches, articles, memos, dictated letters, interviews, etc. During 1919 and 1920 he had avidly sought out the foreign communists visiting Moscow, no matter how young (e.g., Alfred Kurella in 1919) or how politically insignificant (e.g., Lucien Deslinières in 1920), or even how minor or unimportant the parties they belonged to or headed (e.g., E. Rheiland, top communist in Luxembourg), and he engaged them in long discussions, devouring all their news from Europe. But by 1921 he was growing choosier. At the third world congress he refused to receive even delegations of parties then important, like the Yugoslav party, a force to be reckoned with at that time.

Lenin's declining participation in the work of the top-level Comintern agencies was evident from his increasing absence from meetings of the

Executive Committee, of which he was a member. At the second world congress he did take part in some of the meetings, and in one after the congress had ended. He attended those in June of 1921, just before the third world congress, but no more after that congress, not even on important occasions, as when the United Front was inaugurated in December. Nor did he participate in the first plenary session of the expanded Executive Committee the following February. This new tendency to detach himself somewhat from the Comintern was evidenced by another incident. Shortly after the third congress his signature, as that of a member of the Comintern's Executive Committee, appeared on its manifestos and appeals dated July 17 and 30 and August 13 and 26. After the appeal "to the working class of England" of September 28, however, the signatures of Lenin and Trotsky no longer appeared.[89] That it was no accident was recently confirmed by the long-delayed publication (in 1959) of some letters exchanged between Chicherin and Lenin. On October 15, the Soviet Commissar for Foreign Affairs suggested to Lenin several steps that could be taken to improve Soviet relations with capitalist countries. One was that Lenin and Trotsky should quietly cease to be members of the Comintern Executive Committee. Replying the next day, Lenin flatly rejected the idea: "As for Trotsky and me getting off the Executive Committee of the Communist International, that is absolutely out of the question."[90] But no longer did they sign its appeals, and the mere fact that Chicherin, who had taken active part in the preparations for the first congress and had chaired the committee responsible for certifying the delegations attending it (and subsequently withdrew from all Comintern activities himself), would even dream of suggesting that Lenin and Trotsky shed the Executive Committee, was clear evidence of the Soviet Government's growing desire not to be officially identified with the Comintern.

The increased importance assigned to Russian affairs at the expense of Comintern affairs was to work a triple change in the personnel of the Comintern's administrative structure. At the time of the first and second world congresses, in 1919 and 1920, several Bolshevik leaders then serving as Soviet government officials were transferred to the Comintern. Starting in 1921, the process was reversed. Leading Bolsheviks were withdrawn from the Comintern and assigned to the Soviet diplomatic service. Of the first four secretaries of the Comintern in 1919, three had come from diplomatic posts. Berzin and Balabanova had been on the staff of the Soviet embassy in Bern. Vorovsky had been in charge of the negotiations with Finland. Also, between the first and second world congresses, Litvinov and Karakhan attended some Executive Committee meetings, as noted in the Committee's official report presented to the second congress.[91] But after the change of course diplomats like Litvinov and Karakhan took extra care not to be mentioned in any reports on Executive Committee doings, and some of the higher-ups in the initial Comintern setup, men like Kobetsky and Hanetski, then transferred to the Soviet diplomatic service or, like Vorovsky, returned to it.

A second important change in top Comintern personnel resulted from infusion into it of Bolsheviks who had been victims of the purge immediately following the change of course. Piatnitsky, for instance, whose presence was no longer desired on the Moscow Central Committee, in 1921 was appointed head of the Comintern's secret service and finance department. The same was true of Helena Stassova, assigned to the Comintern secret service after losing her executive position in the Bolshevik Party. A similar fate befell G. Safarov, who in 1921 got into a fight with the Party leadership in Turkestan (specifically with Tomsky). At the end of that year he was given a job as secretary to the Comintern Executive Committee. Much the same thing happened to Alexandra Kollontai, figurehead in the "workers' opposition," who was appointed to the Comintern central bureau, where she worked during 1921–22, and later got a diplomatic assignment.

The third innovation after the change of course resulted from the widening scope of Comintern activities, which necessitated more and more personnel. There were just not enough old Bolsheviks, so it became necessary to use the services of the more recent converts—ex-Bundists, ex-Mensheviks, former Party dissidents, etc., people like Manuilsky, Lozovsky, Borodin, Petrovsky-Bennett, Rafes, Guralsky and, a little later, Martynov (under attack by Lenin since the beginning of the century). These ultimately permeated the Comintern administration.

The change of tide in 1921 made clear to Lenin that the wave of revolution and power of attraction of Russia's example had started to ebb. The changed attitude of the various labor parties confirmed this. In 1920 most of the important ones (USPD, SFIO, etc.) had favored joining the Comintern, while by 1921 they were registering majority votes against. In early 1921, too, the Comintern suffered its first crisis of dissidence and disobedience, which cast a menacing shadow over the very principles on which it operated and ended in the break with Paul Levi, chairman of the German Party, the most important after the Russian. If in 1920 Lenin had been partly right in quipping that the Comintern had become "fashionable," the style changed in 1921.

So Lenin's new course, introduced on three fronts—Soviet domestic policy, Soviet foreign policy, and policies and tactics of the Comintern—had different results on each. Within Russia it was successful in that the NEP did succeed in re-establishng a modicum of normality and in consolidating Bolshevik power. But in the realm of foreign policy the success was only partial. Though diplomatic, economic and other formal relationships were constructed with many capitalist countries, the new tactics bore little nourishing fruit. They were least successful with the Comintern. The goals that Lenin set the foreign parties in 1921, to capture a majority of the working class and forge a "United Front" with the Socialists and Syndicalists, were never attained. Yet in all three domains the change of course that he launched that year had a profound and lasting influence—one that long outlasted him.

NOTES TO CHAPTER 9

1. A. Miasnikov in *Lénine tel qu'il fut* (Moscow, 1959), 2:192. In fact even before the Bolshevik seizure of power Lenin was an adversary of the Constituent Assembly. At a meeting of the Bolshevik Central Committee, on October 10 (23), 1917, he condemned in the following words (published for the first time in 1922) the first freely elected assembly in the history of the Russian people: "It is senseless to wait for the Constituent Assembly that will obviously not be on our side, for this will only make our task more involved" (*Polnoe sobranie sochinenii*, 5th ed. [Moscow, 1963], 34:392).

2. Lenin, *Polnoe sobranie sochinenii*, 42:91.

3. *Manifestes, thèses et résolutions des quatre premiers congrès de l'Internationale communiste, 1919–1923* (Paris, 1934), p. 104.

4. Lenin, *Polnoe sobranie sochinenii*, 41:166.

5. P. Levi, *Bericht über die Verhandlungen in Moskau: Rede auf der Zentralausschussitzung am 25.8.1920* (in the author's possession).

6. Clara Zetkin, *Roza Liuksemburg i russkaia revoliutsiia* (Moscow and Petrograd, 1924), pp. 130–31.

7. Lenin, *Polnoe sobranie sochinenii*, 51:236, 438.

8. After his death, his epigones—Zinoviev and Stalin—did just the opposite. Come what might, they proclaimed *their* policies infallible, all proofs to the contrary notwithstanding.

9. Lenin, *Polnoe sobranie sochinenii*, 51:248.

10. Ibid., p. 252.

11. Ibid., p. 260.

12. Ibid., p. 264.

13. Cf. Max Barthel, *Kein Bedarf an Weltgeschichte* (Wiesbaden, 1950), pp. 120–21.

14. "Sitzung der Zentrale mit den Vertreter des Exekutivkomitees für Deutschland," Freitag, den 28. Januar 1921 (in the author's possession). An English translation can be found in M. Drachkovitch and B. Lazitch, *The Comintern: Historical Highlights* (New York, 1966), pp. 285–99.

15. Clara Zetkin, *Erinnerungen an Lenin* (Vienna and Berlin, 1929?), pp. 20–21.

16. Ibid., p. 20.

17. Lenin, *Polnoe sobranie sochinenii*, 41:276.

18. Ibid., p. 282.

19. Ibid., pp. 348–49.

20. "Sitzung der Zentrale."

21. Lenin, *Polnoe sobranie sochinenii*, 41:297; emphasis in the text.

22. Ibid., pp. 416–17.

23. Ibid., pp. 417–18.

24. Ibid., 42:1.

25. Ibid., p. 3.

26. Ibid., pp. 3–4.

27. Ibid., p. 20.

28. Ibid., pp. 20–21.

29. Ibid., p. 22.

30. Ibid., p. 59.

31. Ibid., 43:68, 70.

32. Ibid., p. 248.

33. Ibid., 44:150.

34. Karl Kautsky, *Die Diktatur des Proletariats* (Vienna, 1918), p. 28.

35. Lenin, *Polnoe sobranie sochinenii*, 37:299–300; emphasis in the original.

36. G. Zinoviev, *Die Weltrevolution und die III. Kommunistische Internationale* (Verlag der Kommunistischen Internationale, 1920), p. 17.

37. G. Zinoviev, *Dvenadtsat dnei v. Germanii* (Petersburg, 1920), p. 18.

38. "Communist Saturdays" were introduced by a decision of the Bolshevik Central Committee in May 1919 as a supplementary means in the civil war struggle. In order to enhance production the workers were asked to lengthen their working day by one hour, accumulate these extra hours and put in six extra hours of manual labor on Saturdays.

39. Lenin, *Polnoe sobranie sochinenii*, 39:20.

40. *Manifestes, thèses et résolutions*, p. 32.

41. Lenin, *Polnoe sobranie sochinenii*, 39:330.

42. *Manifestes, thèses et résolutions*, p. 60.

43. *Protokoll des II. Weltkongresses der Kommunistischen Internationale* (Hamburg, 1921), p. 349.

44. *Vestnik 2-ogo kongressa Kommunisticheskoga Internatsionala* (Moscow), no. 1 (July 27, 1920).

45. Lenin, *Polnoe sobranie sochinenii*, 42:72–73. This revised version of the slogan, whose origin Lenin could not recall, had made its first public appearance three months earlier, on September 7, in the speech by Zinoviev closing the Baku congress. He had concluded it with the statement: "Seventy years ago our common teacher, Karl Marx, issued his appeal 'Proletarians of all countries, unite!' We, his disciples and continuers, have the good fortune to be able to implement and broaden that appeal by urging 'Proletarians of all countries and ye oppressed peoples of the entire world, unite!' " (*First Congress of Eastern Peoples* [Baku, 1920], p. 222).

46. Lenin, *Polnoe sobranie sochinenii*, 43:340–41.

47. *Bulletin des III. Kongresses der Kommunistischen Internationale* (Moscow), July 13, 1921, p. 384.

48. Lenin, *Polnoe sobranie sochinenii*, 42:58.

49. Ibid., p. 115.

50. Ibid., 43:191–92.

51. Ibid., 44:160–61.

52. Lenin, *Sobranie sochinenii*, 1st ed. (Moscow, 1923), 17:468.

53. Lenin, *Polnoe sobranie sochinenii*, 43:195.

54. A discussion held at the Historical Institute of the Soviet Academy of Sciences, on June 17 and 18, 1964, at a time of the relatively liberalized and de-Stalinized regime of Khrushchev, confirmed that two of the Soviet archives in the Museum of the October Revolution, devoted entirely to the personality and work of Lenin, were still inaccessible to Soviet historians (cf. *Kultura* [Paris], no. 5 [May 1965]: 122–28).

55. *Novyi zhurnal* (New York), 1961, no. 65 (1961): 146–47. The text was printed verbatim in the *Bulletin of the Institute for the Study of the USSR* (Munich), May 1962. There are three reasons for assuming it authentic: 1) it faithfully reflects Lenin's spirit and style; 2) Annenkov could not conceivably have invented it, an act which would have been utterly inconsistent with his known moral attributes (apart from the fact that he completely lacked the necessary political knowledge); 3) it has been pronounced authentic by Boris Souvarine, who from 1921 to 1925 lived in Moscow in constant close touch with the top Bolshevik Party and Comintern leaders.

56. Lenin, *Polnoe sobranie sochinenii*, 54:444.

57. Cf. *Die Tätigkeit der Exekutive der Kommunistischen Internationale vom 13. Juli 1921 bis 1. Februar 1922* (Petrograd, 1922), meeting of the Presidium on September 6, pp. 163–68. However, *Kommunisticheskii Internatsional* (Moscow, 1969), p. 147, gives this information.

58. *Soviet Documents on Foreign Policy*, vol. 1, *1917–24* (London, 1951), p. 258.

59. Lenin, *Polnoe sobranie sochinenii*, 52:181.

60. B. Souvarine's letter of December 7, 1921 (in the author's possession).

61. Comrade B. Jilek's report on the developments and state of the Czechoslovak Communist Party before the Presidium of the Executive Committee, June 3, 1922 (in the author's possession).

62. *Soviet Documents on Foreign Policy*, vol. 1, p. 229.

63. Lenin, *Polnoe sobranie sochinenii*, 42:95–96.

64. Ibid., 43:57.

65. Cf. ibid., 54:444.

66. Ibid., 45:282.

67. Ibid., 42:360.

68. Ibid., 44:41.

69. Ibid., 42:44.

70. Ibid., p. 56.

71. Ibid., 44:42, 45.

72. Ibid., p. 208.

73. Ibid., p. 204.

74. Ibid., 42:116.

75. *Protokoll des II. Weltkongresses*, p. 706.

76. Lenin, *Polnoe sobranie sochinenii*, 41:282.

77. Ibid., p. 353.

78. Ibid., 42:104, 105.

79. Xenia Joukoff Eudin and Robert North, *Soviet Russia and the East, 1920–1927* (Stanford, 1957), p. 186.

80. Ibid., p. 188.

81. "Just who was ultimately responsible for this act cannot be established with any certainty on present evidence. Ankara may have authorized it as a convenient way to be rid of a potentially dangerous competitor without having to accept responsibility for Subhi's disappearance. Local authorities . . . may have taken it upon themselves to act on their initiative." (George S. Harris, *The Origins of Communism in Turkey* [Stanford, 1967], p. 91.)

82. *Soviet Documents on Foreign Policy*, vol. 1, p. 237.

83. *Bulletin des III. Kongresses*, no. 23 (July 19, 1921): 519–20.

84. *Bulletin du IVe congres de l'Internationale communiste* (Moscow), no. 20 (December 2, 1922): 15.

85. Ibid., no. 17 (November 27, 1922):28–29.

86. Lenin, *Polnoe sobranie sochinenii*, 43:43.

87. Ibid., p. 111.

88. *Leninski sbornik* (Moscow, 1959), 36:208.

89. In the Comintern organ *La Correspondance Internationale* of October 26, 1921 (p. 44), there appeared an appeal bearing the signatures of Lenin and Trotsky, but the date when the appeal was issued was July 17. Likewise, the same source carried on November 2 (p. 359) another appeal with these two signatures, but the date of its issuance was August 26, 1921.

90. Lenin, *Polnoe sobranie sochinenii*, 53:273, 435.

91. Cf. *Bericht des Exekutivkomitees der Kommunistischen Internationale an den zweiten Weltkongress der Kommunistischen Internationale*, 1920, p. 5.

10

STALIN IN
THE DRIVER'S SEAT

The establishment of [Lenin's] one-party regime inevitably reduced the Soviets from a labor parliament to a mere façade through which prior party decisions could be promulgated. It drained the Soviets of all political content and all political power. That left only one tiny vent, one safety valve to check tyranny, combat bureaucracy, criticize error. That last tiny escape valve was democracy inside the Communist Party. So long as party members were free to criticize, not as helpless individuals, but to combine together to form a faction, draft a platform, set up a rival slate, curb or remove officials, attempt to convince the party and win the party away from a given line or leadership, all was not yet frozen—or in the horribly inhuman, even inorganic word which Stalin adopted—all was not yet *monolithic* in the Communist Party of the Soviet Union. The pressure of the masses to which the party appealed might still be reflected inside the party through influence on party members close to the masses and sensitive concerning them.

But during the hard struggles with famine and civil war and chaos, when everything was being settled by command, extraordinary measures, military means, these means became an unconscious skin of habit. Inevitably, the method of command, the employment of coercion, the use of military means, invaded the party.

Still under the leadership of Lenin and Trotsky, with Stalin a mere second-string figure and in no wise responsible, came the first outlawing of the right to form groups and factions within the party. The "Democratic Opposition," the "Workers' Opposition," the "Democratic Centralist Opposition," and others like them, were defeated part by argument, part by the use of "military" methods.

Lenin, and with him Trotsky, resorted to administrative measures to break up and defeat these oppositions and to prevent the further formation of factions. Lenin argued that the outlawing of faction rights was temporary, an emergency measure during a time so grave that discussion was too dangerous a "luxury." But history teaches that it is during such moments that the new regime hardens and that what is first advanced as temporary has a way of becoming permanent. It is wars and emergencies that test democracy and nourish dictatorship.

Lenin dispersed oppositions by deporting their spokesmen. It was, to be sure, a gentlemanly, humane, even comradely mode of deportation, as compared with what has come since. Kollontai, one of the leaders of the "Workers' Opposition," was made an Ambassador. Others were sent to other embassies, or removed from political work and given purely economic tasks, or sent to head enterprises far from the great centers of population and party membership, or assigned to do research in Marxism.

But, before long, one opposition leader, Miasnikov, was sent to Siberia. Apparently he was not adjudged qualified for diplomatic posts abroad, or not "diplomatic" enough so that they could be sure that if they sent him abroad he would keep his mouth shut. Thus, not under Stalin, but under Lenin and Trotsky and the collective leadership of the Old Bolsheviks came the first deportation in a more sinister sense. Such is the logical fatality of error that each step leads to the next one. The outlawing of factions in the Party drained the Communist Party of all democratic political content just as the outlawing of other parties had drained the Soviets.

POLICING THE PEASANT

The same period saw the application of police measures, not merely to the old ruling class and dispossessed proprietors, landowners and intellectuals, but to the overwhelming majority of the Russian people, the peasants. Once more subjective and objective factors combined to bring about this state of affairs. Subjectively, the Russian Marxists (of every faction) had trained themselves to regard the peasantry with reserve and suspicion. It was part of Marxist dogma in Russia that the intense attachment of the peasantry to the soil (so different from the worker's attitude towards the machine) made him "property-minded" and a "petty bourgeois." This made it easy for the advanced workers to justify in their own minds the use of police measures instead of consultation and persuasion in dealing with the overwhelming majority of the toiling masses, the overwhelming majority of the Russian people. The breakdown of industry, so that there was nothing to offer the peasant in exchange for his grain, combined with the hard necessities of famine and civil war, caused the new State to adopt "extraordinary" (that is, irregular, temporary, emergency) measures to requisition crops, determine planting and harvest and seeding, fix prices and conditions of exchange, seize crops by police and communist raids with no more pretense at legality than comes with the possession of power. The result was to beget such a monstrous police apparatus in vast, rural Russia, to use it so continuously and universally against the great majority of Russians, the true "common man," that inevitably the swollen police apparatus reacted on urban life. Ere long it was used against and within the very organizations of the advanced workers who had thoughtlessly sanctioned its use against the majority of the Russian people. In the end the unions were invaded by the secret police, the Soviets were invaded by the secret police, even the party that was supposed to control the police came to be controlled by it.

THE KRONSTADT INSURRECTION

We cannot follow this process in detail, but one more landmark must be noted for its effect upon the nature of the future Soviet and Party life: namely, the Kronstadt Insurrection.

All safety valves having been stuffed up, the inevitable accumulation of discontent with tyranny or arbitrariness or actual error was bound to assume a more dangerous form. Actually, the Kronstadt uprising began as a peaceful, even "lawful" protest (so far as there was law and a constitution in the new Soviet regime) by the Soviet of Kronstadt. But a Soviet, as we have seen, represented both workers' organizations and peasant organizations and, directly through delegates, the armed forces. In Kronstadt, a great fortress town, the armed forces made the Soviet a formidable power. The protesters were declared in rebellion and then their resistance to attack was met by a combination of artillery, economic (but not political) concessions, and frame-up. The importance for our picture lies in the fact that the method of frame-up was used to discredit the Kronstadt Soviet.

Lenin's writings specifically justify the use of frame-up against a rival political faction of his own party after a split has occurred. Such methods had already been used against Mensheviks and Social Revolutionaries. But here the method was used publicly against the masses themselves. From then onward, it became easy for frame-up to develop into a system of fighting one's opponents, and sooner or later this system, too, would invade the party and be turned against those who had themselves sanctioned the use of it. The adoption of the "New Economic Policy" a few months later was an acknowledgment that the Kronstadt Soviet and Garrison had been economically justified in many of their demands, that those demands expressed not only real desires but real necessities of the country. Yet, while parts of their program were adopted, these men were attacked by military force and by frame-up, since—along with their other demands—they challenged the one-party dictatorship. Machine methods were hardening into a system.

LENIN'S LAST FIGHT

With the end of the civil war, Lenin hoped that the harshness, hardness and brutality would decline once more. There would come an expansion of industry, there would be more time to argue, discuss, persuade. Life would become easier. Discontent, justified and unjustified, would alike diminish. The government would become more popular, find it easier to win support and sustain itself. The state of siege could be in part revoked, and some of the things which had been lost could be reintroduced.

Now Lenin became aware of the fact that the relations of the party to the masses, and of the state machine and officialdom to the masses, were in danger. He sensed, rather than fully comprehended, the danger, for by now he had accepted as unalterable some of the chief sources of that danger such as the one-party government. To him the danger was manifested not in its roots but in some of its more noxious surface growths. He began a struggle with what he denominated the tendency to "bureaucratic distortion" of the "workers' state" and the "workers' party." Once more he prepared for battle with the machine which his organization theories and his methods of work and cruel events beyond his control had combined to foster. It was his last fight and was swallowed up in death.

Once more, we are not dealing with an inevitable development. Accident—accident from the standpoint of the things we are discussing—again played its peculiar role. Even as Lenin was turning his still powerful mind to the problem, beginning to become aware of the fact that his machine was turning into a juggernaut, he suffered his first stroke. From the standpoint of biology Lenin's illness was no accident; from the standpoint of sociology it was. And another "biological accident" contributed to the rise of Stalin in the hour of the decline of Lenin. In 1919 there was a worldwide epidemic of influenza. It carried off Sverdlov, the leader of the organization and apparatus of the Bolshevik Party. Sverdlov was an organizing genius. He knew how to carry out orders, get things done, preserve the precious personnel that had taken so many years to form. He was absolutely selfless, free from envy, harshness or rancor. He knew how to convince others to carry out orders, without angering, humiliating or crushing them. All these qualities were badly needed to oil the gears of the machine that necessity and theory between them had created.

When he died, as when Lenin died, there was no one who, in his sphere, could replace him. A secretariat of three was set up: not one of the three was a Sverdlov, nor were the three together equal to him. In 1921 Zinoviev proposed the creation of the new post of General Secretary and nominated Joseph Stalin. Lenin was taken by surprise. Zinoviev broached it during a caucus in connection with a Party Congress. Lenin admired certain qualities in Stalin (ever since the Georgian expropriations), but he knew that Stalin was given to intrigue and hard to get along with. All through the Civil War the imperious temperament of Trotsky and the jealous, secretive, intriguing temperament of Stalin had been in conflict and Lenin had had to intervene constantly to stop members of his party from shooting each other instead of the White Armies. "I am afraid," Lenin responded to Zinoviev, "that he is a cook who will prepare only hot dishes." But Lenin had a serene confidence in his own ability to lead his party and curb his subordinates. He did not press his objections.

It was while the new General Secretary was feeling out the power that lay in controlling appointments and assignments that a blood clot on the brain struck down Lenin and left him paralyzed and speechless for several fateful months. In the year 1922 Bukharin coined one of his meaningful aphorisms: "The history of mankind may be divided into three stages: First, the *matriarkhat*; then the *patriarkhat*; and now the *Sekretariat*." While Lenin lay on his bed of pain, the Secretariat began to prepare the succession.

Lenin rallied several times and tried to return to the battle. His last two years were increasingly concerned with curbing bureaucracy and preventing a clash or a split in his party. There were months in which he could not write or dictate. During those months men who had been unassuming lieutenants were using the powers of appointment and transfer to secure their place in the party in case death should triumph. He became aware of this, too, and much of his last conscious effort was expended on an attempt to fight with "the cook who was preparing hot dishes" and remove him from the key place in the machine that would soon be without the man who had contrived it, and known in the main how to control and direct it. He prepared fragmentary battle campaigns: on bureaucracy; on the Georgian question where Stalin had driven most of the best Georgian Communists into the opposition; on the national question (since this was Stalin's one claim to distinction as a theoretician); on party machine methods. "I am preparing a bombshell for Stalin at the next Congress," he told his personal secretary. When the Congress came, Lenin was no longer able to speak.

LENIN'S TESTAMENT

By the end of the year 1922 he sensed that he would not last much longer, and, when he had rallied sufficiently to be able to talk once more, he dictated to his secretary a letter to the Party which has come to be known as "Lenin's Testament"—a testament which the "best disciple of Comrade Lenin" did his best to conceal from the Party. To this day the Russian people have not been permitted to read it or weigh its warnings or learn of its existence.

The Testament speaks of the danger of a future split. It distinguishes between broader objective factors which might bring about a split, and narrower, more subjective factors. The objective danger sprang from the two-class character of the Party. If the peasantry and proletariat should fall apart, then nothing could stop the formation of two separate parties and a contest between them. But there was another source of danger of a split, which Lenin thought was not an inevitable split, but one which could be avoided by good will and vigilance.

> I have in mind [he wrote] the stability of the Central Committee as a guarantee against a split in the near future, and I intend to examine here a series of considerations of a purely personal character. I think that a fundamental factor in the matter of stability—from this point of view—is the personality of such members of the Central Committee as Stalin and Trotsky. The relation between them constitutes, in my opinion, more than half the danger of that split, which is an avoidable one . . . Since Stalin became General Secretary he has concentrated enormous power in his hands. I am not sure that he always understands how to use power with sufficient care. On the other hand, Comrade Trotsky, as was proved by his struggle against the Central Committee in connection with the question of the People's Commissariat of Ways and Communications, is distinguished not only by exceptional abilities—personally he is without doubt the most able man in the present Central Committee—but also by his too far-reaching self-confidence and by a tendency to be too much attracted to the purely administrative side of affairs. These characteristics of the two most capable members of the present Central Committee might, quite innocently, lead to a split, and, if our party does not take measures to prevent such a split, it might occur unexpectedly.

That was written, or rather, dictated, on December 25, 1922. It showed how well Lenin knew his party and all the people he had gathered around him, and how clearly he could foresee the future.

Ten days later, after he had felt well enough to make inquiries and receive reports on the situation that had developed while he had lain helpless, he became aware that Stalin had carried the machinations for control of the party machine so far that it was no longer sufficient to administer pats and slaps to both sides. He added a postscript, directing as always the main blow where he sensed the main danger.

> Stalin is too rude [reads the postscript] and this fault, entirely supportable in relations among us communists, becomes insupportable in the office of General Secretary. Therefore, I propose to the comrades to find a way to remove Stalin from that position and appoint another man who in all respects is superior to Stalin in this one way only: namely that he is more patient, more loyal and more courteous with the comrades and less capricious. This circumstance may seem an insignificant trifle, but I think that from the point of view of preventing

a split and from the point of view of the relations between Stalin and Trotsky, it is no trifle, or such a trifle as may later acquire a decisive importance.

This postscript bears the date: January 4, 1923.

The letter was withheld from the Party while Lenin sought, in vain, for the strength that might enable him to take up in person the fight against the menacing danger. Though his doctors sought to keep reports from him, he learned more and more of Stalin's further chess moves in the mute struggle for power already raging over the succession to the man who was taking so long in dying. The final "postscript" took the form of dictating a personal note to Stalin "breaking off all comradely relations" with him. That was virtually Lenin's last political act before he lapsed once more into helplessness. It was Lenin's own comment on the future purges. And it was the final form of the triangle, Lenin-Trotsky-Stalin.

11

LENIN AND
THE USES OF POWER

*People who imagined that they had made a revolution always saw next day
that they did not know what they had been doing, and that the revolution
which they had made was nothing like the one they had wanted to make.*—
FRIEDRICH ENGELS TO VERA ZASULICH

INTRODUCTION

It is hard for us, the contemporaries of that great struggle for modernization,
freedom, equality and abundance, known as the Russian Revolution, to
grasp the grandiose process in its entirety, to discover its "law of motion,"
to keep up with its swift and drastic changes of line, leaders, institutions,
spirit, outlook. We humans are by nature lazy-minded: so long as the men
in the Kremlin keep the same labels—Socialism, Communist Party, Soviet—
we are disinclined to look behind the steadily retained labels to the constantly
changing spirit and content. Moreover, as younger people awaken to awareness of the Soviet regime as it is today, they are likely to imagine that it
was substantially the same in its aims and basic nature from the very
beginning.

It would be absurd to expect any revolution to maintain the same state
of effervescence and the same direction of development over half a century.
But as we look behind the stubborn claim of continuity of leadership, purpose
and direction, we are startled to find that in essential respects this "revolution" has reversed itself, described a 180° arc, turned into its opposite. A
few examples will make clear the degree of this transformation, which goes
far beyond the usual "reaction" which has followed every other revolution.

CHANGE IN LEADERSHIP

Of the Council of Commissars, numbering twenty-one at the end of 1936,
only five were left two years later. One died . . . the rest were shot or
disappeared.

In the Central Committee of the Communist Party there were seventy-one
members elected at the beginning of 1934. At the end of 1938 twenty-one

remained alive; three died naturally; one, Kirov, was assassinated; thirty-six disappeared; one committed suicide; nine were announced as shot.

In the city of Kiev between August 1937 and June 1938, more than half of the members of the local Communist Party were officially declared to have been expelled between August 1937 and June 1938. No such announcements were made about the other great cities of Russia, but the proportion is known to have been about the same.[1]

The above statistics are taken from Walter Duranty. They might as well have been taken from any other account of the purges, but I have chosen Duranty's because of his general attitude of friendliness towards Stalin ("I'm betting on Stalin, just the way you say you are betting on Whirlaway or any other horse, and when they've won once or twice you talk of them as 'your' horse . . . Stalin was *my* horse.") But neither Duranty nor any other interpreter has noticed the political meaning of the above figures. Sixteen out of twenty-one members of the Council of Commissars, the heads of the State, means that there has been *a coup d'état in the State.* Fifty out of seventy-one members of the Central Committee purged by the Secretary, who is supposed to be the employee or servant of the Central Committee, means that there has been *a coup d'état in the Party.* The elimination of approximately one-half, or more, of all the members of the Communist Party (with the consequent intimidation of many of the rest) means that the coup ran from the top to the bottom of the Party, and that the Police and Party Secretary, both supposedly under the command of the Party, actually seized power during that coup.

If one adds the fact that, of the original leaders of the Revolution of 1917, most of those who did not die a natural death in good time were purged by Stalin and the secret police, it becomes still more evident that this was a genuine coup d'état. Without attempting to determine who all the leaders of the Bolshevik Revolution of 1917 were, we can take two incontrovertible lists of high-ranking officers and trace their subsequent fate. The first list is that of the members of the Central Committee attending the session of October 23, 1917, the last meeting before the Bolshevik seizure of power. The minutes show that those present were: "Lenin, Zinoviev, Kamenev, Trotsky, Stalin, Sverdlov, Uritsky, Dzierzynski, Kollontai, Bubnov, Sokolnikov, Lomov."[2] Of these, Lenin, Sverdlov, and Dzierzynski died a natural death. Lomov probably died a natural death. Uritsky was assassinated by opponents of the regime. Kollontai was bloodlessly removed from the conduct of Party affairs in Lenin's gentler day, by being sent abroad as an ambassador; Zinoviev, Kamenev, Trotsky, Bubnov, and Sokolnikov were all purged by Stalin.

Similarly, if we take the first Central Committee elected after the successful seizure of power, we find the following people, chosen by the following votes of the Seventh Congress of the Russian Communist Party: "Lenin, 34 votes; Trotsky, 34; Sverdlov, 33; Zinoviev, 33; Bukharin, 32; Sokolnikov, 32; Stalin, 32; Krestinsky, 32; Smilga, 29; Stasova, 28; Lashevich, 27; Shmidt, 26; Dzierzynski, 26; Vladimirsky, 24; Sergeev, 23." The names are given in the order in which they appear in the stenogram of the convention. Of those chosen to lead the Party after the seizure of power, Lenin, Sverdlov, and Sergeev died natural deaths; Vladimirsky and Stasova were still alive in November 1947; and Trotsky, Zinoviev, Bukharin, Sokolnikov, Krestinsky, Smilga, Lashevich, and Shmidt were all purged by their comrade-in-arms.[3]

THE DEVELOPMENT OF THE ONE-PARTY SYSTEM

Observers who have approached Russia for the first time after 1921 tend to take the one-party system for granted as part of Lenin's original program. Yet, on September 28, 1917, we find Lenin making the following proposals for guaranteeing "true freedom of the press":

State power in the shape of the Soviets takes *all* printing presses and *all* papers and distributes them *justly*: in the first place, the State . . . in the second place, the large parties, say such as have polled in both capitals one or two hundred thousand votes. In the third place, the smaller parties, and then every group of citizens which has a certain number of members or has gathered a certain number of signatures . . . This would be real freedom of the press for *all* and not for the rich.[4]

From this it is clear that as late as the autumn of 1917 Lenin had no idea of outlawing all other parties and creating a one-party system. He provided not only for a state press but for a press independent of and critical of the state and of the party in power: for large parties, small parties, and even for "every group of citizens" who might be able to gather a certain minimum of signatures for their special platform.

So swift is the human "forgettory" and so rank the growth of legend that already our generation has forgotten that the first Leninist government was a coalition of two parties: Left Social Revolutionaries and Bolshevik Social Democrats. We have forgotten, too, that for three years other parties existed, put up slates for Soviet deputies, had spokesmen and factions or fractions (we would say "caucuses") in the Soviets and the Central Executive Committee of the All-Russian Soviet Congress. It is now frequently said that Lenin "had to" outlaw all the other working class and non-working class parties beacause, during the Civil War, they all became "counter-revolutionary" and had to be outlawed to win the Civil War, the War with Poland, and the struggle with foreign intervention. Actually the Bolsheviks received the active support of other working-class parties during the Civil War and the War with Poland, and did not venture to outlaw them until both civil and foreign war were safely over. I have in my library a pamphlet published first in Russian, and then by the Communist International in various other languages, in the summer of 1920, which contains speeches not only by Bolshevik spokesmen in the Soviet Congress and Central Executive Committee, but also by the spokesman for the Menshevik deputies and Executive Committee members, Julius Martov.[5]

This was during the midst of the Civil War and at the height of the War with Poland. The Soviet Government and the Comintern were anxious to let the world know that Martov and his Party supported the Soviet Government in that desperate struggle for existence, which explains their readiness to publish a Menshevik speech in many languages. Only after the Civil War and the War with Poland were safely over was the one-party system introduced and the Menshevik party outlawed and proscribed as "counter-revolutionary."

THE ANTI-IMPERIALIST REVOLUTION

The two Russian Revolutions of March and October 1917 occurred in the midst of the bloody, unending stalemate of World War I. It was not a war of movement as was the Second World War, but a war of position. For over three years men had been dug in in bloody and muddy trenches. Every so often, somewhere on the front, a few divisions went over the top, lost a few thousand or hundred thousand men, and won a few yards or "rods" or acres of lands. Then the other side staged a counter-offensive, with the same bloody and indecisive results. The generals seemed powerless to end the war by a military decision, and the diplomats unable and unwilling to end the war by a negotiated peace. It was at this juncture that the Bolsheviks issued their stirring call for the soldiers of all armies to clasp hands and fraternize across No-Man's Land, for the peoples of all lands to take their destinies into their own hands and find a "people's way to peace and freedom." They proclaimed their own revolution to be an anti-war and anti-imperialist revolution. They published the secret treaties they found in the Tsar's archives. They renounced the "war aims" of the Tsar's government. They proclaimed the right of all the peoples who had been forced into that "prison house of peoples," the Russian Empire, to determine their own destinies and to secede from the new Russia. After some vacillation and use of force, they actually permitted Lithuania, Latvia, Estonia, Finland, Poland, Georgia, Armenia, and other marginal lands to secede. They demonstratively renounced the predatory claims of the Tsar's empire upon China, Manchuria, Korea, Port Arthur, Dairen, Mongolia, the Chinese-Eastern Railway.

In April 1917, when Lenin proposed a program for his contemplated uprising against the democratic Provisional Government led by Kerensky and his associates, he wrote:

The Provisional Government has not even published the secret treaties of a frankly predatory nature concerning the partitioning of Persia, the robbing of China, the robbing of Turkey [the Dardanelles], the annexation of East Prussia ... It has confirmed these treaties concluded by tsarism, which for several centuries robbed and oppressed more peoples than did all other tyrants and despots ... disgraced and demoralized the Great-Russian people by trans-forming it into an executioner of other peoples.[6]

The thoughtful reader will immediately perceive that these are precisely the areas claimed or annexed by the Soviet Government today, on the pretext, among others, that the Tsar's government once owned or coveted them. Here too the Revolution has swung through a full arc of 180 degrees. As Lenin once wrote a pamphlet entitled *Imperialism, the Final Stage of Capitalism*, so it would be possible to write a pamphlet today, matching his, analysis for analysis and indictment for indictment (and more than matching his), which could properly be entitled *Imperialism, the Final Stage of Communism*. Indeed, the only great power which made substantial annexations after World War II in violation of the solemn pledges of the Atlantic Charter is this once anti-imperialist, Soviet Government. Here is an incomplete list of its annexations:

	Square Miles	Population
Lithuania	24,058	3,029,000
Latvia	20,056	1,950,000
Estonia	18,353	1,120,000
Eastern Poland	68,290	10,150,000
Bessarabia and Bukovina	19,360	3,748,000
Moldavia	13,124	2,200,000
Carpatho-Ukraine	4,922	800,000
East Prussia	3,500	400,000
Karelo-Finland	16,173	470,000
Petsamo, Finland	4,087	4,000
Tannu Tuva	64,000	65,000
Southern Sakhalin	14,075	415,000
Kurile Islands	3,949	4,500
Total	273,947	24,355,500

The reader will note that this includes several areas—Galicia, East Prussia, Tannu Tuva, Carpatho-Ukraine—which the Tsars coveted but never possessed. And it does not include the much larger territory of Mongolia, the naval bases in Port Arthur and Dairen, the re-seizure of the Tsarist Chinese railway, the occupation plus puppet control of Northern Korea, Bulgaria, Rumania, Albania, Czechoslovakia, Eastern Germany, or any other area not openly annexed but dominated by a combination of military force with financial and political penetration, in the areas collectively known as "behind the iron curtain." Once more we see a swing from an originally anti-imperialist revolution to a much more vigorous expansion than the Tsar's feebler state and military apparatus was able to manage. The new state which appears on every frontier which the last tsars held, claimed or coveted, is a state that has been rejuvenated and strengthened and endowed with a new dynamism by revolution.

THE STATE THAT WAS TO WITHER AWAY

Lenin's writings of 1917 are full of promises and apocalyptic prophecies of the "withering away of the State," a formula which he took from Marx and Engels. Even before he took power, he was urging the abolition of the police force and the army, as formations separate and apart from the people. For it he wished to substitute:

> a real people's militia, i.e., firstly, one that consists of the entire population, of all adult citizens of both sexes; secondly, one that combines the functions of a people's army with those of the police . . . This is the type of 'state' that we need! This is the kind of militia that would be in fact and not only in name a 'people's militia.' This is the road we must follow if we wish to make impossible the re-establishment of a special police or a special army, separated from the people.[7]

Lenin made exemplary calculations to prove that even if one allowed for the sick, the too young and the too old, and had each able-bodied workman leave his job for but one day every two weeks to serve in this popular militia, Petrograd could thus furnish an "army" and "police" indistinguishable from the people, of at least 50,000.[8] He was convinced that a uniformed, specialized, professional army and a uniformed, specialized, professional police were a perpetual threat to democracy and freedom, an accursed heritage from class society and capitalism, which could be abolished at once. Otherwise, he warned, the new Russian Revolution would end in reaction as "following very brief revolutionary periods, *all* the bourgeois and bourgeois-democractic republics of the world had organized or re-established precisely that kind of police—a special organization of armed men, separated from and opposed to the people . . ."

It is not my purpose here to evaluate the soundness of Lenin's vision. What I want to establish is that this was his true program for the State. He was convinced that his revolution, like every revolution in history, would have to retain some elements of force to prevent the newly defeated former rulers from staging a counter-revolution. But he was no less convinced that "from the first day" the new regime would rest on a broader democratic basis and that the State could begin "at once" to wither away. This withering process would be gradual and would culminate in the complete disappearance of the state:

> When the resistance of the capitalists has been completely broken, when the capitalists have disappeared, when there are no classes (i.e., there is no difference between the members of society in their relation to the social means of production), *only then* does "the state cease to exist" and does it "become possible to speak of freedom." Only then will a really full democracy, a democracy without exceptions, be possible and be realized. And only then will democracy itself begin to *wither away*, due to the simple fact that . . . people will gradually become accustomed to the observations of the elementary rules of social life that have been known for centuries . . . They will *become accustomed* to observing them without force, without compulsion, without subordination, without the *special apparatus* for compulsion which is called the state.[9]

In the early thirties, it became official theory that "the capitalists have disappeared, there are no classes, no difference in the relation of the various members of society to the means of production," and that all the other preconditions that Lenin had spoken of for "the state's ceasing to exist" had already come into being. But at the same time that Stalin announced that Socialism and a classless society had been attained in Russia, he proclaimed that the State was destined not to wither away, but to grow "stronger than ever," at least until the Soviet system had spread throughout the world. Vyshinsky proclaimed that Stalin had made various enrichments and corrections of the theories of Marx, Engels and Lenin. Among these were (1) the rejection of the idea of equality as proper to a socialist society; and (2) the rejection of the idea of the withering away of the state.

> A characteristic aspect of the dynamics of wages in capitalist lands is the levelling of wages as between the unskilled and the skilled . . . Petit-bourgeois equalization [or equalitarianism; the Russian word is *uravnilovka*, levelling] in the compensation of labor is the worst enemy of socialism. Marxism-Leninism in the course of long years has been carrying on a relentless war against equalitarianism.[10]

And in 1944 Vyshinsky wrote:

> The so-called doctrine of the withering away of the state has been the favorite subject of petty-bourgeois chatter on Marxism . . . What we need is a strong state and an energetic repressive power.[11]

This talk of "petty-bourgeois chatter on Marxism" is a little hard on the dead Lenin and his still officially cherished writings, but it is an accurate register of the fact that the State which was to wither away has actually expanded into (1) the greatest police state in history, and (2) the greatest and most complete example in history of a total state system or totalitarian state.

Totalitarianism is a philosophy of government which asserts that the state is identical with society as a whole and coextensive with it. Therefore it denies autonomy to the individual, his purposes, judgment, conscience. It denies autonomy to non-state societies or social organizations—to unions, clubs, churches, parties, or any voluntary organization whatsoever. All these social organizations must be coordinated into the apparatus of the State (the German world is *gleichgeschaltet*; the Russian word is "made into transmission belts"). If they cannot be thus transformed into transmission belts to transmit to the ruled the will of the rulers, then they must be charged with treason, dissolved, outlawed, crushed. It is this which explains the outlawing of the various political parties, the framing-up of their leaders, the arrest and frame-up of the leaders of the Protestant and Catholic and Jewish church organizations, the reduction of unions to state organizations, wherever the total state is being introduced.

Actually, of course, statified trade unions are no trade unions at all, since they are no longer instruments of the workers to defend themselves against their sole employer who is now the state. They become, instead, agencies of labor management, speedup and increased production.

The total state penetrates into every aspect of life, assumes control of every activity, takes over the direction and systematic organization of every interest. It aims to convert every individual activity and interest, and every social activity and interest, into a state activity and interest. Once more it is the inimitable Vyshinsky who shows how far this process has gone and how unconscious and taken-for-granted it has become. When on June 30, 1947, Vyshinsky was approached by some Canadian boys who, while soldiering or serving in Russia during the war had married Russian girls and founded families there and who now longed to bring their wives and children to Canada, or to England, he answered them:

> We have no racial prejudice as to whom our women may marry. But it is up to us whether or not they leave the country. . . . The duty of a Russian woman is to produce Soviet children—not children *for the Canadian government.*[12]

From the universal penetration of every social activity, work, play, leisure, organization, thoughts, emotions, comes the phenomenon of universal policing. If every social organization, every union, every party local, every club, every church, has to be penetrated, directed, coordinated by the state, the state agent must be everywhere and the police must be ubiquitous. Every science, from astronomy to linguistics, every art, from the cinema to the symphony, must become an object of state regulation under the control of state agents.

The total state should not be confused with earlier forms of despotism. The nature of earlier despotism was to be absolute in certain chosen spheres, and in them to crush all opposition, but the older great-state despotisms had neither the resources nor the mechanics nor the will to regulate every aspect of life on a vast territory. Thus not only democracy is distinguished by restrictions or limitations upon the powers of government ("Congress shall make no law . . ." runs the classic formula of our Bill of Rights). But ancient despotism was also, at least when it ruled over large areas, a limited state, in contradistinction to this new total state. For a total state modern machinery is necessary: modern means of communication so that orders can be telegraphed or telephoned or broadcast in a jiffy from one end of the land to the other, so that police and army can be transported and concentrated anywhere; modern loudspeakers on every square so that everyone may hear, even be obliged to hear, the same slogan at the same moment; modern universal literacy so that everyone may, nay must, read the same version of every event; a modern conscript army and conscript labor; an ideology of the glorification of the state above all else; modern propaganda techniques for conditioning all minds. Without this twentieth-century apparatus, the total state, a truly twentieth-century phenomenon, would be impossible.

The forces that make for totalitarianism are at work everywhere. Because of the magnitude of modern industry, because of the universality of modern warfare, because of the size, scope and complexity of modern social organization, because of the growth of modern collective enterprise, there is observable everywhere a tendency of the state to enlarge its spheres, to enter into operations formerly left to private initiative or non-state organization. Indeed, this enlargement of the spheres of activity of the state is in some measure inevitable. Who today would advocate the return of unemployment insurance to private insurance companies or to old sock or mattress savings? What private enterprise can undertake the flood control and consequent hydroelectric development made possible by modern technology, as necessary to the Tennessee Valley as to the gorges of the Yang-tse?

In simple fact, all countries, in varying ways and at varying tempos, are moving towards greater collectivism and towards greater statism (these are not necessarily synonymous terms). The United States, facing backwards and shouting "free enterprise" as it moves into social security, federal deposit insurance, stock market regulation, floors under farm prices, flood control, federal aid for health and education, and a score of other such activities, is well up in the vanguard of the countries moving towards entry of the state, and of large, voluntary, collective, non-state organizations, and quasi-state organizations, into ever new fields. Indeed, when the historian of the future looks back upon our age, he will say: "The thing which agitated them most—capitalism or socialism—wasn't the issue at all. While all countries moved towards greater degrees of state and socialized activity, the real question was: Would the people continue to control the state, or would the state gain control over the lives of its people? Would the state become coextensive with society and reduce society to a mere instrument of the state, or would society, as it entered into new fields, plan for freedom along with its planning for security and abundance, so that the state, however significant, might still remain only one of the instruments of society, obeying the will of the complex of non-state organizations: political parties; trade unions; clubs; churches; cooperatives; consumers' and producers' societies?"

We live in an age when it is easy to drift, or planfully move, into a system of total statism: "all for the state, nothing against the state, nothing outside the state." It will take deeper understanding and more conscious planning than. we have so far shown to keep alive our complex of voluntary, non-state organizations and to keep the state subordinated to their will, as one among various of society's instruments.

NOTES TO CHAPTER 11

1. Walter Duranty, *U.S.S.R.* (New York, 1944), p. 228.

2. These minutes are reproduced in the Appendix to John Reed, *Ten Days That Shook the World*, with introduction by V. I. Lenin, Modern Library edition (New York, 1934), p. 327.

3. The names, their order and the vote for each are taken from the stenographic minutes of the Seventh Congress (*Sedmoi s"ezd rossiiskoi kommunisticheskoi partii: Stenograficheskii otchet, 6–8 marta 1918 g.* [Moscow and Petrograd: Gosudarstvennoe izdatelstvo, 1923], pp. 193–94). The list of leading Old Bolsheviks still living in November 1947 is taken from *Pravda* of that date, in which the pitiful remnant, 538 Old Bolsheviks out of the tens of thousands that orginally made up the Party that seized power, sign their names to a letter "To the Leader of the Bolshevik Party and the Soviet People, Comrade Stalin, I. V.," thanking him for what he has done to and for the Party.

4. Lenin, *Collected Works*, English translation authorized and edited by the Marx-Engels-Lenin Institute (Moscow: International Publishers, 1932), vol. 21, book 1, p. 175; emphasis in the original.

5. "In the Soviet elections of 1920, the Menshevik Social Democratic Labor Party won 46 deputies in Moscow, 205 in Kharkov, 120 in Ekaterinoslav, 78 in Kremenchug, 50 in Tula and 30 each in Smolensk, Odessa, Poltava, Kiev and Irkutsk" (Martow und Dan, *Die Geschichte der russischen Sozialdemokratie* [Berlin, 1926], p. 318).

6. Lenin, *Collected Works*, authorized English translation (Moscow: International Publishers, 1929), vol. 20, book 1, p. 131.

7. Ibid., p. 52.

8. Ibid.

9. Ibid., vol. 21, book 2, pp. 219–20; emphasis in the original. This is taken from a general study of the State, called "State and Revolution," the central theme of which is the beginning of the withering away of the state and its specialized power institutions on the day after the Bolsheviks seize power.

10. *Soviet Labor Law*, textbook of the People's Commissariat of Justice (Moscow, 1939).

11. Vyshinsky, *The Patriotic War and the Soviet Government* (Moscow, 1944).

12. *New York Times*, July 1, 1947 (emphasis mine).

12

THE INFLUENCE OF LENIN
ON THE HISTORY OF OUR TIMES:
THE QUESTION
OF TOTALITARIANISM

OUR TIME OF TROUBLES

The century in which I was born has gone into the history books as *la belle époque*, the "Grand Century of Peace and Progress." Our own century, I think, will be recorded as our *smutnoe vremya*, our time of troubles.

From the fall of Napoleon in 1815 to the First World War in 1914 there was no general war in Europe. My generation was taught to believe that the twentieth century would be too civilized for war. And look at it now!

We have had two total wars, in which every man, not excluding criminals and crackpots, has learned to use a rifle with a telescopic sight, to make bombs, to throw grenades, to try to persuade men and settle issues by assassinating a John F. or a Robert Kennedy, or a Martin Luther King. A new generation of well-to-do young terrorists is fouling its nest by tossing bombs into libraries and university buildings, by cutting off power from laboratories, classrooms and hospitals, as it did in Berkeley recently. In the thirties storm troopers smashed all the shop windows of Berlin belonging to Jews in the Night of Crystal. Similar violent minorities are satisfying their passions and trying to force their views upon our universities by smashing thirty-four windows under cover of darkness in a single night, as occurred in Stanford.

THE AGE OF THE DICTATORS

Ours is an age of force and violence, of barbed wire running through the heart of a great city from which sentries shoot to kill their own countrymen going from one part of their own land to another.

Reprinted by permission of the publisher, from *Lenin and Leninism*, edited by Bernard W. Eissenstat (Lexington, Mass.: Lexington Books, D. C. Heath and Company, Copyright 1971, D. C. Heath and Company).

The first cause of this brutalization and dehumanization of man is the crisis in the civilization of Europe during which the ancient continent stumbled, all unconsciously, into the age of total wars. In my own lifetime I have seen two such total wars followed by two periods of false peace. The First World War broke down into lesser wars, civil and national. Then the lesser wars built up into the second total war. Today we hold our breaths lest they now beget a third. If the First World War can be ascribed to men's blunders, the second was unleashed by the pact for the redivision of the world entered into by the two giant totalitarian states born in the fiery womb of the First World War.

The heroes or antiheroes of our age are the *men of might* produced by an age of blood and death: Lenin, Mussolini, Hitler, Stalin, Khrushchev, Brezhnev, Mao Tse-tung and lesser two-bit dictators over their own peoples, like Franco and Castro and Ho Chi-Minh. Total war has been their progenitor and their opportunity. The war which Wilson proclaimed would make the world safe for democracy begot the age of dictatorships. For this first total war that opened our age's Time of Troubles, neither Lenin nor his disciples and imitators can be blamed. True, he was the only leading socialist who felt so little apprehension at the war clouds gathering in the Balkans that he did not trouble to attend the two emergency sessions of the Socialist International, the Congress on War in Basle in 1912, and the special session of the International Socialist Bureau in London in 1913. In 1913 he could coolly write to Gorky: "A war between Austria and Russia would be a useful trick for the revolution in all of Eastern Europe, but it is not likely that Franz Joseph and Nikolasha will give us that pleasure. . . ."[1] Lenin instinctively recognized that a general war originating in the Balkans might be "a useful trick" for him but this does not give him any responsibility for the crisis in European civilization that gave him his opportunity.

Given this opportunity, however, Lenin used it to initiate the manners and morals, and the machinery of power, that constitute the second factor in the formation of our Time of Troubles. It is this factor which I shall now examine as my contribution to the observance of Lenin's centenary.

THE SELFLESS EGOIST

What kind of man was this "event-making man," V. I. Lenin?

He was—I have written elsewhere—a selfless egoist. We never catch him glancing into the mirror of history. He lived austerely. He was selfless, too, in that he never sought either the perquisites and privileges, or the cult of adoration that often go with the absolute power he sought and achieved.

But this selflessness was only the outer shell. At the core of Lenin's spirit was an abnormally powerful, unquestioning belief in himself, and an absolute certitude that the Marxism he believed in was an infallible doctrine, and that he was the only true master and expounder of this science.

THE INFALLIBLE DOCTRINE

"Out of every hundred Bolsheviks," he wrote in the margins of a book he was reading, "70 are fools and 29 rogues, and only one a real socialist."

And in his *Philosophical Notebooks*: "After half a century, not a single Marxist has understood Marx." Implicit but unspoken is the thought that there was the one exception.

He possessed a certitude of his rightness in every controversy, large or small. Indeed, given his dogmatic, domineering temperament, there were no small controversies. When you differed with him, you were cast into outer darkness, both intellectually and morally. When he spoke, it was Marxism, Science, and History that spoke, the working class, the vanguard, the Party, the infallible interpreter of the infallible science that teaches its high priest what history wants man to do, to think and feel, to be, and to become.

From this belief followed the conviction that he must have authority and power in whatever sphere he happened to be operating: the troika, the editorial board, the Central Committee, the Party, power in Russia; power in the international movement, power in the world. Whatever organization he could not control, he split. "Split, split, and again split," was the order he gave the faithful. The Russian word he used in his command was *raskol*, a word which signifies both split and sect. Both meanings fit perfectly for he was both an inveterate splitter and an inveterate sectarian.

THE DICTATOR

When did Lenin become a dictator? There is reason to answer: As soon as he became a "Leninist."

In 1902 when he was still one of the six editors of *Iskra*, to the other five he sent a memorandum explaining that "we should show every kindness to the peasantry" but "not yield an inch" in "our maximum program." "If the peasants do not accept socialism when the dictatorship comes, we shall say to them: 'It's no use wasting words when you have got to use force.' " On the margin of this memorandum Vera Zasulich wrote, "Upon millions of people? Just you try!" When he came to power, that is just what he tried. In the end he shrank back from the consequences, but his disciple and successor, Joseph Stalin, fulfilled his injunction.

Also in 1902 he wrote:

> The committee should lead all aspects of the local movement and direct all local institutions, forces and resources. . . . Discussion of all party questions,

of course, will also take place in the local circles, but the deciding of all general questions of the local movement should be done only by the committee. The independence of local groups would be permitted only in questions of the technique of transmitting and distributing. The composition of the local groups should be determined by the committee which designates delegates to such and such a district and entrusts these delegates with setting up the district group, all the members of which must in turn be confirmed in their positions by the committee. The district group is a local branch of the committee that ·receives its powers only from the latter.

In 1903, when at last a Congress met to unify the splintered Social Democratic Party under the aegis of *Iskra*, at the first defeat he suffered (on a strict definition of the word *member* in the by-laws), Lenin split the unity congress in two. He called an *Iskra* caucus to consolidate the split but posted guards to keep all the other *Iskra* editors except Plekhanov out of the *Iskra* caucus. Soon he would split with Plekhanov too for it was from his first clash with Plekhanov that he derived his guiding motto: "To regard all persons without sentiment, to keep a stone in one's sling. . . ."[2]

At the same Congress, when a delegate spoke in liturgical language of the projected Central Committee as a "Spirit omnipresent and one," Lenin cried out from his seat, *"Ne dukh, a kulak!"* (Not spirit, but fist—the whole of Lenin's organization philosophy is in that cry, always providing the "Fist" is his.)

If splitting with Plekhanov gave him a wrench because Plekhanov had been his master, splitting with Martov wounded his heart because, even on his deathbed, Lenin showed that he still felt affection for Martov.

DOWN WITH ALL SOFTHEARTEDNESS

But to Krzhizhanovsky he sent instructions: "Write to Martov, appealing for the last time to reason . . . and prepare for war with the Martovites. Do not look on Martov as before. The friendship is at an end. Down with all softheartedness."

Down with All Softheartedness could be posted over the laboratory in which Lenin was to make his living experiment to impose his blueprint on the Russian people.

At the Party Court of Honor, where he was put on trial for slandering his own comrades during the electoral campaign of 1906, Lenin coolly admitted that he had chosen "obnoxious terms calculated to evoke hatred, aversion, contempt . . . calculated not to convince but to break up the ranks of the opponent, not to correct the opponent's mistake but to destroy him, to wipe his organization off the face of the earth." His excuse? He had taken it for granted that a difference on how to nominate candidates for

Duma Deputy would become a "splitting point." Since he expected a split, that meant war, and in war one acted as if one were at war. "And I shall always act in that way whenever a split occurs . . . in the event of the development of a split, I shall always conduct a war of extermination." When Lenin said extermination he meant it. When the occasion arose, it must be said that he was faithful to his pledge.

Lenin was thus the organizer of his own faction and party. He was its self-chosen leader, he personally selected his own lieutenants in high places and low, he was its commander-in-chief exacting from his followers the discipline of an army. He defined and redefined its doctrines and its tactics. He instilled into it his own total rejection of all existing institutions. He was its will and its intellect. I would be tempted to say its heart as well, were he not by grave and serious conviction opposed to all sentimental considerations, all emotions save the emotion of class hatred, all general moral rules applying to the treatment of one's fellow man merely because he is human. To the Young Communist League he would say in 1920:

> Our morality is completely subordinated to the interests of the class struggle. . . . For Communists, morality consists entirely of compact united discipline and conscious mass struggle against the exploiters. We do not believe in a timeless morality and we expose all fairy tales about such a morality.[3]

This ruthlessness and cynicism were partly natural to Lenin, partly the result of a blueprint he had devised for himself in accord with what he thought a revolutionist should be like. It was this amorality that made it possible for him to arrange the counterfeiting of Russian rubles and direct holdups by his followers to obtain funds for his action, though public opinion was shocked and a congress of his Party had expressly forbidden such acts. This it was that made it possible for him to use such unscrupulous lieutenants as Victor Taratuta, Joseph Stalin, and Roman Malinovsky and defend them against exposure. This it was that made it possible for him to use the funds and physical aid made available to him by the German General Staff from 1915 to 1918, so long as the source was properly disguised.[4]

LENIN'S CENTRALISM

The first striking peculiarity in Lenin's organization doctrine is its extreme centralism, coupled with an extreme distrust of the rank and file of his party and the local organizations. When Lenin was in control of the central organ of the Party, he asked defiantly: "What is bad about the complete dictatorship of the central organ?"[5] Chided with suppressing party democracy, Lenin answered for himself and his band of professional revolutionaries: "They have no time to think of the toy forms of democracy . . . but they have a lively sense of their *responsibility* and they know by experience that to get rid of an undesirable member, an organization of real revolutionaries will stop at nothing."[6]

This is surely one of the most unresponsive answers in political literature. Lenin argues that under the conditions of police spying in Russia, party democracy is a "useless and harmful toy." But the context reveals that even in a free country the chief function of party "democracy" to him is to provide "the general control, in the literal sense of the term, that the Party exercises over every member," a control which enables the Party to decide whether to assign to a member one function or another, or to get rid of him altogether as unfit. He believes that, in the context of illegality, democracy can be replaced completely by the mutual trust of Socialists in each other, the absolute trust of all in the self-selected leading committee, and faith in the ability of the latter to get rid of those who cannot be trusted.

Even more uncompromising is Lenin's championing of "bureaucratic centralism" as against the democratic autonomy of the primary and local organizations and their control over the center. This bureaucratic centralism he considers as appropriate to a Socialist party in any country. The language of his celebration of "bureaucratism" is prickly and rough-hewn, but its meaning is startlingly clear:

> Bureaucratism *versus* autonomy, such is the principle of revolutionary social democracy as against that of the opportunists. . . . The organization of revolutionary social democracy strives to go from the top downward and defends the enlargement of the rights and plenary powers of the central body.[7]

Of course it was hard, indeed impossible, for this power-centered man to imagine that he would not be in control of the center. To Lunacharsky he said:

> "If we have in the CC or in the central organ a majority, then we will demand the firmist discipline. We will insist on every sort of subordination of the Mensheviks to party unity . . ."
>
> I asked Vladimir Ilyich: "Well, and what if it should turn out after all that we are in a minority?"
>
> Lenin smiled enigmatically and said: "It depends on the circumstances. In any case we will not permit them to make of unity a rope around our necks. And under no circumstances will we let the Mensheviks drag us after them on such a rope."[8]

Not until Lenin had been chided by his opponents for more than half a decade for his rejection of Party democracy did he finally seek to conceal somewhat his arch centralism and aversion to any local autonomy or to control from below. For the purposes of his concealment, he coined his celebrated term, *democratic centralism*! Even after he was in power and no longer could give as his justification the tsar's police, in the third year of his rule he defined that self-contradictory term as "meaning only that representatives from the localities gather and choose a responsible organ. . . . The responsible organ must do the administering."

When Lenin's concept of democratic centralism was transplanted to the Communist International, it was formulated this way:

> The main principle of democratic centralism is that of the higher cell being elected by the lower cell, the absolute binding force of all directives of a higher cell to a cell subordinate to it, and the existence of a commanding [*vlastnogo*; i.e., endowed with, or clothed with, power] Party center [the authority of which] is unchallengeable for all leaders in Party life, from one congress to the next.[9]

Lenin's division of spheres between what should be "centralized" and what "decentralized" would be comical were it not for its tragic implications for Russia and for communism. In his "Letter to a Comrade on Our Organizational Tasks," Lenin wrote:

> We have arrived at an extremely important principle of all Party organization and Party activity. In regard to ideological and practical *direction* the movement and the revolutionary struggle of the proletariat need the *greatest possible centralization*, but in regard to *keeping the center informed* concerning the movement and concerning the Party as a whole, in regard to *responsibility* before the Party, we need the *greatest possible decentralization*. The movement must be led by the smallest possible number of the most homogeneous groups of trained and experienced revolutionaries. But the largest possible number of the most varied and heterogeneous groups drawn from the most diverse layers of the proletariat (and of other classes) should take part in the movement. And in regard to each such group the center of the Party must have always before it not only exact data on their activities but also the fullest possible knowledge of their composition.[10]

If we add to this the rule prescribing that the "committee should lead *all* aspects of the local movement and direct *all* local institutions, forces . . . decide all general questions" and leave "independence of the district groups . . . only in the questions of the technique of transmitting and distributing," then Lenin's conception of hierarchical centralism becomes terrifyingly clear. All power, all command, all decision should be with the center ("the district group receives its powers only from the latter"), but the duty to carry out, obey and report should be "decentralized" and accorded as a "privilege" to every local organization and individual member, and even to party sympathizers.

Afraid that his readers might not get its full implications, Lenin repeated it all again, as was his wont, with only slight variations and different underscorings:

> We must centralize the direction of the movement. We must also (and we must *for this reason*, for without the informing of the center its leadership is impossible) decentralize as much as possible the *responsibility before the Party* of each circle which forms part of the Party or inclines to it. This decentralization is the necessary condition for revolutionary centralization and *its necessary corrective*. In order that the center may not only give advice, persuade, and argue (as has been done up to now), but may really direct the orchestra, it is essential to know exactly who is playing which fiddle and where; who, where, is learning to master which instrument or has mastered it; who, where and why, is playing out of tune (when the music begins to grate on the ear); and who, how, and where should be transferred to correct the dissonance, and so on.[11]

From the outset Lenin's "center" was self-appointed. He began with himself, then gathered around him those who agreed with him. Again and again he removed players from his orchestra when their playing grated on his ears, gathering others more in harmony with his directing. Thus his "Leninist" center was self-perpetuating.

The same ideas reappeared in the years of comparatively open activity between 1907 and 1914, when *Zvezda* and *Pravda* were legal journals and the Bolsheviks could campaign openly and elect deputies to the Duma. They continued during the six months of 1917 when Russia, in Lenin's words, was "the freest country in the world." And they continued when Lenin held power in party and country. At first he sought to justify his centralism before its critics by pointing to the harsh conditions of a conspiratorial underground movement, but in time it became clear that his centralism sprang from the deepest necessities of his temperament, his confidence in himself, and his pessimistic view of his fellow men. He has been compared to a schoolmaster commanding his pupils (by Edmund Wilson) and to a general commanding an embattled army (in his own figures of speech on military discipline). Here, in any case, is a revolutionary of a rare type: a revolutionary with a military-bureaucratic mind, to whom the complete centralization and control of all activities is—of all things—the road to a stateless, partyless utopia!

Hence Lenin's Archimedean cry for an organization of revolutionaries "to turn Russia upside down" did not cease when Russia was turned upside down. As before, Lenin continued to repeat the cry for "organization, organization, organization." In power, as when fighting for power, he said: "Our fighting method is organization." But now he had something new to add. To the old dream of centralized organization of the Party, which he did not for a moment abandon, he added the new dream of total organization by the Party. Of what? Why, of Russia. Its industries and its agriculture, its feelings and its thoughts, its habits, even its dreams—total organization of slackness, of the waywardness of will, of all deeds and desires. "We must organize everything," he said in the summer of 1918, "take everything into our hands."[12]

THE NATURE OF TOTALITARIAN DICTATORSHIP

When Lenin said class war, he meant war. It would, of course, be a war for the good of humanity, but for the good of humanity, a good part of humanity would have to be dealt with according to the rules of war. Even on fellow socialists, when they differed with him, he waged "a war of extermination."

> When we get power [Lenin wrote in 1916] we will establish a dictatorship of the proletariat, although all evolution moves toward the elimination of rule by force of one part of society over another. Dictatorship is the rule of a part of society over the whole of society, and, moreover, a rule basing itself directly on force.

This he wrote in 1916 when he was but dreaming of his possible dictatorship. But on December 5, 1919, after he had been dictator in fact for two years, he wrote: "Dictatorship is a harsh, heavy, and even bloody word." And on October 10, 1920, near the end of the third year of his rule, he bade advocates of democracy remember: "The scientific concept of dictatorship means neither more nor less than unlimited power, resting directly on force, not limited by anything, not restricted by any laws, nor any absolute rules. Nothing else but that."

This formulation is beautiful in its pedantic clarity, for the first giant step in the establishment of a totalitarian power is the destruction of all the restraints that limit power, the restraints of religion, morality, tradition, institutions, constitutions, and laws, that may place any restrictions upon the atomization of a people. The history of all totalitarian regimes has proved the rightness of Lenin's "scientific definition." If one adds to that Lenin's total rejection of the existing world and his conviction that he was the infallible interpreter of an infallible doctrine that told him what mankind should be like, to what blueprint it must be made to conform, and what "history" wants man to do; and further the ambition expressed by Lenin in the summer of 1918, "We must organize everything, take everything into our hands," we have a fair definition of totalitarianism.

This ambition to organize everything tidily, accurately, and totally was actually inherent in Lenin's doctrine from the start. We have only to read attentively his outburst against the first and chief of the cardinal sins in his Decalogue: *stikhiinost* (elementalness, spontaneity, initiative from below). To him it was the opposite of *soznatelnost* (consciousness, the instruction or direction that comes from above from the "vanguard" or "center"). In his first characteristic credo of 1902, he declared war on *stikhiinost*. In early 1918, when he was already in power, he pronounced the elemental, uncontrollable spontaneity of the "million-tentacled hydra" of the "petty bourgeois" peasantry and the workers affected by them to be "the main enemy." And in 1922 and 1923, after he had been four years in power and was discovering that the great "machine refuses to obey the driver's hand," he reiterated the denunciation, adding the grim corollary: "Petty bourgeois spontaneity is more terrible than all the Denikins, Kolchaks, and Yudeniches put together."

LENIN'S IDEA OF THE CLASS WAR

The operative word in what Lenin called the class war was not class but war. This involved not merely an acceptance of terror and a loving concern with the idea of its application but also a pedantic elaboration of terroristic methods that distinguished him from other socialist leaders.

In 1901, he wrote in the Marxist theoretical journal, *Zarya*, an apostrophe to lynch law: "Trial by the street breathes a living spirit into the bureaucratic formalism that pervades out government institutions."

In 1905, he did not hurry back to Russia while tsarism was reeling, as did Martov, Leon Trotsky, and Rosa Luxemburg, but he showered his followers with detailed and bloody instructions from afar. In January 1905, he wrote his "Plan of the Battle of Saint Petersburg": "Revolution is war. . . . The workers will arm themselves. . . . Each will strain with all his might to get himself a gun, or at least a revolver."

Subtly he recalled the cry of Zaichnevsky: "To the Axe! No, with axes you won't be able to do anything against sabres. With an axe you can't get to him; perhaps with a knife, but that is even less. No, what we need is revolvers . . . still better, guns."

In a call for a Congress of his party, he suggested as the order of business: "Organization, relation to the periphery, uprising, arming of the workers— setting up workshops for making dynamite." Workshops for making dynamite on the order of business of a socialist Congress—who but Lenin could write that?—and his draft "Resolution on Armed Uprising" said: "The Congress resolves . . . that by preparation of the uprising it understands not only the preparation of weapons and creation of groups, etc., but also the accumulation of experience by means of . . . individual armed attacks on the police and army . . . on prisons, government institutions, etc."

For these armed groups he exceeded himself in the ardor of his incitements and the detailed pedantry of his instructions: "The bomb is a necessary part of the equipment for arming the people. . . . Bombs can be prepared everywhere and in all places. . . . In this, frenzied energy is needed, and yet more energy. With consternation, by God, with consternation, I see that there has been talk of bombs for more than a half year, and not a single bomb has been made. . . ."

In his "Tasks of the Detachments of the Revolutionary Army," written at the moment when the tsar was promising a constitution and large sections of the opposition were calling off their activities to see what the promise meant, Lenin instructed his revolutionary detachments to "engage in actions on their own and assume leadership over mobs." They must:

> arm themselves as best they can (guns, revolvers, bombs, knives, brass knuckles, cudgels, rags soaked in kerosene to start fires, rope or rope ladders, spades for erecting barricades, barbed wire, tacks against cavalry, etc., and so forth). . . . Select leaders or officers, work out signals . . . cries, whistles, passwords, signs to know each other in darkness or in tumult. . . . Attack a policeman or cossack who has gotten separated and take away his weapons. . . . Climb on roofs or upper floors to shower stones on troops, boiling water, etc. [Always there was that etc. for fear that they would do nothing without his instructions, and perhaps he had forgotten something.]

He gave directions for securing the help of friendly officers, for procuring explosives, learning the layout of prisons, police stations, ministries, arms deposits, banks, instructions for employment of the aged, the weak, women, and children. These directives, and the train of thought they bespoke, are unique in the history of modern socialism. The ruthlessness of Nechayev, the romantic exaltation of criminals and barricades by Bakunin, the call of Zaichnevsky to the axe, are mere violent posturing in comparison.

Up to August 1914, the overwhelming majority in every socialist party and of Russian workingmen and revolutionary intellectuals rejected both Lenin's view of dictatorship over the working class and other classes, his methods of organization, and his prescriptions for waging the class war. They were outraged by his quarrelsome splitting, his bank holdups, his money counterfeiting. Had they understood more fully what he was saying and believed he meant it literally, they would have been still more outraged. These methods isolated him and reduced his following to a little band of "rockhards"—a word he loved to echo—of men who admired him for this ruthlessness and cynicism, plus men in key posts, who, as it turned out when the police files were opened, were agents of the police.

TOTAL WAR WAS LENIN'S OPPORTUNITY

But in August 1914 began the terrible years—four long years of a frozen war of position, brutalizing years in which statesmen and generals treated their male citizens as so much human materiel to be expended without stint or calculation in the pursuit of undefinable and unattainable objectives. Men learned to accept as commonplace the mud and blood of the trenches and the ruthless logic of mutual extermination. They learned to master their fear of death and their revulsion against inflicting it. They developed a monstrous indifference to suffering, their own as well as that of others. Universal military discipline made Lenin's vision of military discipline in his party and public life seem less alien. Total war, which saw in entire nations a total enemy, made Lenin's idea of exterminating entire "hostile classes" less shocking. Universal war so brutalized European man that, as Reinhold Niebuhr wrote: "It became possible to beguile men into fresh brutalities by the fury of their resentment against brutality." Now that all things were being subjected to the arbitrament of bullet and bayonet, why not war and peace and the "system" that was declared to have made the sterile carnage possible and, according to Lenin, "inevitable." (It would take Lenin's disciples fifty years and an awareness of the atomic stalemate before they would grudgingly admit that universal war might not be inevitable.)

"Since it was a time of horrors," Raymond Aron would write in retrospect, "at least violence might have peace as its objective." If Lenin still rejected peace in favor of prolonging war until it could be transformed into a universal civil war,[13] this fine point of distinction was now less noticeable, for was he not "rejecting" the imperialist war and declaring war on "the system that begot it"?

Thus, war was Lenin's opportunity, since it made his fantastic prescriptions on military discipline and class war seem less unnatural. For, before there could come the reign of what Churchill would one day call "the bloody-minded professors of the Kremlin," there had first to be the bloody mess of Flanders Field, in which, as England's wartime leader, Lloyd George, himself would write, "Nothing could stop Haig's compulsion to send thousands and thousands to their death against the enemy's guns in the bovine and brutal game of attrition."

THE BEGINNINGS OF TOTAL POWER

The completeness of Lenin's belief in himself was matched by the completeness of his distrust of everybody else, from the proletariat to his own lieutenants, local bodies, and rank and file. Once in power he tried to define and prescribe everything, give detailed orders and write detailed decrees and instructions on everything, check upon everything's execution. His correspondence is filled with such detailed prescriptions and reports.

Uncomfortable as always in the presence of spontaneity, complexity, ambiguity, partial truths, shadings, pluralism, openness, the not-yet-known, the imperfectly known, or the unknowable, Lenin treated all questions of government and human conduct as if they had only one right answer, one simple, definite solution. The striking exception was his retreat in 1921 from the complete nationalization of everything down to the last bit of wool out of which a housewife might otherwise have knitted a sock or sweater, the last typewriter, scrap of paper, and inkwell, and the last exchange of rural grain for city-made hammers or nails, an impossible procedure partly brought on by the exigencies of civil war and partly by the primitive and credulous nature of Lenin's original "Marxist" dogmas. The retreat gave Russia Lenin's "New Economic Policy," or N.E.P., from which Stalin was to return to all-out nationalization.

Apart from this, Lenin's answer to whatever failures and irrationalities arose from his fantastic blueprint and his excessive centralization and control was yet more control and yet more administrative machinery.

A "terrible simplifier" in his remedies, he tended to cut through any complexity or muddle with the simplest of remedies: *arrest*! Set up another overseer committee to oversee the remiss or defective one, and "arrest a few scoundrels as an example."

A perpetual conspirator himself, before he came to power one of his weapons of confusion and demagogy was to bombard the Provisional Government with demands for the arrest of the "wealthy conspirators," the "ten capitalist ministers," and a stipulated number of bankers, manufacturers, and millionaires.

When the Provisional Government, simultaneously attacked by Lenin from the "left" and Kornilov from the "right," guiding itself by the false maxim *pas d'ennemi à gauche*, armed the Bolsheviks along with the other socialists and democrats against Kornilov, Lenin privately told his followers, "We will support Kerensky as the rope does the hanged man." But publicly he "supported" Kerensky with the demand, "Arrest Miliukov, arrest Rodzianko." In the "Threatening Catastrophe and How to Combat It," written a little over a month before he seized power, Lenin demanded "the abolition of commercial secrets [Is there any country with more secrets today than the totalitarian regime he founded?] and the firing squad for hiding anything."

But it was after he took power in the state that was "to begin at once to wither away" that his imagination ran riot. On November 18, 1917, he called upon the people of Petrograd and Moscow to show initiative by "arresting and handing over to revolutionary tribunals" all those guilty of "damage, slowing up, undermining production . . . concealment of supplies . . . any sort of resistance to the great cause of peace," to the policies of "land to the peasants" and "workers' control of production and distribution." Every man his own judge!

Then he proposed that every man be his own executioner, too, provided only that he was one of the mob and not one of the "scoundrels, loafers, rich." The instruction came in a draft article entitled, with unconscious irony, "How to Organize Competition." Each commune, each village, each town, should show "initiative and inventiveness" in devising ways of "cleansing the Russian land of all noxious insects, scoundrel fleas, bedbug rich, and so forth and so forth."

When I read this passage afresh with its "insects, fleas, and bedbugs," it gave me a start. I had always imagined that the vocabulary for the dehumanizing of men to make them easier to kill had been invented by Vyshinsky in the great purge trials. There the former Menshevik took special pleasure in denouncing the Old Bolsheviks who only yesterday had looked down on him. He called them "a foul-smelling pile of human garbage, vultures, serpents in human form, jackals, the last scum and filth of the past. . . . They must be shot like dirty dogs," he said. "Our people are demanding one thing: Crush the accursed reptiles."

Vyshinsky's choice vocabulary and the grim and depressing study of the trials had made me sensitive to this device. Hence, when I read one day, that a group of Americans had chosen for themselves the name, Black Panthers, I exclaimed, "These people are resigning from the human race. They are giving notice that they will spring from ambush, shoot from behind shrubs and trees, and from the rooftops of buildings." Alas, I was correct. And when they chose to call the police and administration and other officials "pigs" I knew that they were dehumanizing their intended targets. But it has astonished me to learn that Lenin, too, invented this, and gave to his successors from Stalin to Vyshinsky, the inhuman terms, "noxious insects, scoundrel fleas, bedbug rich."

"In one place they will put into prison a dozen rich men, a dozen scoundrels, a half-dozen workers who shirk on the job. . . . In another place they will set them to cleaning outside toilets. In a third they will give them yellow tickets [as identity cards] after a term in prison . . . so that the entire people . . . will act as the overseers of them as harmful people (wreckers). In a fourth they will shoot on the spot one out of every ten guilty of sloth . . . the more varied, the better . . . for only practice can work out the best measures of struggle."

Clearly, Lenin was being unjust to himself when he wrote: "We will suppress the resistance of the possessing classes by the methods they used," since "other means have not been invented." In the speech in which he thus belittled his own inventiveness, he invented the term "enemies of the people" for an entire political party, the Kadets, and outlawed them and their elected Deputies to the Constituent Assembly. In three weeks he had invented the

Extraordinary Commission (*Cheka*) along with the experimental "shooting of one in ten."

On January 27, 1918, he demanded that the entire working class join the terror. Workers who did not want to join in the hunt against "speculators" must be "forced to . . . under threat of the deprivation of their bread cards." Every factory and every regiment must pitch in to set up "several thousand raiding parties of ten to fifteen people each." "Regiments and workshops that do not accurately set up the required number of detachments [the word accurately is typical of this pedant of terror] will be deprived of bread cards and subject to revolutionary measures of persuasion and punishment. . . . Speculators caught with the goods . . . will be shot on the spot by the detachments. The same punishment for the members of the detachments convicted of bad faith."

As a socialist, Lenin had voted for the resolution of the parties of the Second International in favor of abolishing the death penalty for any crime. No one dreamed then that in the twentieth century the death penalty would be restored for theft, crimes against property, or "speculation."

But Lenin was furious with his lieutenants for abolishing the death penalty in October 1917. Even before the civil war began—a war provoked largely by such arbitrary acts as here described, by Lenin's insistence on one-party rule and the outlawing of other parties, and by his dispersal by force of the Constituent Assembly when he found that the Russian people in their first (and last) free election had not given him a majority—he had restored the death penalty and was calling for "shooting on the spot." "As long as we do not apply terror—shooting on the spot—" Lenin told the representatives of organizations for procuring food on January 14, 1918, "we won't get anywhere." When the civil war ended, the death penalty was abolished (on January 17, 1920) but restored in May of the same year. The first Criminal Code of the RSFSR provided the death penalty for seventy crimes. With ebbs and flows, the regime Lenin set up, returning now to "Leninist norms," has once more restored the death penalty for the various types of "aggravated speculation," theft, forgery, and crimes against the one real property, state-owned property.

Ce n'est que le provisoire qui dure. Lenin did not intend this "accurate" application of terror to chaos to be more than temporary. But there is an embarrassment of riches in Lenin's subsequent writings and speeches in the same vein. Let us skip to the Eleventh Congress, held during the gentler age of the N.E.P., in April 1922, the fourth and last year of his rule, when Lenin was talking of the problem of "purchasing canned goods in a cultured manner." Then he said: "One must think of this elementary culture, one must approach a subject thoughtfully. If the business is not settled in the course of a few minutes on the telephone, collect the documents and say: 'If you start any of your red tape, I shall put you in prison.'"

Ce n'est que le provisoire qui dure. Perhaps Lenin was in earnest when he wrote: "As soon as the new order has been stabilized, all administrative restrictions [on the press] will be abolished and a complete liberty of the press, subject only to the limitations of juridical responsibility, will be instituted in conformity with the most liberal and progressive legislation."[14]

The decree promised that each group of citizens would get printing plants and a supply of newsprint according to its numbers of adherents.

But after more than a half century the monopoly of the press continues, and even the Party is by Lenin's fiat denied the right to organized discussion and groupings to advance proposals or correct errors.

The one-party state is owner of all the means of communication, all printing plants, all journals, all bookstores, all libraries, all critics, and all criticism, decides what should be published and in how many copies, and what censored, what rewritten, what falsified over the author's signature, what should be sold, and what destroyed.

It is possible that Lenin's promise is not mere demagogy nor an attempt to silence critics. Lenin carried with him some of the intellectual baggage of nineteenth century socialist humanism and democracy and it took some little time to shake it off. But his heirs began without the encumbrance of this heritage from the nineteenth century. They were born and forged in the age of iron totalitarianism. All they need is to find some quote from Lenin to justify any dictatorial act and those quotations exist in abounding profusion to make pious and infallible their deeds.

ON THE INTERNATIONAL ARENA

When Lenin entered the international arena, he carried the same methods with him. Thanks to the persuasiveness of power and victory, he felt that everything he had done in Russia in his war with the Mensheviks, the "Economists," and the Socialist Revolutionaries, all his unending splits on matters large and small, his rigid "night watchman" organization principles (as Rosa Luxemburg had ironically called them), his extreme centralism—had been legitimatized by victory and proved correct by history. Now he prepared to enforce on every party which approached his "Holy of Holies," all these views and procedures, in order to banish "Menshevism" from the ranks of the new International from the outset.

At this moment he was completely possessed by the legends or myths within which he lived his political life. He was sure that the world war was the *"final crisis of capitalism"*; that the Russian Revolution and his *coup d'état* which that Revolution had made possible were but the first act in the "*world revolution*" which must now spread swiftly through Europe and the world.

"A quite small party is sufficient to attract the masses," Lenin told the great Italian Party when he was naming the leaders and groups that it must expel. "In certain moments there is no need for a large organization. . . . You are in a preparatory period. The first stage of that period is a break with the Mensheviks like that we carried out in 1903." Lenin had his way with the Italian Party, splitting open the powerful workers' front in Italy; through the breach, Mussolini "marched" triumphantly on Rome, traveling all but the last few miles in a Pullman sleeping car. The same pattern was repeated by Lenin's "best disciple," Joseph Stalin, at the end of the twenties, enabling Hitler's storm troopers to march through the breach Stalin created between Socialists and Communists by his dogma that the main enemy was not the fascists but the "social fascists," the "Mensheviks" of the period.

Thus, V. I. Lenin, and his disciple and successor, Joseph Stalin, were the midwives of the birth of Mussolini's incomplete totalitarianism, and of Hitler's ruthless totalitarian rule. "The revolution is an idea that has found bayonets," Mussolini said. And Mao, more crudely, stressed power rather than ideology with his "Power comes out of the barrel of a gun." Indeed, the ideology Lenin had devoutly borrowed from Marx, he had already hammered thin. His classless elite, recruited from students and intellectuals who are children of the possessing classes, might well seize power not, as Marx expected, where the economy was most advanced and the working class most "conscious," cultured, organized, numerous, and politically most active; it might seize power just as easily, nay, even more easily, where the economy was backward, the workers neither mature nor conscious nor politically active, and all political parties of all classes rudimentary or non-existent. Indeed, the more fragmented and the less organized and educated a society, the easier for a little classless band of the discontented to seize power in the name of socialism and the proletariat.

This vanguard-elite theory would later make it possible for restless students, officers, or intellectuals to seize power in the name of the proletariat even where the proletariat was in its infancy. In the name of this doctrine, Mao could seize power "for the proletariat" by means of peasant armies. Ho Chi-Minh might do the same in a land where the only workers were plantation hands and handicraftsmen plying their ancient trades. All that was needed was a power vacuum; a supply of arms (the Second World War took care of that); a supply of malcontents (and where are there no malcontents?); an *apparat* to seize power; some fragments of Lenin's doctrine; and Stalin's example. Once in power they can do as Lenin, Stalin, and Khrushchev have done: use the "proletarian power" to rule society as a whole, to put all industry, all weapons, all means of communication, into the hands of the ruling "party," to develop a power as total as the wayward spirit of man and the development of technology and controls permit.

The trouble with this system is that permanent dictatorship spells permanent illegitimacy. History has known several types of legitimacy: hieratic or religious legitimacy, monarchical hereditary legitimacy, constitutional democratic legitimacy. When a given type of legitimacy is ruptured by revolution, the only wholesome government that can issue from the breakdown is a prelegitimate government, one that has the grace to call itself *provisional* and to recognize that its chief task is to summon the nation to elect a constitutional or constituent assembly to write a new constitution and provide a new legitimacy. In our age, this is most likely to be a democratic legitimacy.

But permanent dictatorship does not provide for an expression of the popular will. Such a regime can last for fifty years and yet not dare to submit its acts to its subjects for approval or correction. Every time a dictator dies, it faces a new crisis of succession, for there is no legitimate procedure to determine a successor. As Rosa Luxemburg tried to tell Lenin in her friendly warning:

> Dictatorship, certainly! But this dictatorship consists in *the manner of applying democracy*, not in its *elimination*, it means resolute attacks upon the well-entrenched rights and economic relations of bourgeois society without which a socialist transformation cannot be accomplished. But this dictatorship must be the work of a *class*, and not of a little leading minority in the name of the class. Freedom for the supporters of the government alone [she wrote in a truly memorable passage of her criticism of Lenin's revolution], freedom only for the members of one party—however numerous they may be—that is no freedom at all. Freedom is always freedom for the one who thinks differently. Not because of any fanatical conception of "justice" but because all that is instructive, wholesome, and purifying in political freedom depends on this essential characteristic, and its effectiveness vanishes when "freedom" becomes a special privilege.
>
> . . . with the repression of political life in the land as a whole, life in the soviets must also become more and more crippled. Without general elections, without unrestricted freedom of press and assembly, without a free struggle of opinion, life dies out in every public institution, becomes a mere semblance of life, in which only the bureaucracy remains as the active element. Public life gradually falls asleep, a few dozen party leaders of inexhaustible energy . . . direct and rule . . . an elite of the working class is invited from time to time to meetings where they are to applaud the speeches of the leaders, and to approve proposed resolutions unanimously—at bottom then a clique affair . . . not the dictatorship of the proletariat but the dictatorship of a handful of politicians. . . . Such conditions must inevitably cause a brutalization of public life: attempted assassinations, shooting of hostages, etc.[15]

After fifty years, she is a prophet still.

As we review the hundred years of Lenin's life and the seven decades of our century, it seems to me that we must begin with a mea culpa. Our age has been brutalized by the psychology and habits of total war. Totalitarianism is only one by-product of this brutality. Its practitioners forgot that man, being capable of evil, cannot be trusted with unrestricted power.

We must learn afresh a sense of man's limitations, of the precariousness, uncertainties and mysteries of life, the unexpected possibilities of our every act, the disorderliness and irrationality and discontinuity of history. The attempt to remake the world totally by force has manifestly collided with insuperable obstacles. Our boasted technological progress, too, is coming into a collison with what seems to be a stone wall at the end of a blocked street.

Saint-Just rises from the ashes of his dream to remind us that "when all the stones are cut to build the structure of freedom, from the self-same stones you can build a palace or a tomb," even as economically "from one cross, two scaffolds can be made."

However, since today we are reviewing Lenin's life and work and not our age as a whole, I shall give the last word to a fellow historian in England, Max Beloff, who has written in *Encounter*, "The world has been a poorer and bleaker and more dangerous place because Lenin lived."

NOTES TO CHAPTER 12

1. V. I. Lenin and A. M. Gorkii, *Pis'ma, vospominaniia, documenti* (Moscow, 1958), p. 91.

2. Lenin, *Collected works*, English translation from the 4th Russian ed. (Moscow, 1960), 4:342.

3. Address to the Young Communist League, October 2, 1920.

4. The scope of the present analysis prevents the documentation of these matters. On aid from the German government and General Staff, see George Katkov, "German Foreign Office Documents on Financial Support to the Bolsheviks in 1917," *International Affairs* (London), April 1956, pp. 181–89; Werner Hahlweg, *Lenins Rückkehr nach Russland, 1917* (Leiden, 1957); Z. A. B. Zeman, *Germany and the Revolution in Russia, 1915–1918* (Oxford, 1958). On the revolutionary holdups, see the chapter "Arms and the Man," in this writer's *Three Who Made a Revolution*. On Lenin's blueprint for his own spirit, see my "Leninism," in Milorad M. Drachkovitch, ed., *Marxism in the Modern World* (Stanford, 1965), pp. 51–54.

5. Leon Trotsky, *Lenin* (New York, 1925), p. 43.

6. *Sochineniia*, 4th ed., 5:448.

7. Ibid., 7:365–66.

8. *Vospominaniia o Lenine* (Moscow, 1956), p. 313.

9. Lenin to the Ninth Party Congress in April 1920; and *II Kongress Kommunisticheskogo Internatsionala*, p. 576.

10. *Sochineniia*, 6:221–23; 7:355–56.

11. Ibid.

12. *Sochineniia*, 27:477.

13. Actually when Lenin got back to what he pronounced "the freest country in the world in wartime" and sought to overthrow its new freedoms, for the first time in his life he found himself face to face with mass meetings of real peasants and workingmen in uniform. Then he found it convenient to urge peace and not prolongation of the war, and limited his slogans to suggestions of fraternizing in the trenches, grounding arms, turning arms on your own officers, desertion of the imperialist war to seize land in one's native village. The transforming of the imperialist war into universal civil war proved so impractical for the seizure and holding of power that within two months of his *coup d'état* he was threatening to "appeal to the sailors of Kronstadt" against his own Central Committee if they continued to vote for "revolutionary war" in place of a separate peace with Germany.

14. Decree issued on November 10, 1917, by Lenin: "On the Press of the Party and the Soviets," *Collection of Documents* (Moscow, 1954), p. 173.

15. Rosa Luxemburg, *The Russian Revolution* and *Leninism or Marxism?* (Both in one volume) (Ann Arbor, 1961), pp. 69–78.

Index